Masculinities
in Chinese History

ASIA/PACIFIC/PERSPECTIVES

Series Editor: Mark Selden

Crime, Punishment, and Policing in China, edited by Børge Bakken

Woman, Man, Bangkok: Love, Sex, and Popular Culture in Thailand, by Scot Barmé

Making the Foreign Serve China: Managing Foreigners in the People's Republic, by Anne-Marie Brady

Marketing Dictatorship: Propaganda and Thought Work in China, by Anne-Marie Brady

Collaborative Nationalism: The Politics of Friendship on China's Mongolian Frontier, by Uradyn E. Bulag

The Mongols at China's Edge: History and the Politics of National Unity, by Uradyn E. Bulag

Transforming Asian Socialism: China and Vietnam Compared, edited by Anita Chan, Benedict J. Tria Kerkvliet, and Jonathan Unger

Bound to Emancipate: Working Women and Urban Citizenship in Early Twentieth-Century China, by Angelina Chin

The Search for the Beautiful Woman: A Cultural History of Japanese and Chinese Beauty, by Cho Kyo

China's Great Proletarian Cultural Revolution: Master Narratives and Post-Mao Counternarratives, edited by Woei Lien Chong

North China at War: The Social Ecology of Revolution, 1937–1945, edited by Feng Chongyi and David S. G. Goodman

Little Friends: Children's Film and Media Culture in China, by Stephanie Hemelryk Donald

Beachheads: War, Peace, and Tourism in Postwar Okinawa, by Gerald Figal

Gender in Motion: Divisions of Labor and Cultural Change in Late Imperial and Modern China, edited by Bryna Goodman and Wendy Larson

Social and Political Change in Revolutionary China: The Taihang Base Area in the War of Resistance to Japan, 1937–1945, by David S. G. Goodman

Islands of Discontent: Okinawan Responses to Japanese and American Power, edited by Laura Hein and Mark Selden

Masculinities in Chinese History, by Bret Hinsch

Women in Early Imperial China, Second Edition, by Bret Hinsch

Chinese Civil Justice, Past and Present, by Philip C. C. Huang

Local Democracy and Development: The Kerala People's Campaign for Decentralized Planning, by T. M. Thomas Isaac with Richard W. Franke

Hidden Treasures: Lives of First-Generation Korean Women in Japan, by Jackie J. Kim with Sonia Ryang

North Korea: Beyond Charismatic Politics, by Heonik Kwon and Byung-Ho Chung

Postwar Vietnam: Dynamics of a Transforming Society, edited by Hy V. Luong

From Silicon Valley to Shenzhen: Global Production and Work in the IT Industry, by Boy Lüthje, Stefanie Hürtgen, Peter Pawlicki, and Martina Sproll

Resistant Islands: Okinawa Confronts Japan and the United States, by Gavan McCormack and Satoko Oka Norimatsu

The Indonesian Presidency: The Shift from Personal toward Constitutional Rule, by Angus McIntyre

Nationalisms of Japan: Managing and Mystifying Identity, by Brian J. McVeigh

To the Diamond Mountains: A Hundred-Year Journey through China and Korea, by Tessa Morris-Suzuki

From Underground to Independent: Alternative Film Culture in Contemporary China, edited by Paul G. Pickowicz and Yingjin Zhang

Wife or Worker? Asian Women and Migration, edited by Nicola Piper and Mina Roces

Social Movements in India: Poverty, Power, and Politics, edited by Raka Ray and Mary Fainsod Katzenstein

Pan Asianism: A Documentary History, Volume 1, 1850–1920, edited by Sven Saaler and Christopher W. A. Szpilman

Pan Asianism: A Documentary History, Volume 2, 1920–Present, edited by Sven Saaler and Christopher W. A. Szpilman

Biology and Revolution in Twentieth-Century China, by Laurence Schneider

Contentious Kwangju: The May 18th Uprising in Korea's Past and Present, edited by Gi-Wook Shin and Kyong Moon Hwang

Thought Reform and China's Dangerous Classes: Reeducation, Resistance, and the People, by Aminda M. Smith

Japan's New Middle Class, Third Edition, by Ezra F. Vogel with a chapter by Suzanne Hall Vogel, foreword by William W. Kelly

The Japanese Family in Transition: From the Professional Housewife Ideal to the Dilemmas of Choice, by Suzanne Hall Vogel with Steven K. Vogel

The United States and China: A History from the Eighteenth Century to the Present, by Dong Wang

The Inside Story of China's High-Tech Industry: Making Silicon Valley in Beijing, by Yu Zhou

Masculinities
in Chinese History

Bret Hinsch

ROWMAN & LITTLEFIELD
Lanham • Boulder • New York • Toronto • Plymouth, UK

Published by Rowman & Littlefield
4501 Forbes Boulevard, Suite 200, Lanham, Maryland 20706
www.rowman.com

10 Thornbury Road, Plymouth PL6 7PP, United Kingdom

Copyright © 2013 by Rowman & Littlefield

British Library Cataloguing in Publication Information Available

Library of Congress Cataloging-in-Publication Data
Hinsch, Bret.
  Masculinities in Chinese history / Bret Hinsch.
     pages cm. — (Asia/Pacific/perspectives)
  Includes bibliographical references and index.
  ISBN 978-1-4422-2233-5 (cloth : alk. paper) — ISBN 978-1-4422-2234-2 (pbk. : alk. paper) — ISBN 978-1-4422-2235-9 (electronic) 1. Masculinity—China—History. 2. Men—China—Identity. 3. Men—China—Social conditions. I. Title.
  HQ1090.7.C6H56 2013
  305.310951—dc23

2013017662

∞™ The paper used in this publication meets the minimum requirements of American National Standard for Information Sciences—Permanence of Paper for Printed Library Materials, ANSI/NISO Z39.48-1992.

Printed in the United States of America

Contents

Introduction   1

1   Zhou Dynasty (1046–256 BCE): Separation of the Sexes   13

2   Han Dynasty (206 BCE–220 CE): Honor Culture   29

3   Jin Dynasty (265–420 CE): Buddhism and Changing Masculinity   47

4   Tang Dynasty (618–907 CE): Masculine Honor and Women   71

5   Song Dynasty (960–1279 CE): Cultural Capital and Manhood   91

6   Ming Dynasty (1368–1644 CE): Marginal Heroes   111

7   Late Qing and Republican Eras: Modernizing Masculinity   131

8   Revolution, Reform, and Beyond   151

Glossary   171

Bibliography   177

Index   193

About the Author   199

Introduction

Is a book about men in Chinese history even necessary? Common sense would suggest that the history of men is far from understudied, whether in China or anywhere else. Any conventional history of China is almost entirely about men—their actions and ideas, inventions and battles, intrigues and achievements. By focusing on the public realm, which mostly excluded women, historians have traditionally used one half of the population to represent all of China. Only in recent decades has the rise of women's history begun to remedy this glaring omission, revealing rich and fascinating alternate realms of experience that had previously escaped the historian's selective gaze.[1]

Nevertheless, even when we add women to the picture, accounts of gender in China's past remain incomplete. In the 1960s and 1970s, research into "gender" was virtually synonymous with the study of women and their relations with men. This limited view of the subject implies that maleness is somehow normative and hence instantly comprehensible, whereas the feminine is exceptional and demands explanation. To correct this imbalance, scholars have been turning their attentions back to men. But instead of accepting the male realm uncritically and masculinity as normative and neutral, a more analytical approach now sees men as gendered agents and investigates how male identity influences thinking and behavior.

This flourishing field of study is called the history of masculinities. Pluralizing "masculinities" emphasizes the multiplicity of masculine roles, images, and values. Of course, normative manhood has changed enormously over time. A Bronze Age warrior of the Shang dynasty would have felt distinctly out of place in the art deco ambience of 1930s Shanghai. Even in a particular time and place, manifestations of manhood could vary considerably. Different masculine norms informed the respective behaviors of emperor, literatus, merchant, eunuch, soldier, and peasant.

The history of masculinities does not focus on individual men, as scholars have already studied them in depth; rather, it seeks to understand manhood itself. Perceptions of what constitutes a good and successful man have always been varied, mutable, and somewhat contradictory. Despite this inherent ambiguity, masculinity exerts an enormous impact on every aspect of human affairs, making it an important topic worthy of sustained inquiry.[2] Viewing the history of China from the standpoint of varied masculinities provides novel perspectives for reexamining familiar people and events, evoking a more comprehensive understanding of the past.

In many respects, the achievements of women's history have inspired the rapid growth of the history of masculinities. Scholars have actively explored the history of women since the 1960s, pioneering many approaches to gender that are equally applicable to the study of manhood. Beyond their methodologies, studies of women and manhood share deeper similarities as well. Rather than seeing the masculine and feminine as independent opposites, the history of gender is now revealing how ideals of manhood have influenced womanhood and vice versa. Gender is not hermetically sealed. To the contrary, views of the male and female have always dynamically interacted, each influencing the other. Sometimes a man understands his maleness in opposition to womanhood, while a woman takes the opposite approach to constructing her own gendered selfhood. And the sexes often interact in predictable ways, creating normative gender identities.

Individual men's views of male identity have shaped them in myriad ways, exerting an immense impact on the overall course of Chinese history. How many wars were sparked by monarchs and generals who wanted to prove themselves manly? How many acts of vengeance arose out of an insult to a man's honor? Many Chinese initially mistrusted Buddhism not just because of its alien dogmas but also due to unease with the foreign custom of male celibacy. In the modern era, many men turned to reform and revolution to redeem collective Chinese manhood from a prevailing sense of disgrace. The list of masculinity's influences goes on and on. Masculinity has always been a major influence on the behavior of both key historical actors and ordinary men. Bringing it into the historical narrative can enrich any account of China's past.

DEFINING MASCULINITY

To study the historical significance of masculinity, it is first necessary to understand what this term implies. Every society has gender norms, but not all of them have a word precisely equivalent to the English term "masculinity." Imperial China is one culture that lacked a specific word for manhood. But just because people do not have a particular word does not mean that they are unfamiliar with the underlying idea. Even in Western culture, where the study of manhood first became a topic for research, the concept of masculinity is only a few hundred years old.[3] Previously there was no need to define masculinity overtly because, even when gender norms were debated and in flux, most people nevertheless thought they knew quite well what it meant to be a man.[4]

Nor is this term unproblematic. For example, the concept of masculinity seems to imply that manhood is standard when it is in fact both diverse and endlessly contested. Not only do people in various times and places view manhood differently, but opinions about what constitutes a successful man can vary considerably within a single community. Many voices put forward assorted views of masculinity, each raising somewhat different opinions and concerns. Nor do various masculinities hold equal weight. People consider some men successful, they accept others but admire them less, while they often deem manhood at the margins strange or shameful.

Because masculinity is so fundamental, it covers a vast range of ideas, symbols, and actions. Masculinity encompasses the body, institutions, politics, ritual, work, and everything else that men think and do. This irreducible complexity makes it difficult to come up with a satisfying but brief definition of masculinity. Even so, it is certainly possible to identify key ideas and practices of male experience that constitute the core of masculinity and to analyze how these have changed over time.

Such an elaborate problematization of the issue would puzzle most people. Common sense equates gender with biology, making masculinity seem obvious to everyone but academics.[5] However, the shortcomings of blunt biological reductionism are readily apparent. Even if physical differences were always binary and clear-cut (which is not always the case), individuals nevertheless express masculinity and femininity in dizzyingly varied ways. For example the gentle Chinese scholar and rugged Native American, although seemingly opposite in many ways, both represented successful masculine archetypes in their respective cultures. How can a single view of masculinity encompass such different views of the normative man?

Although scholars have put forward many definitions and models of masculinity, a solid consensus on the matter has yet to emerge.[6] One problem is that masculinity encompasses multiple social phenomena. Anthropologists frequently use the term to refer to four different conceptions: male identity, manhood (what men think and do as men), manliness (being a better man than other men), and the spectrum of normative male social roles.[7] Nor can men simply take their masculine identity for granted. Challenging Simone de

One ideal man . . .

Beauvoir's famous assertion that manhood is natural and womanhood artificial, anthropologist David Gilmore has argued to the contrary that in most cultures people automatically accept a woman's innate femininity, whereas a man has to actively prove his manhood.[8] This provocative thesis has become a cornerstone of masculinity studies. The need for a man to publicly affirm his masculinity gives rise to considerable anxiety. He must either construct an acceptable masculine identity or suffer the stigma of failure.[9]

Because there exist multiple ways of expressing masculinity, individuals and groups advocate conflicting views of manhood. Although a society can encompass a plurality of masculinities, some are regarded as more prestigious than others, and views on the matter inevitably conflict. The irreducibly agonistic character of masculinity lends it endless dynamism. Researchers have already studied some masculine hierarchies in great detail. For example, athletics embody the most prestigious type of masculinity in some contemporary high schools, and boys proudly flaunt their membership in an athletic subculture to gain respect.[10] This sort of "hegemonic" masculinity serves as a means not only to assert superiority over women but also to dominate other men.[11] In reaction, as men on the lower rungs of the masculine hierarchy struggle to raise their own status, they sometimes strategically create alternate expressions

. . . and another.

of manhood. Whenever new expressions of masculinity emerge, practitioners must strive to make an unfamiliar style of manhood respectable, challenging and perhaps altering prevailing views of what constitutes a successful man.

Masculinity gets expressed in social relations, becomes enmeshed with cultural expressions, and is formalized in authoritative institutions and economic structures. Gender norms influence kinship, work, politics, education, and ideology, in turn shaping our ideas about the masculine and feminine. Given the complex interaction among so many elements, the relationship between masculinity and its myriad influences is dialectical.[12] Examining one piece of the puzzle in isolation distorts its meaning, as we can only adequately understand each component within the framework of an interlocking dynamic whole.[13] By looking at the particularities of each manifestation of manhood, taking into account all the relevant factors regarding context and individual agency, it is possible to gain a better understanding of the masculinities that have evolved over time.

CHINESE MASCULINITIES

To appreciate this topic within the Chinese context, we must break free from a long history of facile Western stereotypes. During the nineteenth century, as the West surged economically, European and American views toward China hardened into outright contempt. Intellectual luminaries such as G. W. F. Hegel, Karl Marx, and Max Weber all dismissed China as a stagnant backwater isolated from the mainstream of historical progress. Of course, writing off China implied that the nation's manhood had failed as well.[14] Orientalist assumptions that Chinese men are innately effeminate, as seen in the fascination with androgyny, have conditioned Western scholarship.[15] A patronizing

English gentlemen shocked by Chinese manhood. *Source:* John Merson, *Roads to Xanadu: East and West in the Making of the Modern World* (London: Weidenfeld and Nicolson, 1989), 145.

attitude toward Chinese manhood has also infiltrated Western popular culture. Books and movies have long portrayed Chinese men as decadent, prissy, or evil. Until recently, Hollywood usually cast Chinese men as either servile domestics speaking pidgin English or malevolent personifications of Yellow Peril.[16]

Of course, we cannot reduce the numerous manifestations of manhood in such an ancient and complex society to simplistic stereotypes, whether negative or positive. Chinese masculinities have always been highly diverse and mutable. Moreover, the scale of Chinese civilization is immense in both time and space. In temporal terms, an unbroken legacy of literate culture extends back thousands of years to high antiquity. Ideas and writings from the distant past continuously influenced the behavior of later generations, just as ancient paragons of manhood continue to inspire men today. The spatial scope of Chineseness is equally vast. Sichuan is just one of more than thirty province-level administrative units in China; yet, it is far more populous than Germany, the largest European country. Viewed from the standpoint of world history, China stands out for its size, antiquity, and diversity. This exceptional scale must inform any discussion of the history of Chinese masculinities, as it provided ample room for an impressive variety of male identities. Some manifestations of maleness remained confined to a small area or soon disappeared, while others flourished and exerted widespread influence.

A comprehensive list of various Chinese masculinities would be impossibly long. Nevertheless, a few key factors can help point the way to understanding some widespread practices. One of the most salient traits of Chinese society is the importance of kinship. Of course bonds of blood and marriage hold together every society. But whereas these ties usually fray as a society increases in complexity, in China kin relations remained uncommonly strong even with urbanization and economic development. Chinese valued kin relations so much that they frequently extended them by creating fictive kinship bonds, pretending that nonrelatives were kinsmen to expand the circle of trusted intimates.[17] Men treated close friends as brothers, gang members swore blood oaths to create fictive families, and a same-sex couple might forge a ritual kinship bond.[18] Historical Chinese manhood is inseparable from this dense network of real and fictive kinship ties. Normative masculinities had to fit into these kinship structures to gain acceptance.

Perhaps the greatest influence of kinship on maleness has been the importance of filial piety. Ever since antiquity, deference to senior kin, especially parents, has constituted a paramount virtue. The elevation of filial piety to a preeminent masculine ideal marks a radical distinction between manhood in China and the West.[19] Although originally directed toward one's father, over time this virtue expanded to include the mother as well.[20] As long as a man's parents were alive, the community expected him to treat them with respect and a degree of deference and even to continue living with them in a multigenerational family. Filial piety has had an immense impact on what it means to be a man in China. In many cultures, a man proclaims his entry to adulthood by aggressively asserting independence from his parents. In contrast, to some extent the Chinese man always remains a child in relation to his parents.[21] He proves his maturity by subsuming his desire for autonomy, thereby demonstrating a manly strength of will.

Some scholars have argued that the unusually strong links between adult men and their parents constitute the premier hallmark of Chinese male identity.[22] As long as a parent is alive, a man remains confined to a juvenile role within the family. Of course the exigencies of filial piety create tensions, as adult men inevitably chafe at parental whims. On the other hand, the savvy man can manipulate the image of the virtuous son to his advantage. Filial piety is not just a duty but also an opportunity. Some men become celebrated for their filial piety, winning not only fame but also social advancement. Publicly sacrificing oneself for the sake of one's parents has long been a standard strategy for gaining prestige and approbation.[23]

Another striking characteristic of Chinese masculinities has been the engagement between manhood and the state, for elite men in particular. Starting in antiquity, men of status and talent hoped to obtain a post in government. Besides bringing wealth and power, acceptance into official service publicly confirmed successful manhood. While men elsewhere might earn the greatest respect by participating in religion or commerce, traditionally Chinese men saw a government post as the best way to construct and display an ideal male image. In consequence, elite men and the state developed an intense symbiotic relationship. Men used government service to prove their manhood, and the state helped them cultivate an aura of successful masculinity in return for their aid in controlling a fractious society. The benefit of this close relationship to each side helps explain one of the greatest puzzles of Chinese history—how such an enormous polity remained intact for so many centuries. Large states in other regions often rapidly imploded under their own weight. But in China, buttressing the masculine public image of the state's key backers helped win the support of the elite, thereby maintaining stability for centuries at a time.[24]

In fact, identification with the state was so strong among the elite that they deemed a highly qualified man's decision to forgo government service a considerable hardship. Although Confucianism discouraged criticism of government policies by those outside officialdom, a qualified candidate could implicitly protest the current state of affairs by refusing office. This practice became common in the Eastern Han dynasty, as the quality of administration declined and the government lost support among the landowning elite. Every subsequent era of discontent saw a similar withdrawal of talented men from public life. The accomplished would declare themselves recluses and refuse to seek office, often turning to personal cultivation for consolation. Recluses put forth an alternate vision of successful masculinity, emphasizing the overriding importance of moral courage and unsullied rectitude. Pained discussions of the importance of flawless personal integrity versus duty toward the state, which inevitably required ethical compromises, were in fact debates over the nature of elite manhood.[25]

Yet another major theme in the history of Chinese manhood is the significance of economic change. Sociologists note that economic organization has a heavy influence on manifestations of masculinity. As the economy changes, expressions of manhood inevitably respond.[26] For example, the rise of the commercial economy in China produced new social groups, such as wealthy merchants and poor urban day laborers. Many of the previous ideals of manhood, grounded in agriculture and government service, were irrelevant to these men's lives. They had no choice but to seek new ways to construct a favorable masculine image. Ultimately the rise of capitalism led to an even greater transformation of gender ideals. The Confucian gentleman was a completely inappropriate role model for the new middle class that flourished in Shanghai during the 1930s. Ambitious businessmen rejected many aspects of traditional Chinese manhood, embracing westernized ideals amenable to commerce and middle-class life.

Foreign influence is a final major theme in the history of Chinese masculinities. Chinese have traditionally held a contradictory view of their place in the world. Although they considered China the center of the world, they often regarded other peoples with suspicion and repeatedly tried to shut themselves off. Even so, successive waves of foreign influence have washed across China, repeatedly provoking reassessments of what it means to be a man. Invasions by nomadic peoples were particularly traumatic, as their alien masculine ideals were deeply at odds with those of a literate, agricultural, urban people. The adoption of Buddhism was equally destabilizing, as Chinese confronted disorienting views of masculinity emanating from an equally sophisticated civilization. More recently, Western imperialism and global capitalism have challenged Chinese manhood. China's initial failure in confronting the West in the nineteenth century led to a vigorous reassessment of traditional views of manhood. Chinese deliberately abandoned many time-tested beliefs about maleness as backward and inconsistent with the modern world, replacing them with masculine models imported from the West, as well as homegrown versions of masculinity appropriate to China's new circumstances.

This brief summary of some of the forces conditioning Chinese manhood can only introduce a few of the most important themes. Even so, the masculinities to which these factors gave rise have been fantastically diverse. Because there have been so many different expressions of masculinity in China, it would be both futile and tedious to try to catalog them all in one volume. Instead, this book provides a general overview of manhood in Chinese history by focusing on a handful of carefully chosen masculinities. Each chapter concentrates on a particular type of manhood situated in a different era of China's past, thereby providing both temporal and thematic focus. By sampling different practices and periods, the reader can gain a sense of the range of Chinese masculinities and appreciate how changing conditions in economy, society, religion, and politics repeatedly gave rise to innovative ideals of manhood.

NOTES

1. Joan W. Scott, "Gender: A Useful Category of Historical Analysis," *American Historical Review* 91, no. 5 (1986): 1053–75, provides an eloquent justification for stressing gender in historical analysis.

2. For an overview of the rise of masculinity studies, see Rachel Adams and David Savran, "Introduction," in *The Masculinity Studies Reader* (Malden, MA: Blackwell, 2002), 1–8; R. W. Connell, *Masculinities*, 2nd ed. (Berkeley: University of California Press, 2005), xiv–xxiv.

3. Connell, *Masculinities*, 68.

4. W. J. F. Jenner, *A Knife in the Ribs for a Mate: Reflections on Another Chinese Tradition* (Canberra: Australian National University, 1993), 10.

5. Even some scholars have argued that gender identity is firmly grounded in the physical differences between male and female. Alice S. Rossi, "Gender and Parenthood," in *Gender and the Life Course*, ed. Alice S. Rossi (New York: Aldine, 1985), 161. Others take a related approach and emphasize gendered characteristics in the mind, arguing that the basis of gender identity lies in universal male and female psychological essences. Nancy J. Chodorow, "Gender as a Personal and Cultural Construction," *Signs* 20, no. 3 (1995): 516–41.

6. For a critique of various definitions of masculinity, see R. W. Connell, "The Big Picture: Masculinities in Recent World History," *Theory and Society* 22, no. 5 (1993): 598–603.

7. Matthew C. Gutmann, "Trafficking in Men: The Anthropology of Masculinity," *Annual Review of Anthropology* 26 (1997): 386. Connell, *Masculinities*, 68–70, puts forward a critical typology of the main approaches. Also see Scott, "Gender," 1067; R. W. Connell, "Theorizing Gender," *Sociology* 19, no. 2 (1985): 263.

8. David D. Gilmore, *Manhood in the Making: Cultural Concepts of Masculinity* (New Haven, CT: Yale University Press, 1990), 11–12.

9. Martin W. Huang, *Negotiating Masculinities in Late Imperial China* (Honolulu: University of Hawaii Press, 2006), 8.

10. Connell, *Masculinities*, 37.

11. Mike Donaldson, "What Is Hegemonic Masculinity," *Theory and Society* 22, no. 5 (1993): 655. For the origins of the concept of hegemonic masculinity, see R. W. Connell and James W. Messerschmidt, "Hegemonic Masculinity: Rethinking the Concept," *Gender and Society* 19, no. 6 (2005): 830–32.

12. Connell, *Masculinities*, 37.

13. Robert A. Nye, "Kinship, Male Bonds, and Masculinity in Comparative Perspective," *American Historical Review* 105, no. 5 (2000): 1656.

14. Harvey Goldman, "Images of the Other: Asia in Nineteenth-Century Western Thought—Hegel, Marx and Weber," in *Asia in Western and World History: A Guide for Teaching*, ed. Ainslie Thomas Embree and Carol Gluck (Armonk, NY: M. E. Sharpe, 1997), 146.

15. Gilmore, *Manhood in the Making*, 170.

16. Philippa Gates, *Detecting Men: Masculinity and the Hollywood Detective Film* (Albany: State University of New York Press, 2006), 78.

17. Philip C. Huang, *The Peasant Economy and Social Change in North China* (Stanford, CA: Stanford University Press, 1985), 261.

18. David Ownby, *Brotherhoods and Secret Societies in Early and Mid-Qing China: The Formation of a Tradition* (Stanford, CA: Stanford University Press, 1996), 41; Xu Xiaowang, "Cong 'Mindu bieji' kan gudai dongnan de tongxinglian wenti," *Lishi yuekan* 133 (February 1999), 101–7.

19. Donald Holzman, "The Place of Filial Piety in Ancient China," *Journal of the American Oriental Society* 118, no. 2 (1998): 185–99; Keith Nathaniel Knapp, *Selfless Offspring: Filial Children and Social Order in Medieval China* (Honolulu: University of Hawaii Press, 2005).

20. For one example, see Alan Cole, *Mothers and Sons in Chinese Buddhism* (Stanford, CA: Stanford University Press, 1998).

21. David Y. F. Ho, "Fatherhood in Chinese Culture," in *The Father's Role: Cross-Cultural Perspectives*, ed. Michael E. Lamb (London: Routledge, 1987), 240.

22. Gilmore, *Manhood in the Making*, 170, notes that some Western observers believe that in China, filial piety subsumes masculinity. Even in the martial culture of ancient China, achievement in war came second to filial piety as an expression of admirable manhood. Yiqun Zhou, *Festivals, Feasts, and Gender Relations in Ancient China and Greece* (Cambridge: Cambridge University Press, 2010), 127.

23. Wu Hung, *Monumentality in Early Chinese Art and Architecture* (Stanford, CA: Stanford University Press, 1995), 196, discusses how elite Han dynasty men cleverly used the construction of a funerary monument for a parent to celebrate their own filial piety, shifting focus away from the parent they were supposedly commemorating and toward their own filial virtue. Also see Angela Zito, *Of Body and Brush: Grand Sacrifice as Text/ Performance in Eighteenth-Century China* (Chicago: University of Chicago Press, 1997), 204.

24. Benjamin A. Elman, "Political, Social, and Cultural Reproduction via Civil Service Examinations in Late Imperial China," *Journal of Asian Studies* 50, no. 1 (1991): 7–28.

25. Alan J. Berkowitz, *Patterns of Disengagement: The Practice and Portrayal of Reclusion in Early Medieval China* (Stanford, CA: Stanford University Press, 2000).

26. Tim Carrigan, Bob Connell, and John Lee, "Toward a New Sociology of Masculinity," *Theory and Society* 14, no. 5 (1985): 551–604, discusses the impact of economic change on ideas about masculinity.

1

※※

Zhou Dynasty (1046–256 BCE)
Separation of the Sexes

In the wake of feminist politics, it has become the convention to downplay differences between the sexes as much as possible and assert that women and men are fundamentally similar. However, in historic China the opposite view prevailed. From high antiquity, thinking about gender was conditioned by the assumption, deeply held and virtually universal, that men and women are extremely different. Corollaries to this supposition profoundly shaped the contours and development of society. Chinese considered it mere common sense that men and women ought to differ in almost every aspect of life, including kinship roles, jobs, duties, and privileges, as well as education, legal status, and control over wealth. Elaborate bodies of ritual, elite thought, religion, law, and popular custom systematically enforced these starkly delineated gender identities, which went far beyond any differences grounded in physiology.

During the Zhou dynasty (ca. 1046–256 BCE), rhetoric about gender differentiation reached a high degree of sophistication. Separation of the sexes (*nannü youbie*) implied not only that men and women should receive different treatment but also that they ought to maintain a degree of physical separation for the sake of propriety. Originally grounded in practical concerns, such as gendered work roles, this pragmatic custom of separation grew over time into a valorized keystone of ethics, justified by parallels drawn to the natural world via cosmology and metaphysics.[1] Discourse about the differences between men and women served as the fundamental prolegomenon for emerging ideas about masculinity.

WORK ROLES

It seems that separation of the sexes dates back far beyond the historian's ken, developing alongside gendered work patterns in remote prehistory. Anthropological fieldwork has shown that division of labor based on sex is the norm in economically simple societies throughout the world. Gendered division of labor boosts productivity by increasing work specialization, while allotting fixed roles to each person fosters social stability. Generally speaking, women take on those tasks they can perform in tandem with child care. These include cooking and cleaning, tending a kitchen garden, weaving cloth, plaiting baskets, coiling pottery, and so on. Activities conducted farther away from the home, such as hunting and tending grain fields, become customary male labor.[2] When men and women perform different routine tasks, separate work roles tend to keep the sexes apart for much of the day.

Such seems to have been the case in the northern region of China during prehistory. For example, graves from the Neolithic Peiligang culture dating to between 6000 and 5000 BCE contain quotidian items used by the deceased. Some graves have hunting weapons as well as agricultural tools, while others hold the implements used to remove millet husks prior to cooking. Archaeologists have concluded that these different grave goods reflect gendered labor, with men hunting and growing grain while women worked near the home.[3] This archaeological evidence suggests that long before the advent of written records, men and women were already spending much of the day apart because they often worked in different places. The pragmatic allocation of work roles along gender lines formed the earliest substrate of what later became an enforced separation of the sexes.

During the Eastern Zhou era (771–256 BCE), the division of labor underwent an important shift. Whereas the gendering of work roles had previously been nothing more than a mundane custom, the strict division of labor between women and men became elevated into a moral ideal. Moralists now saw it as virtuous for women and men to perform the tasks appropriate to their sex and considered a society oriented around stereotypical gendered work roles to be ethically grounded and guaranteed to succeed. Although this culture specifically delegated many kinds of work either to women or men, moralists seized on one task as normative for each sex, stressing that in a well-ordered society, men plow the fields while women weave cloth. Of course men also planted, weeded, irrigated, and harvested, while women cleaned, cooked, and looked after children. Nevertheless, just one task came to symbolize the proper work of each sex, so the shorthand phrase "men plow, women weave" (*nangeng nüzhi*) came to stand for gendered labor in general.[4] As men and women performed these two key tasks in different places, extolling gendered labor also infused the physical separation of the sexes with an air of implicit virtue. In this way, the

Man plowing. *Source*: Wang Jianzhong, *Handai huaxiangshi tonglun* (Beijing: Zijincheng, 2001), 389.

gendered division of labor gradually developed into a far more comprehensive ideology serving as a fundamental framework for gender relations.

The fifth-century BCE thinker Mo Di, better known as Mozi, was one of the first thinkers to elevate stereotypical gendered work roles into a lofty social principle worthy of elite discourse.[5] Mozi argued that because plowing and weaving are fundamental occupations, men and women should be encouraged to devote themselves to these tasks so that society can become prosperous. Abandoning these key economic roles to pursue marginal work, such as producing useless luxury goods, would bring shortages and hardship.

This practical reasoning appealed to Legalist thinkers, who referred to plowing and weaving as the basic occupations (*benye*). According to the *Writings of Lord Shang* (*Shangjun shu*), traditionally attributed to Shang Yang (d. 338 BCE), division of labor served as an important engine of social development.[6] In the distant past, the natural environment had been far more salubrious, so human beings initially lived simple and easy lives. As conditions deteriorated, however, people faced terrible hardship. In response to the worsening environment, the wise mythical sage ruler Shennong taught men to plow and women to weave, thereby giving them the means to survive and even prosper. So to the Legalists, gendered labor allowed humanity to emerge from savagery and develop an industrious civilization. Although this ideal of a society grounded in male plowing and female weaving originated with Mohist and Legalist discourse, thinkers of virtually all orientations eventually adopted it, and it became a standard point of reference for discussing well-ordered gender relations.

GENDERED SPACE

The assumption that men and women ought to pursue different work steadily extended in scope, eventually giving rise to the belief that physical separation of the sexes is inherently virtuous. It seems that Chinese culture originally lacked an ideal of gender segregation. The ancient *Classic of Poetry* (*Shijing*) depicts a naive rural society in which women and men mingled freely,[7] a spirit of openness gradually lost over time. Because men and women tended to perform gendered tasks in different areas and practicing these normative occupations expressed virtue, it came to be considered righteous to keep men and women apart. As a result, "separation of the sexes" expanded to denote not just work roles but physical segregation as well. The *Classic of Changes* (*Yijing*) succinctly sums up this moral principle: "Among family members, women's proper place is inside and man's proper place is outside."[8]

During the Eastern Zhou and early Han eras, ritualists redacted hundreds of disparate rules and theories about standard behavior into several collections that became integrated into the Confucian tradition.[9] Ritual specialists held that performing standardized ceremonies grounded in ethical principles fostered social order while also transforming a person's moral inclinations. By regulating behavior from youth onward, the rites turned virtuous behaviors into deep-seated habits and reflexive emotions, thereby molding character. In embracing separation of the sexes and propounding specific rules for its enforcement, this body of writing had an immense impact on the relations between men and women.

Ritual works described in great detail how to keep women and men apart. Control of the body, particularly the female body, was the primary means for enforcing gender separation. These rules, seen most clearly in the *Records of Rites* (*Liji*), were sweepingly comprehensive, dictating that even siblings or spouses should keep some space between them. If followed to the letter, these instructions would surely have had the desired effect.

> Male and female should not sit together (in the same apartment), nor have the same stand or rack for their clothes, nor use the same towel or comb, nor let their hands touch in giving and receiving . . . Outside affairs should not be talked of inside the threshold (of the women's apartments), nor inside (or women's) affairs outside it. . . . When a married aunt, or sister, or daughter returns home (on a visit), no brother (of the family) should sit with her on the same mat or eat with her from the same dish. (Even) the father and daughter should not occupy the same mat.[10]

If married couples were supposed to remain physically separate, except in their most intimate moments, restrictions on interactions between unrelated women and men would of course be even greater.

As it was inappropriate for the sexes to mingle freely, women became increasingly confined to the home. Women of lesser means were to retreat inside when not engaged in unavoidable work that took her outside. In mansions of the wealthy, where some areas functioned almost as public spaces, men expected their wives and daughters to remain cloistered within the inner recesses of the home forbidden to unrelated males. Isolating women deep inside the domestic quarters became a deeply held cultural ideal that endured to the end of imperial history.[11]

The burden of gender segregation fell mostly on women. Whereas men enjoyed access to the outside world with all its opportunities, women remained sequestered inside. Of course, for the majority of women, who lived in families of humble means, keeping completely apart from men was impractical. They had to perform necessary activities such as drawing water from a public well, washing clothes in a nearby stream, or tending a vegetable patch, all in public under the potentially humiliating male gaze. For women of higher status, who did not have to work outside, staying hidden from men was a source of pride for them and their families. Chinese society admired elite households that kept their women in isolation, and it celebrated a woman who expressed her determination to keep away from unrelated men as a paragon of female virtue.

With women largely confined to the home while men pursued a variety of activities elsewhere, different locations became associated with each sex. Although the early classics did not emphasize the connection of specific places with gender, during the late Zhou it became common to contrast feminized

Woman weaving. *Source:* Wang, *Handai huaxiangshi tonglun*, 393.

"inner" (*nei*) space with the masculine "outer" (*wai*) realm beyond the home.[12] The association of gender with place became so important that "inner" became a common epithet to describe women in general. Of course the division of space worked to the benefit of men. While sexual segregation confined women to hidden regions apart from centers of economic, cultural, and political power, men spent much of their time in important "outer" spaces. Physical segregation became one of the most important distinctions between the sexes and a crucial source of enduring male privilege.

While women often chafed at their confinement, the requirement to venture outside safe and familiar domestic spaces sometimes imposed a burden on men. In response, men stressed homosocial bonds as relationships among men intensified in response to the difficulties of navigating the outside world.[13] With women removed from the loci of public life, relations among men became critical to masculine identity. Instead of positioning male identity vis-à-vis invisible women, a man lived out his life for the most part in a segregated world composed of other men. Winning the approval of a male audience was vital for constructing an honorable masculine identity.

SEGREGATION AND MORALITY

Confining half the population indoors was an extreme ambition and so required persuasive rationalizations. Although separation of the sexes began as a pragmatic economic practice, Eastern Zhou thinkers made this ancient custom a moral imperative, justifying what began as a convenient arrangement of gendered work roles as separation of the sexes for the sake of ethical purity. They assumed that although men and women could both be good, the ideal behavior of each sex varied due to their different proclivities, normative social roles, and ways of life. The ritual canon is replete with picayune rules governing the proper behavior of women and men, not just in daily life but also on special occasions such as funerals and religious sacrifices.

Although few people ever observed these rules to the letter, many believed that maintaining such distinctions set one apart as a particularly good person. Even when not systematically observed, ritual rules governing gender separation served as a point of reference that shaped gender relations down through the centuries. Historical narratives argued that free mingling between the sexes invariably brought about enervating decadence that could ruin a state; one such narrative attributed the infamous ruin of King You of Zhou (r. 781–771 BCE) to "women causing chaos inside and barbarians attacking outside."[14] Failure to regulate space properly according to gender could lead to catastrophe.

To avoid this terrifying outcome, ritual specialists sought to impose ethical social norms on women and men. This detailed body of rules attracted considerable contemplation and debate as the embodiment of the behavioral models guaranteeing a good and successful society. Ritual theory assumed that behavior ought to vary according to social station, and a major goal of the rites was enforcing proper hierarchies between people of different status. Given this supposition, it is not surprising that the ritual canon sought to compel men and women to interact in an unequal manner, with the good woman voluntarily hiding herself in the inner recesses of the household and assuming a submissive demeanor toward her husband and senior in-laws.

Separation of the sexes justified the suppression of female autonomy, implicitly raising male status in the gender system. For example, the *Records of Rites* demands immense sacrifices on a woman's part if she is to be considered a good family member.

> No daughter-in-law, without being told to go to her own apartment, should venture to withdraw from that (of her parents-in-law). Whatever she is about to do, she should ask leave from them. . . . If anyone gives the wife an article of food, or dress, a piece of cloth or silk, a handkerchief for her girdle, an iris or orchid, she should receive and offer it to her parents-in-law. If they accept it, she will be glad as if she were receiving it afresh. If they return it to her, she should decline it, and if they do not allow her to do so, she will take it as if it were a second gift, and lay it by to wait till they may want it.[15]

The author of this passage knew that few women would ever actually practice such superhuman humility. But ritualists did not intend to describe real behavior. Instead they sought to set down the highest possible standards to which ordinary people ought to aspire. The message of this and similar passages is clear. A woman should ideally hide herself within the recesses of the home, sacrifice her desires so she could cater to her husband and his kin, and obey her spouse and senior in-laws. Conversely, a man was free to leave the home and enter the wider world, pursue personal interests apart from his family, and exercise authority over his wife. Separation of the sexes had become a justification for wide-ranging masculine privilege.[16]

COSMOLOGY

When we think of men and women as fundamentally different, it is a short mental step to assume that a unique essence defines each sex. This way of thinking does not conceive of people as unique individuals characterized by a wide range of traits. More fundamentally, in this view gender profoundly conditions each person, providing core identity and character. So instead of emphasizing individuality, Chinese convention traditionally saw a person as a representative of his or her gendered inclinations, social roles, and expectations. Of course the division between the sexes was not always clear-cut, and many people acknowledged that men and women could share certain traits and behaviors.[17] Nevertheless, elite thinkers far more frequently argued that the sexes are fundamentally different.

Because it was customary to understand people in terms of their gender, early thinkers came to think of the concepts of man (*nan*) and woman (*nü*) (or male/female) as essences that one could discuss in isolation. Instead of viewing female and male through real people, with their complexities and contradictions, theses thinkers often conceived of gender as a simple binary essence. Essentializing gender made it possible to discuss male and female in highly theoretical terms, untroubled by the complex personalities of actual people, and to project the resulting intellectual constructs into elaborate metaphysical systems. Abstracting gender discourse to such a high degree allowed early thinkers to understand masculinity through artificial intellectual systems with little reference to real circumstances.

Once it had become conventional to simplify male and female into abstract binary terms, Zhou thinkers began to project gender onto the metaphysical pairings integral to major intellectual systems of the day.[18] Binary thought was a fundamental trait of early Chinese philosophy. Regardless of academic orientation, thinkers of various schools shared an assumption that dualistic phenomena underlie the visible world and condition its workings, and they struggled to resolve the messy ambiguities of the real world into aesthetically pleasing pairs.[19] Enormous effort went into identifying and analyzing these dualities, with debates erupting over their basic definition, characteristics, influence, and relative priority.

Binary does not necessarily imply equal. As elite thinkers relentlessly divided the cosmos into numerous component pairs, they usually imagined them as hierarchies, with one element exercising priority or dominance over the other. According to the prevailing reasoning, one element of the gender dyad must be superior to the other. The masculine, whatever its identity in a particular system, thus became elevated into a favored term. When applied to politics and society, these hierarchical cosmological systems could readily justify male privilege and female subservience.

Aside from the paradigmatic pair of male (*nan*) and female (*nü*), three other concepts central to early metaphysics also assumed gendered identities: Heaven/Earth, yin/yang, and *qian/kun*. Although the identities and functions of these terms differ somewhat, each pair occupied a central place within a major intellectual system, thereby injecting gender into the heart of discourse about the nature of the cosmos. Although these discursive frameworks emerged during the Zhou, their popularity remained undiminished over time. For centuries, elite thinkers and ordinary people used these concepts as points of reference for understanding and navigating the world. These paired ideas have continued to influence popular and religious thinking down to the present and impact Chinese gender discourse even today.

Although Heaven (*tian*) and Earth (*di*) are obviously concrete realities, these basic cosmological elements took on abstract identities as well, allowing thinkers to incorporate them into metaphysical systems as representatives of abstract concepts. Metaphysicians presumed that this pair is both the source of and engine driving the vital force (*qi*) constituting the "ten thousand things" of the material world. Interaction between Heaven and Earth continuously influence every aspect of the material world. As these interfaces tend to be regular, nature exhibits a high degree of stability and predictability.

In the earliest texts, Heaven and Earth are usually unrelated to gender. Ancient Chinese worshipped Earth as a deity associated with fertility, giving it a vague association with the feminine. Heaven, by far the greater element in the pair, had been revered as a supreme god since high antiquity. Initially, Earth and Heaven were not discussed in tandem, as they were regarded as completely separate forces or deities.[20] During the Eastern Zhou, however, thinkers began to discuss the two as a dyad, using their interaction to explain key aspects of the natural and human worlds. When they came to be thought of together as a pair, the terms took on an overtly gendered identity. Heaven was by far the more important term, so it assumed the senior position in the hierarchy. As earlier thought had linked Earth to the feminine, sometimes envisioned as a mother, Heaven became its paternal masculine counterpart.[21]

This pair also interacted with humanity, not only influencing human beings but also serving as a template for human ethics and relationships.[22] Influential writers asserted that people ought to imitate Heaven and Earth. Of course mere people are very different from these grand cosmic entities, so literally resembling Heaven or Earth was physically impossible. Instead this exhortation pursued a far more modest goal of modeling social relationships on the orderly hierarchy of Heaven and Earth. Ritual regulations were sometimes based on celestial regularities, hence applying the stately patterns underlying the cosmos to social regulation.[23]

The assumption that society should emulate this cosmic pair had a major influence on gender norms.[24] For example, the *Laozi* declares that human beings should imitate Earth, Earth should imitate Heaven, and Heaven should be modeled after the ineffable Way (*dao*) underlying all reality.[25] The arrangement of these three terms into a hierarchy demonstrates the assumption that masculine Heaven is superior to feminine Earth. Accordingly, it stood to reason that in proper management of the human world, men should take precedence over women.

Another binary construct that assumed gendered characteristics, known as *qian* and *kun*, is a product of the intricate divination system of the *Classic of Changes* (*Yijing*).[26] This work gradually accreted around sixty-four abstract symbols, known as hexagrams, composed of different combinations of six broken or unbroken lines. The hexagrams in turn comprise eight simpler trigrams, each with three broken or unbroken lines. As the basic building blocks of this complex system, each trigram evolved a complex identity subject to enormous amounts of commentary amassed layer by layer over the centuries. By far the most important of the trigrams are the two simplest and most basic: *qian* (three unbroken lines) and *kun* (three broken lines).

The *Classic of Changes* system had many uses. When used as a straightforward divination tool, the trigrams provided profound insights into the basic nature of the universe, worthy of sustained reflection. As scholars elaborated the original ideas in the classic, they applied the system to compelling ethical and social concerns. Over time the two most important trigrams became steadily associated with male and female, bringing gender into the heart of this symbolic system. This is not to say that *qian* simply means man and *kun* means woman. The system of the *Classic of Changes* is so abstract that one cannot draw direct one-to-one links with gender. Instead, the commentarial tradition educed subtle relations between these two trigrams and gender while evoking numerous other qualities as well.

The elusiveness of these concepts helps explain their perennial appeal. Irreduceable to simplistic definitions, *qian* and *kun* evoke a wide range of connotations depending on the user's predilections. Although opposites, the meanings of this interlocking pair were often relational. This binary structure made them seem similar to male and female, to which the system's users regularly compared them.[27]

These two terms form a hierarchy, with masculine *qian* always coming before feminine *kun*. Each exhibits traits highlighting their fundamental inequality. As *Qian* is strong, it rules and initiates. In comparison, *kun* is relatively weak and merely shelters and completes.[28] These characteristics conformed to prevalent gender stereotypes, making *qian/kun* a convenient analog for gender. The *Changes* system also integrated many aspects of Confucian ethics, using this abstract cosmology to bolster an ethical tradition that privileged the interests of patrilineal kinship institutions and men in general.[29]

The third abstract pair at the foundations of Chinese metaphysics, yin and yang, began as little more than terms referring to the lighter and darker parts of a landscape.[30] For example, one might describe the shaded northern slope of a mountain as yin and the southern exposure as yang. As neither bright nor dark is absolute, early thinkers understood the two in contrast to one another, thereby as forming an inseparable dyad. Zhou thinkers pondering the nature of the universe adopted and redefined this pair to encompass a range of abstract meanings and connotations. As tradition had understood yin and yang in tandem as descriptions of relative brightness, Zhou metaphysicians could readily adapt them to express cosmic phenomena that appear together yet alternate in relative intensity.

The trigrams: *qian* (top) is specifically related to yang, and *kun* (bottom) to yin.
Source: Lai Zhide 來知德, *Zhouyi jizhu* 周易集注, annotated by Zhang Wanbin
張萬彬 (Beijing: Jiuzhou, 2004), 840.

Early Chinese thinkers commonly redefined standard key concepts in innovative ways to make them fit a favored intellectual system. One of the greatest intellectual projects of the Zhou was the search for an abstract schema of interactive elements that could account for the regularities observed in the natural and human worlds. Binary terms were a focus of this quest, with yin and yang particularly popular. Thinkers of Confucian, Daoist, Huanglao and other persuasions all referred to yin and yang in their writings, each using them a bit differently. Most famously, the third-century BCE thinker Zou Yan made yin and yang the centerpiece of a comprehensive cosmological system, elevating the terms to unprecedented importance and explicating them with unprecedented clarity.

As with the other paired elements, yin and yang represented a wide range of physical, medical, moral, psychological, and cosmological phenomena. Because these two characters are inherently ambiguous, they can describe almost anything divisible into two interactive parts that alternate in influence, including male and female.[31] However, yang does not simply mean male; nor does yin have a simplistic correspondence with woman or female. While obliquely associated with gender, the two abstractions concurrently maintain myriad other implications as well.

As abstract systems of thought proliferated and increased in complexity, the link between yin/yang and gender came to influence how elite thinkers and ordinary people thought about the ideal relations between the sexes. Of course people living in an agricultural society consider sunlight far preferable to darkness, so from the beginning yang was the more positive term. Seeing dark female yin as inferior to bright male yang provided yet another metaphysical justification for patriarchy. Thinkers such as the influential Dong Zhongshu (179–104 BCE), who blended yin/yang theory together with Confucian discourse, used metaphysics to legitimate man's domination of woman.[32]

Not only were yin/yang, Heaven/Earth, and *qian/kun* the axes of different metaphysical systems, but thinkers also sometimes discussed these three pairs together or inserted them into even larger conceptual schemes. For example, some asserted that *qian* and *kun* imitate Heaven and Earth.[33] As metaphysicians came to think of these three dyads as cosmic templates for the masculine and feminine, it seemed reasonable to assume that they were also parallel to each other. Combining these three pairs or referring to them within the same work gave authors a rich arsenal of rhetorical tools for asserting masculine privilege.

We cannot exaggerate the significance of these intellectual constructs. Cosmological dualism became the basic template for the intellectual substrate underlying gender discourse. As seen from the various pairs that evoked gender within abstract systems of thought, thinkers saw masculine and feminine as fundamentally different yet locked together as an interactive pair. They understood the identity of each not just according to a fixed essence but also in relation to the other element in the dyad. Although both male and female are necessary, one takes primacy. Just as the three major pairs of metaphysical concepts were hierarchies, so were men the social, intellectual, and physical superiors of women. Throughout imperial history, numerous prominent thinkers referred to these three fundamental binary constructs to justify male superiority.

The practice of using portents to criticize female influence shows the concrete power of these intellectual abstractions.[34] According to early Chinese historiography, Heaven employs unusual natural events such as earthquakes, eclipses, and floods to communicate its displeasure with the state of human affairs. Theorists assumed that these catastrophes were caused by malfunctions in the normally smooth interactions between binary cosmic pairs such as yin and yang. Because these forces were associated with gender, it became common for officials to use natural disasters to argue that an excess of female influence (yin or *kun*) had put the cosmos out of balance. A calamity could therefore be interpreted as a divine portent utilized by Heaven to express cosmic displeasure toward the excessive influence of a powerful imperial consort. If one assumes that the world is controlled by interlocking series of abstract systems built around interactive dyads, it seems reasonable to conclude that an excess of the female element can lead to disaster. Through this sort of reasoning, portent theorists turned gendered metaphysics into a sophisticated ideology that could be deployed to keep powerful women in check.

These metaphysical pairs are not entirely negative portrayals of the feminine. In each case, the feminine element is as necessary as its masculine counterpart, and each complements the other within both the natural order and society. Nor did Chinese thinkers base the separation of the sexes on a view that women were unimportant. They believed women had vital social duties but should be treated differently from men. Both gender separation and dualistic cosmology imply that the female is not just normative but crucial for the proper functioning of the world. And just as the gendered elements in cosmological systems alternate in intensity, so too can the dividing line between male and female at times seem nebulous. As these beliefs see the feminine as a vital element integral to the proper functioning of the cosmos, we cannot dismiss them as crude misogyny. The overall message is far subtler: although the female element is good and necessary, it remains inferior to the male.

These prominent cosmological schemata, set down during the formative axial age of Chinese thought, provided basic templates for thinking about manhood and laid the ideological framework used to discuss how men ought to relate to women. Dualistic intellectual systems implied that men ought to remain aloof from women and restrict female access to the loci of wealth and power. Just as Heaven, yang, and *qian* hold priority over their feminine counterparts in the cosmological realm, so man ought to be superior to woman in society. This elaborate ideological substrate, based on natural metaphors and idealized social roles, constituted the basic intellectual stencil upon which subsequent ideas about masculinity emerged.

NOTES

1. For a general overview of the subject, see Bret Hinsch, "The Origins of Separation of the Sexes in China," *Journal of the American Oriental Society* 123, no. 3 (2003): 595–616.

2. Judith K. Brown, "A Note on the Division of Labor by Sex," *American Anthropologist* 72 (1970): 1073–78.

3. An Jinhuai, *Zhongguo kaogu* (1992; rpt. Taipei: Nantian, 1996), 76. Many types of labor are still associated with gender in China. Tamara Jacka, *Women's Work in Rural China* (Cambridge: Cambridge University Press, 1997), 194.

4. Xu Jieshun, "Hanzu gudai nangeng nüzhi jingji jiegoulun," *Liaozhou Shifan xuebao* 16, no. 4 (2001): 80–84.

5. Tan Jiajian, *Mozi yanjiu* (Guiyang: Guizhou jiaoyu, 1995), 125–32; Yang Kuan, *Zhanguoshi* (Taipei: Taiwan shangwu, 1997), 85.

6. Anonymous, *Shangjun shu* (Taipei: Taiwan shangwu, 1988), 18:142.

7. Paul Rakita Goldin, *The Culture of Sex in Ancient China* (Honolulu: University of Hawaii Press, 2002).

8. Jia Gongyan, annotator, *Zhouli zhushu* (1815; rpt. Taipei: Yiwen, 1955), 4:89.

9. Michael Nylan, *The Five "Confucian" Classics* (New Haven, CT: Yale University Press, 2001), 168–71.

10. Robin R. Wong, *Images of Women in Chinese Thought and Culture: Writings from the Pre-Qin Period through the Song Dynasty* (Indianapolis: Hackett, 2003), 49–50.

11. Francesca Bray, "The Inner Quarters: Oppression or Freedom?" in *House Home Family: Living and Being Chinese*, ed. Ronald G. Knapp and Kai-yin Lo (Honolulu and New York: University of Hawaii Press and China Institute in America, 2005), 259–79.

12. Lisa Raphals, *Sharing the Light: Representations of Women and Virtue in Early China* (Albany: State University of New York Press, 1998), 195–206; Fan Ye, *Hou Hanshu*, annotated by Liu Zhao et al. (Beijing: Zhonghua Shuju, 1965), 84:2786n3.

13. Susan L. Mann, *Gender and Sexuality in Modern Chinese History* (Cambridge: Cambridge University Press, 2011), 45–46, 142–43, lists some of the important homosocial relationships in the late imperial era. Also see Kenneth E. Folsom, *Friends, Guests, and Colleagues: The Mu-fu System in the Late Ch'ing Period* (Berkeley: University of California Press, 1968).

14. Ban Gu, *Hanshu*, annotated by Yan Shigu (1962; rpt. Taipei: Dingwen, 1979), 27B1:1452, also 27B2:1502, 1518; Wai-yee Li, *The Readability of the Past in Early Chinese Historiography* (Cambridge, MA: Harvard University Asia Center, 2007), 147–60.

15. Wong, *Images of Women in Chinese Thought and Culture*, 57.

16. Jiao Jie and Geng Guanjing, "Cong 'Liji' kan zhanguo yihou fuquan de qianghua," *Funü yanjiu luncong* 4, no. 106 (2011): 59–64.

17. Charlotte Furth, "Androgynous Males and Deficient Females: Biology and Gender Boundaries in Sixteenth- and Seventeenth-Century China," *Late Imperial China* 9, no. 2 (1988): 1–3; Tani Barlow, "Theorizing Women: Funü, Guojia, Jiating," in *Body, Subject and Power in China*, ed. Angela Zito and Tani E. Barlow (Chicago: University of Chicago Press, 1994), 259.

18. Alison H. Black, "Gender and Cosmology in Chinese Correlative Thinking," in *Gender and Religion: On the Complexity of Symbols*, ed. C. W. Bynum et al. (Boston: Beacon, 1989), 166–95.

19. Liu Jingshen, "An Exploration of the Mode of Thinking in Ancient China," *Philosophy East and West* 35, no. 4 (1985): 387–96.

20. Guo Moruo, "You guan Yijing de xin," *Zhongguoshi yanjiu* 1 (1979): 5.

21. Fang Liqing and Wu Weigen, "Daojia 'tian fu di mu' yinyu ji qi shengtai zhihu jiedu," *Zhejiang Nonglin Daxue xuebao* 28, no. 4 (2011): 640–43.

22. Peng Zhongde, "'Xiao tian fa di', ru 'yi' zhi men," *Hubei Daxue xuebao (zhehui shehui kexue ban)* 38, no. 4 (2011): 82–86.

23. Shi Lei, "Li yi shun tian: 'Liji' zhong de tiandao sixiang shulun," *Jinan xuebao (zhexue shehui kexue ban)* 156 (2012): 134–39.

24. Hu Zifeng, *Xian Qin zhuzi yishuo tongkao* (Taipei: Wenshizhe, 1974), 127–60; Peng, "'Xiao tian fa di' ru 'yi' zhi men," 82–86.

25. He Rongyi, *Daodejing zhuyi yu xijie* (Taipei: Wuna, 1985), 73:587; D. C. Lau, *Laotsu: Tao Te Ching* (Harmondsworth, UK: Penguin, 1963), 135; Robert G. Henricks, *Lao-Tzu Te-Tao Ching: A New Translation Based on the Recently Discovered Ma-Wang-Tui Texts* (New York: Ballantine, 1989), 172–73.

26. A comprehensive introduction to *Yijing* can be found in Nylan, *The Five "Confucian" Classics*, 202–52. For the origins of the character *kun* and its relation to *qian*, see Liu Chunxue, "'Yi' zhi kun yanjiu," *Xingtai Xueyuan xuebao* 26, no. 1 (2011): 113–14.

27. Chen Menglei, *Zhouyi qianshu* (Shanghai: Guji, 1983), 7:4a; Richard Wilhelm and Cary F. Baynes, *The I Ching or Book of Changes* (Princeton, NJ: Princeton University Press, 1977), 285.

28. Chen, *Zhouyi qianshu*, 6:2b, 7:4b, 7:39a, 7:59b, 7:89a, 8:7a, 8:13a, 8:36a; Wilhelm, *The I Ching*, 267, 273, 285, 311, 327, 332, 353.

29. Cheng Jiangong, "'Yi—Yanwen' de lunli jiazhi ji qi xianshi yiyi," *Hexi Xueyuan xuebao* 26, no. 6 (2010): 38–42; Wei Hui, "Nüxing pinde xiuyang yanjiu: cong 'Zhouyi' zhi buyi nüde fenxi," *Xuzhou Gongcheng Xueyuan xuebao (shehui kexue ban)* 3 (2010): 88–92.

30. Duan Yucai, *Shuowen jiezi zhu* (Shanghai: Guji, 1981), 14B:1b; Sun Guangde, *Xian Qin liang Han yinyang wuxing shuo de zhengzhi sixiang* (Taipei: Jiaxin shuini Gongsi Wenhua Jijinhui, 1969), 2–3.

31. Bao Jialin, "Yinyangxue shuo yu funü diwei," in *Zhongguo funüshi lunji xuji*, ed. Bao Jialin (Taipei: Daoxiang, 1991), 37–42.

32. Lai Yanyuan, *Chunqiu fanlu jinzhu jinyi* (Taipei: Taiwan Shangwu, 1984), 12:314, 315, 317.

33. Peng, "'Xiao tian fa di' ru 'yi' zhi men," 83.

34. Bret Hinsch, "The Criticism of Powerful Women by Western Han Dynasty Portent Experts," *Journal of the Economic and Social History of the Orient* 49, no. 1 (2006): 96–121.

2

༘

Han Dynasty (206 BCE–220 CE)

Honor Culture

Although Chinese like to think of themselves as a peaceful people who cherish humility and forbearance, the culture also has a confrontational side. Early Chinese masculinity was closely bound up with ideas of personal and group honor, often expressed through violence. The influence of honor on male behavior demonstrates its importance. In antiquity, otherwise ordinary men sometimes felt compelled to commit spectacular acts of violence to defend their honor. Even today, many men pay scrupulous attention to appearances and go to great lengths to present a respectable facade to the world. The origins of ideas about honor, the ways men proved their honorability, and the social functions of honor expose some of the fundamental underpinnings of historic Chinese manhood.

HONOR CULTURE

The dynamics of early Chinese masculine honor were far from unique. People can organize gender norms in a limited number of ways, so the same general patterns appear in numerous cultures.[1] In some respects, basic Chinese ideas about manhood seem strikingly similar to those found in many other places around the world. Although humanity has devised many ways to manifest masculinity, we construct masculine identity in two basic ways: suddenly or gradually. Manhood is realized suddenly in cultures that require a youth to undergo a difficult coming-of-age ritual to prove himself worthy of the cherished status of adult male.[2] Because this rite is so important, it must be difficult. An adolescent

29

passes through some sort of ordeal to publicly prove himself good enough to be called a man. Ordeals can be extremely painful, even involving extreme physical torments, such as ritualized beatings or circumcision.[3] Adolescents must endure these tribulations, however arduous, stoically. Society forever after considers the youth who successfully completes the rite of passage a man, regardless of any future failings. Anyone who falls short, however, is disgraced for life.

China never had a dramatic coming-of-age ceremony of this sort. Although the elite held a capping (*guan*) ritual to mark the official commencement of adulthood, this ceremony posed no difficulties and certainly entailed no ordeal.[4] In the absence of a challenging rite of passage, Chinese men had to acquire a reputation for successful manhood gradually over the course of their lifetimes. Historic Chinese masculinity was cumulative, not sudden.

Anthropologists have studied this sort of gradualist masculine honor in detail, particularly as manifested in cultures bordering the Mediterranean Sea. Although the many cultures lining the Mediterranean exhibit numerous differences, decades of fieldwork have revealed that some basic ideas about manhood are nonetheless very common throughout the region.[5] Honor is the most important trait associated with masculinity. Because anthropologists studying this area conducted some of the earliest discussions on this topic, honor-based masculinity has come to be known as the Mediterranean model.[6] This name is somewhat misleading, however, as masculinity is closely associated with honor in many other places around the world, from Latin America to the Indian subcontinent. "Honor culture" is a more neutral appellation for this social pattern.

In contrast to cultures in which youths achieve manhood suddenly through a difficult adolescent rite of passage, in an honor culture the successful man builds up his masculine reputation piecemeal over the course of a lifetime. He carefully directs his actions, values, and overall bearing toward constructing an honorable facade, making manhood a long-term public performance critically

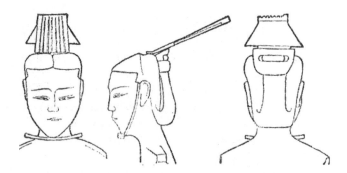

Formal Han dynasty caps. *Source:* Sun Ji, *Handai wuzhi wenhua ziliao tushuo* (Beijing: Wenwu, 1991), 231.

assessed by the community.[7] If judged a success, a man will enjoy the respect and privileges attending his normative social role. However, even a minor flaw in the performance can have catastrophic consequences. A man knows that a single slip can ruin him for life. Because the code of masculine honor is so demanding and success is subject to the caprices of public opinion, a man faces a lifetime of unrelenting stress in maintaining his masculine bearing.

While an intimate connection between honor and manhood appears in societies throughout the world, the precise constituents of honorable behavior vary from place to place. In the Mediterranean region, the honorable man of popular stereotype "drinks heavily, spends money freely, fights bravely, and raises a large family."[8] He must face up to physical, moral, and psychological challenges with stoicism and courage to prove himself worthy of respect. William Ian Miller sums up the general masculine mind-set in an honor culture:

> Honor is above all the keen sensitivity to the experience of humiliation and shame, a sensitivity manifested by the desire to be envied by others and the propensity to envy the success of others. To simplify greatly, honor is the disposition which makes one act to shame others who have shamed oneself, to humiliate others who have humiliated oneself. The honorable person is one whose self-esteem and social standing is ultimately dependent on the esteem or the envy he or she actually elicits in others.[9]

Masculine honor is inescapably agonistic. Not only must men compete with each other for public approbation, but exposing a rival as insufficiently manly elevates one's own reputation in comparison. Men constantly bait and test each other, hoping to goad rivals into unwittingly shaming themselves. They also become acutely sensitive to snubs and criticism, as the slightest hint of shameful treatment undermines masculine identity. Men in many honor cultures are eager to exact revenge on anyone who has shamed them to erase the stain of past humiliation. These cultures do not perceive violent revenge as a sign of immaturity, criminality, mental illness, or uncontrolled temper. In this value system, vengeance becomes a pragmatic strategy for restoring a man's honor.

EARLY CHINESE HONOR CULTURE

Male obsession with reputation is not confined to the distant past. Contemporary anthropological fieldwork has found that honor remains an important motivation for many men.[10] However, this mind-set has ancient roots. An acute sensitivity to honor conditioned the development of early Chinese masculinity. Obsessed with reputation, men strove to create and maintain a respectable public image. Standard honor culture traits, such as courage (both physical and moral), loyalty, endurance, and a willingness to requite shame, were cardinal male virtues emblematic of honor.[11] Ritualized public displays of status, such as receiving the seat of honor at a feast, bows of obeisance, or polite address, could confirm a man's good reputation. Material abundance stood as further proof of honor. A luxurious house, rich vestments, ornate carriages, gifts from prominent people, and a well-appointed tomb could all bolster a man's reputation. The right profession, such as state service, teaching, and scholarship, also brought honor, while association with commerce was generally disgraceful, however great the monetary rewards.

China's enduring culture of masculine honor seems to have emerged initially in antiquity in reaction to the internecine chaos plaguing the period. According to one influential theory, Mediterranean-style values of masculine honor develop when a weak state cannot contain endemic low-level violence.[12] In the absence of strong formal institutions to protect family and property from constant threats, ordinary men have no choice but to take matters into their own hands. As a result, normative masculinity becomes associated with whatever behaviors and values can provide a man and his family with a degree of security.

A related anthropological theory explains honor as linked to the exigencies of property ownership. According to this interpretation, we should see masculine honor as an ideology that emerges as a way of protecting and perhaps enlarging a kin group's property holdings. Societies with partible inheritance, such as China, usually end up with highly fragmented landholdings. Competition among neighboring families, each struggling to survive on a scrap of land, becomes particularly intense, as each contends for space, water, and other scarce resources. A code of masculine honor can serve as a useful way to legitimize violence in defense of family interests.[13]

Eastern Zhou (771–256 BCE) society suffered from the anarchy conducive to the formation of honor culture masculinity. As feudalism slowly decayed, new social and political institutions were slow to emerge, resulting in a long period of disorienting chaos known as the Warring States era (475–221 BCE). In response to this turmoil, an ethos of manhood grounded in typical honor culture values evolved. For example, warfare was largely a trial of honor between groups of men, and a desire for either glory or revenge motivated numerous wars.[14] On a more mundane level, society encouraged men to conduct themselves in ways that would safeguard those around them. Lauding these sorts of behaviors as honorable reinforced advantageous male conduct.

Of course the early Chinese terminology of honor differed from modern social science jargon. A number of Chinese terms conveyed the general concept of honor. Speakers of contemporary Mandarin most often describe honor through the physical metaphor of face (*mianzi*).[15] In antiquity, however, Chinese made recourse to the abstract language of morality and social station. An honorable reputation (*rong*) was the goal of any self-respecting man.[16] A high or low social position, expressed as exalted (*gui* or *liang*) or base (*jian*), expressed the degree of one's honor. An insult (*ru*) brought shame (*chi*), the negation of honor. Nor was shame limited to personal disgrace. As in other honor cultures, any insults suffered by members of a man's inner circle could also mar his reputation. "When a son or mother is insulted, people feel shame (*chi*)."[17]

The most important term related to Chinese honor is *yi*, usually translated as "righteousness." Early Chinese frequently evoked *yi* in antiquity to describe a range of virtues characterizing the good and successful man. The sustained efforts of elite thinkers to clarify *yi* and explore its broader implications attest to its importance. Confucian-inspired thinkers often understood *yi* in relation to *li* (ritual propriety), another key ethical concept. The elite rites codified during the Western Zhou dynasty (ca. 1046–771 BCE) consisted of detailed rules for how to behave in key situations. But no matter how many rules the ritual canon propounded, most of the events encountered in daily life remained beyond its scope. In the absence of a specific rule, an individual had no choice but to rely on general moral guidelines. So in Confucian ethical theory, righteousness (*yi*) refers to the normative values guiding behavior in situations not governed by the rites, with the intent of keeping each person within the bounds of his or her proper social station.[18]

Success or failure in abiding by *yi* redounded on one's reputation, making this ideal virtually synonymous with honor. Upholding the standards of righteousness in daily life earned a man public recognition for his honorable behavior, while failure brought shame. Confucians hoped that by defining honor as righteousness, an overweening desire for honor and fear of shame would steer people toward morality. Even if a man did not believe that virtue was its own reward, he might still do the right thing for the sake of his reputation. Over time, love of honor and fear of shame might gradually mature into genuine righteousness.[19]

Despite the importance of honor and its expropriation by Confucian ethics, this value was not uncontroversial. Confucius (traditionally 551–479 BCE) himself feared that the senseless pursuit of honor might encourage immorality. Because established views of honor sometimes differed from Confucian ideals, elite ethics and mainstream masculine values could readily conflict. A man might win popular commendation by doing something abhorrent to Confucian sensibilities. For example, the fact that people considered high office and wealth tokens of honor might tempt the ambitious man to win them by immoral means.[20] When honor conflicted with formal ethics, a man had to choose between virtue and reputation. Given the importance of honor to masculine identity, it was far from certain that he would side with the good.

Mencius (c. 372–c. 298 BCE) tried to work around this contradiction by redefining masculine honor. He claimed that one gains honor not through wealth, power, or vengeance but by displaying Confucian benevolence (*ren*).[21] However, given the yawning gap between the Mencian reinterpretation of honor and traditional masculine mores, this idealistic viewpoint clearly lacked wide appeal. However much elite thinkers might try to channel masculine honor in a more beneficent direction, less lofty priorities continued to prevail.

VENGEANCE AND HONOR

The honor culture of early Chinese masculinity is most readily apparent in the obsession with vengeance characterizing the era. The frequency of revenge will immediately strike anyone perusing historical records of the late Zhou and Han (206 BCE–220 CE) dynasties. The calculus of honor and shame inspired numerous acts of violence, mob vengeance, and even outright warfare. Early historians recognized vengeance as a major motivation for the behavior of powerful men and made it a stock theme in their writings. Although readers today might look down on the vengeful mind-set as petty and irrational, at the time a willingness to pursue revenge not only seemed perfectly reasonable but could even endow one with an air of dignity. By exacting revenge for a disgrace, a man publicly proved his devotion to honor and thereby restored his reputation.

A minor incident recorded in *Records of the Later Han* (*Hou Hanshu*) illustrates the psychology of vengeance. A clerk under a local official repeatedly harassed a man named Cai Zun. After a time, unable to endure this humiliation any longer, Cai gathered together a group of companions, and together they killed the bully. Reaction to this crime reveals contemporary values. Far from being condemned as a cold-blooded murderer, Cai Zun gained stature in the eyes of the community. "Originally people of the county considered him weak, but then they were in awe of him."[22]

As people regarded defense of honor so highly, stories about revenge were far more than just interesting action tales. Aside from the aesthetic and emotional resonance vengeance narratives evoked in readers, they also imparted invaluable wisdom. Men looked to these stories for guidance on how and when to restore lost honor. Because vengeance narratives had such practical utility, they became a staple topic of early historiography.

The earliest roots of Chinese vengeance probably date back to prehistory. Anthropologists have found that large kinship groups, such as those that dominated the earliest agricultural societies in the northern region of China during the Neolithic era, often practice revenge. Violent feuding can even become an important component of an enduring social structure.[23] Moreover, in high antiquity people believed that the dead continued their existence in noncorporeal form, remaining members of the kinship group. As a consequence, in their view blood justice benefited not only the living but the dead as well.[24]

Given the importance of filial piety to Chinese manhood, it is not surprising that vengeance became associated with this virtue. Many people came to believe that "a son who will not exact revenge is not a son."[25] Far more than merely an arbitrary duty owed to one's parents, filiality came to be considered an essential prerequisite for a thriving society. Just as loyalty to the ruler holds together a well-functioning state, so filial piety toward elders maintains the family.[26] In this manner, moral teachings grounded the two main levels of social organization in parallel virtues. Following this line of reasoning, a culture could justify vengeance for the sake of filial duty as an expression of loyalty akin to the fealty the virtuous official feels toward his ruler.[27] "The son must exact revenge on behalf of his father. Regarding the ruler and father, the righteousness (*yi*) of official and son are the same."[28] As Confucianism holds hierarchical political bonds to be a model of normative human relations, casting filial vengeance as analogous to political loyalty not only legitimized this sort of violence but elevated it to a sacrosanct obligation. Far from violating social norms, righteous revenge was necessary for maintaining moral order. Even so, according to the logic of filial piety, a man must pursue vengeance prudently and avoid serious harm to himself and his family. Were he to incur serious injury, he would be unable to take care of his elderly parents or conduct the ancestral sacrifices.[29]

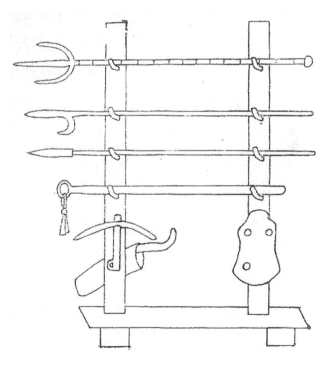

Han dynasty weapons. *Source:* Sun, *Handai wuzhi wenhua ziliao tushuo*, 137.

Over time vengeance became tightly integrated into increasingly sophisticated ethical systems. Although parts of the ritual canon encouraged revenge
under certain circumstances, the most influential and sustained elaboration of
violence for the sake of honor is found in the *Gongyang* commentary to *Springs
and Autumns of the State of Lu* (*Chunqiu*), one of the most revered classics of
antiquity and a pillar of both Chinese historiography and ethics.[30] This key
text not only defends vengeance as a respectable means of attaining justice and
clearing one's reputation but even commends righteous murders and wars of
vengeance as moral achievements, celebrating vengeance as an expression of
the recompense (*bao*) underpinning justice.[31] When undertaken within the
framework of the rites, revenge became a moral virtue. In literature, *bao* also
served as an important aesthetic ideal. Because readers found recompense emotionally satisfying, it was a worthy theme for compelling narrative.

The story of Duke Xiang of Qi highlights the central place of revenge within
the moral universe of the *Gongyang*. Overall the work portrays the duke as a
terrible person. He committed incest with his sister, killed the ruler of another
state, and met a well-deserved violent end. Nevertheless, the *Gongyang* still
praises him for seeking revenge when appropriate.[32] His willingness to resort
to revenge proved that despite his many flaws, he still possessed a modicum
of honor. The case of Duke Xiang shows that according to the standards of
the day, even a deeply flawed person could use righteous vengeance to redeem
himself to some degree.

The life story of a man named Zhou Dang, as recounted in *Records of the
Later Han*, demonstrates the influence of the *Gongyang* on the educated elite of
the Han dynasty. A local official had insulted Zhou in his youth. Even though
he dared not retaliate, the young man never forgot this slight. While away at
school, Zhou studied the commentarial traditions surrounding *Springs and
Autumns*, including "the righteousness of vengeance." After completing his
studies he returned home and, inspired by what he had learned, picked a fight
with the powerful man who had insulted him. During the altercation, Zhou was
injured. Nevertheless, Zhou's devotion to righteousness so moved his intended
victim that the man brought Zhou home and nursed him back to health.[33]

This account is particularly revealing in two respects. First, it is significant
that Zhou Dang was initially not interested in seeking revenge for the insults he
had suffered. He only began to value vengeance as a moral ideal after he became
a student of the classics, presumably the *Gongyang*. Moreover, the man whom
Zhou attacked adhered to a similar ethical system. Even though a young man
had tried to kill him, he nevertheless admired his attacker's motivations as an
expression of the righteousness characterizing manly honor. So although Zhou
lost the fight and suffered serious injuries, according to the ethical system of the
time he had nevertheless achieved his goal. Even an abortive attempt to seek
vengeance was sufficient to earn him respect as an honorable man.

Students attending a lecture. *Source:* Wang Jianzhong, *Handai huaxiangshi tonglun* (Beijing: Zijincheng, 2001), 285.

As this vignette shows, even though early imperial China was a steeply hierarchical society, revenge was not limited to action against someone of a lower order. To the contrary, numerous cases tell of government functionaries singled out as targets of vengeance. Sometimes these attacks were unrelated to the conduct of office. In one case, after a local official insulted the mother of one Yang Qiu, the aggrieved man gathered together a mob of youths, who killed the disrespectful offender and then wiped out his entire family. One might expect widespread condemnation of a massacre of the local elite. To the contrary, Yang received broad praise for exceptional filial loyalty and eventually received the reward of an official posting for his honorable behavior.[34]

Vengeance ethics were so deeply ingrained that sometimes a man sought revenge against a government minister who had ordered the execution of a lawbreaking family member. Although execution of a convicted criminal constituted an impersonal bureaucratic act, honor ethics nevertheless required taking revenge on the presiding functionary to restore the reputations of the deceased and his social circle. The *Records of the Han* (*Hanshu*) notes that at the beginning of the dynasty, when governance was still tentative, assassinations in the name of honor were particularly common. Sometimes the aggrieved killed an official himself, or else a family might assemble a gang of assassins.[35] Alternatively, the vengeful might exact retribution on a target's family member.[36]

OFFICIAL REACTIONS TO VENGEANCE

Despite the danger that vengeance posed to the powerful, the political elite nevertheless usually saw it as a legitimate moral obligation. Influential scholar Dong Zhongshu (179–104 BCE) helped fashion a framework of jurisprudence amenable to vengeance by advocating the use of *Springs and Autumns* and its commentarial traditions to assay justice. Dong argued that in addition to consulting the law code, an official should seek guidance from *Springs and Autumns* regarding the general nature of justice and ethics. As the *Gongyang* was the most influential *Springs and Autumns* commentary at the time, Dong was essentially insinuating this work's distinctive ethical views, including approval of righteous vengeance, into the justice system.[37] Dong believed that to determine true justice, one must sometimes go beyond the law to ponder the profound moral insights revealed in the ancient classics. This reasoning sanctioned revenge in the name of honor, even though the law specifically prohibited this sort of extrajudicial violence. Given the blatant contradiction between law and ethics, officials found themselves torn between conflicting priorities. Which took precedence—righteous blood justice or the rule of law? Reactions to this conundrum were ad hoc. As each magistrate handled matters as he saw fit, considerable uncertainty plagued the Han dynasty justice system.[38]

Not everyone took such a sanguine view of vengeance. Assassination and murder were not just morally troubling; they also threatened the state's monopoly on violence, which always serves as the sine qua non of political stability. Some officials tried to bolster state institutions by limiting the scope of vengeance in politics. For example, the *Zuo* commentary argues that the family of an official executed for wrongdoing should not seek revenge as the ruler has simply exercised his legitimate judicial prerogative.[39] Even the *Gongyang* discourages revenge against those enforcing the law. Although the text generally encourages a son to exact vengeance for a father's murder, it does not consider revenge justifiable if the father was executed for a crime.[40]

Some officials punished honor killings in an attempt to discourage freelance justice.[41] Nevertheless, vengeance often went unpunished. Whether through institutional weakness, negligence, or sympathy with the honorable avenger, men regularly got away with murder. In fact, historical records often depict vengeful murderers as proud of their violent actions. They clearly felt that their righteous deeds, however bloody, deserved the state's forbearance.

While many officials turned a blind eye to acts of vengeance, in some eras tolerance became the norm. After a man killed someone who had insulted his father, Emperor Han Xiaozong (r. 75–88) pardoned the murderer, thereby setting an influential precedent.[42] The subsequent Wei dynasty (386–534) took an even stronger stand on the issue and actively encouraged revenge. The Wei parted from legal tradition to explicitly sanction vengeance against bandits who had killed a family member.[43] In a time of chaos, when the state was particularly weak, this measure served as a practical tactic to fight persistent brigandage.

Even in the absence of official guidelines mandating forgiveness for honorable murder, numerous Han dynasty cases demonstrate widespread official tolerance for vengeance killings. For example, after a man from the same district killed the brother of one Yin Yuan, Yin stabbed the murderer to death. Even though Yin came from a poor family, he was pardoned for this honor killing and returned home. Later he even served in government, demonstrating that murder in the name of righteousness held no stigma.[44] An almost identical case involved a man named Wei Lang. After the murder of his brother, Wei took revenge on the killer and turned himself in to authorities. Wei was not completely forgiven, as he was ordered to leave the area and exiled to another district. However, this punishment was not much of a hardship, as he was still able to study the classics and eventually embarked on a successful career in service to the state.[45]

Nor were honor killings limited to retribution for insults to blood kin. The case of Chen Gang helps define the outer limits of vengeance. Chen was so enraged by the murder of a close friend and classmate that when he came across the murderer asleep in a drunken stupor, Chen woke him up and killed him. He then turned himself in to the local magistrate and confessed to the murder. After admitting his crime, he received a pardon and escaped punishment.[46] Significantly, Chen Gang did not commit murder in response to a slight toward himself or a kinsman. This case demonstrates that authorities might even forgive vengeance on behalf of a friend considered part of the vigilante's in-group. Seeing the murder of a close friend as an assault on Chen's own honor, the magistrate excused his righteous vengeance in response.

Of course, sanctioning murder put everyone in danger. If sufficiently cynical, a man could potentially enhance his manly reputation by killing a rival in cold blood, then demand forgiveness for the crime by claiming his victim had insulted him. Some people had no choice but to flee their homes in terror, knowing that the government would not protect them from vicious rivals.[47] Even the wealthy and powerful lived in fear. The prevailing sense of insecurity forced the elite to turn their houses into defensive enclosures resembling small

Fortified house. *Source:* Sun, *Handai wuzhi wenhua ziliao tushuo*, 191.

fortresses. The home of a wealthy landowner was typically encircled by high walls, defended by one or more towers, and equipped with a large drum to summon aid in case of attack.[48]

Retribution could incite large-scale vendettas that turned some areas into virtual battlegrounds. An incident from the early Eastern Han shows how the cycle of revenge could escalate to threaten the stability of the state. During the reign of Emperor Han Guangwu (r. 25–57), various princes living in the capital jealously vied for prominence by striving to assemble the largest band of retainers. When members of one gang felt insulted by another, loyal retinues could instantly turn into violent mobs. Marquis Li of Shouguang resented the former pretender Liu Penzi, as he felt that Penzi had harmed his father. After the retainers of Li and his allies exacted revenge on Penzi's brother, fighting broke out on all sides. The resulting melee ended in a bloodbath with more than a thousand casualties.[49]

Of course, brawling between gangs of toughs was absolutely intolerable. Insightful thinker Huan Tan (43 BCE–28 CE) called for authorities to take strong countermeasures.

Today people kill and injure each other. Even if they have already pleaded guilty and been executed, there is still private enmity. Sons and grandsons exact vengeance on each other with enmity steadily increasing until the murdered corpses lie in coffins and they are popularly referred to as bold and strong. In the past, although someone was cowardly and weak, he would still exert himself and commit vengeance. This is a case of hearing about people taking matters into their own hands and no making recourse to the law and prohibiting it. Now it is appropriate to state the old statutes.[50]

Huan recommends a simple solution to the problem. As premeditated murder was illegal, simply enforcing existing laws would be sufficient to allow each magistrate to forbid honor killings in the area under his jurisdiction.

Even those taking a hard line against honor killing did not argue for the execution of all murderers. For example, the state could prosecute a vengeful murder as an involuntary manslaughter. This would not be out of keeping with the jurisprudence of the time, as killing was sometimes permissible under early law. For example, according to the Qin dynasty code, a father could request that authorities kill a son or slave on his behalf. Infanticide of a deformed newborn was also acceptable.[51] In other words, early imperial jurists assumed that some murders were permissible. Given this acceptance of certain types of justifiable homicide, it was difficult to argue that there was a blanket prohibition on murder that precluded honorable vengeance. Nevertheless, general prohibitions against premeditated murder gave authorities the legal tools to fight violence

Fighting. *Source:* Sun, *Handai wuzhi wenhua ziliao tushuo*, 128.

when necessary. Chinese jurisprudence never solved the perennial conflict between law and sentiment (*qing*), but at least a legal mechanism for containing violence existed if officials chose to employ it.

Classical scholarship inspired another strategy to limit vengeance. Conveniently for those who wanted to bolster social stability, the revered *Rites of Zhou* (*Zhouli*) took a skeptical stance toward the morality of revenge. This influential work did not recommend execution for those who committed murder for honor's sake, but it did declare that the offending party should suffer exile to a distant place as punishment for disturbing social harmony.[52] Banishment represented something of a compromise position. According to the *Rites of Zhou*, even though a man might understandably commit vengeful murder to erase shame, he should still suffer the consequences for disturbing the peace. In interpreting this passage, scholar Xun Yue (148–209) noted that even though society might tolerate certain forms of revenge, the practice had to remain within the framework of the law.[53]

Despite these attempts to limit or outlaw vengeance, honor killings remained common up until the end of the Eastern Han dynasty and beyond. Even today Chinese newspapers regularly describe violent revenge in response to insults and injustices. Over time, however, the frequency of vengeance steadily declined. Although honor or "face" remained a key component of masculine identity, men came to express this value in more peaceful ways. After the fall of the Eastern Han, vengeance ethics underwent a gradual decline, especially among the elite, and the state steadily assumed a monopoly over the use of violence. Although authors continued to discuss and even romanticize revenge, the number of cases reported in historical records steadily decreased.

The decline of violent revenge is attributable in part to academic trends, as texts encouraging violence lost popularity. The most important source of legitimacy for revenge was the *Gongyang* commentary. Of all the classics, this work went furthest in sanctioning violence for honor's sake. After the Western Han, however, the influence of this text declined precipitously, and the *Zuo zhuan* replaced it as the premier interpretation of *Springs and Autumns*. Although both based on events in the laconic *Springs and Autumns*, the *Zuo* commentary and *Gongyang* commentary differ considerably in style and content. As study of the *Zuo* became fashionable during the Eastern Han, scholars of the time remarked on how much the values of this text differed from the *Gongyang* and *Guliang* commentaries it had superseded.

In particular, the *Zuo* puts much more emphasis on respect for authority.[54] Under this new value system, which attributed political power to the mandate of heaven, it was much more difficult for an underling to justify assassinating an official or ruler in the name of honor. In the moral universe of the *Zuo*, it is even doubtful whether taking revenge against a superior was ever legitimate. Although changing fashions in classical studies might seem like a fairly arcane development, in a society in which the elite looked to these canonical texts for practical guidance, the social consequences of a shift from the *Gongyang* to the *Zuo* commentary were in fact quite profound. As the elite steadily turned away from violence as a means to prove honor, vengeance became increasingly associated with lower-status manhood. Elite men found new ways to peacefully assert their honor and compete for status. The history of masculinities in China is thus in large part a chronicle of the changing strategies men have used to prove their honor.

NOTES

1. Connell and Messerschmidt, "Hegemonic Masculinity," 850.

2. Arnold van Gennep, *The Rites of Passage*, trans. Monika Vizedom and Gabrielle L. Caffee (Chicago: University of Chicago Press, 1960).

3. Gilmore, *Manhood in the Making*, 13; van Gennep, *The Rites of Passage*, 85–86.

4. Grant Hardy, "The Reconstruction of Ritual: Capping in Ancient China," *Journal of Ritual Studies* 7, no. 2 (1993): 69–90; Zhou, *Festivals, Feasts, and Gender Relations in Ancient China and Greece*, 149–50.

5. João de Pina-Cabral, "The Mediterranean as a Category of Regional Comparison: A Critical View," *Current Anthropology* 30, no. 3 (1989): 399–406, rejects the assertion of a pan-Mediterranean culture. However, most anthropologists working on manhood in the region believe that cultures bordering the Mediterranean share enough basic similarities to allow them to be discussed as a group.

6. For some classic descriptions of the Mediterranean model of masculinity, see Michael Herzfeld, *The Poetics of Manhood: Contest and Identity in a Cretan Mountain Village* (Princeton, NJ: Princeton University Press, 1985); Jean G. Peristiany, ed., *Honour and Shame: The Values of Mediterranean Society* (London: Wiedenfeld & Nicolson, 1965); David D. Gilmore, *Honor and Shame and the Unity of the Mediterranean* (Washington, DC: American Anthropological Association, 1987).

7. Julian Pitt-Rivers, "Honour and Social Status," in *Honour and Shame: The Values of Mediterranean Society*, ed. J. G. Peristiany (Chicago: University of Chicago Press, 1966), 21.

8. Gilmore, *Manhood in the Making*, 16.

9. William Ian Miller, *Humiliation* (Ithaca, NY: Cornell University Press, 1993), 84. Also see J. K. Campbell, *Honour, Family, and Patronage: A Study of Institutions and Moral Values in a Greek Mountain Community* (Oxford: Clarendon Press, 1964), 269. Kwame Anthony Appiah, *The Honor Code: How Moral Revolutions Happen* (New York: Norton, 2010), 175–78, provides a cogent summary of the main characteristics of honor.

10. Heidi Fung, "Becoming a Moral Child: The Socialization of Shame among Young Chinese Children," *Ethos* 27, no. 2 (1999): 180–209; Joo Yup Kim and Sang Hoon Nam, "The Concept and Dynamics of Face: Implications for Organizational Behavior in Asia," *Organization Science* 9, no. 4 (1998): 522–34.

11. Kam Louie, *Theorizing Chinese Masculinity: Society and Gender in China* (Cambridge: Cambridge University Press, 2002), 36, 82, 92.

12. Anton Blok, "Rams and Billy-Goats: A Key to the Mediterranean Code of Honour," *Man* (New Series) 16, no. 3 (1981): 434–36.

13. Jane Schneider, "Of Vigilance and Virgins: Honor, Shame and Access to Resources in Mediterranean Societies," *Ethnology* 10, no. 1 (1971): 2.

14. Mark Edward Lewis, *Sanctioned Violence in Early China* (Albany: State University of New York Press, 1990), 37.

15. David Yau-fai Ho, "On the Concept of Face," *American Journal of Sociology* 81, no. 4 (1976): 867–84. Physical metaphors reifying honor as part of the body are common in Mediterranean cultures. Blok, "Rams and Billy-Goats," 432–34.

16. Jane Geaney, "Guarding Moral Boundaries: Shame in Early Confucianism," *Philosophy East and West* 54, no. 2 (2004): 132.

17. Fan, *Hou Hanshu*, 64:2101.

18. Benjamin I. Schwartz, *The World of Thought in Ancient China* (Cambridge, MA: Belknap Press of Harvard University Press, 1985), 79; David Schaberg, *A Patterned Past: Form and Thought in Early Chinese Historiography* (Cambridge, MA: Harvard University Asia Center, 2001), 155.

19. Schwartz, *The World of Thought in Ancient China*, 267. (Changing *i* to *yi*).

20. Antonio S. Cua, "The Ethical Significance of Shame: Insights of Aristotle and Xunzi," *Philosophy East and West* 53, no. 2 (2003): 156–57.

21. Cua, "The Ethical Significance of Shame," 162–63.

22. Fan, *Hou Hanshu*, 20:738.

23. E. E. Evans-Pritchard, "The Nuer of the Southern Sudan," *Kinship and Family: An Anthropological Reader*, ed. Robert Parkin and Linda Stone (Malden, MA: Blackwell, 2004), 74–77; He Jianping, "Shizu shehui yu 'xieqin fuchou,'" *Guizhou shehui kexue* 136, no. 4 (1995): 40–44.

24. Wang Li, "Xiezu Fuchou yu guiling chongbai," *Shanxi Daxue xuebao* 24, no. 4 (2001): 11–15.

25. Fan, *Hou Hanshu*, 44:1503.

26. *Hsiao Ching* (Taipei: Confucius Publishing, n.d.), 10–11 (*shizhang*).

27. It was common to equate political loyalty and filial piety. In fact, filial piety was sometimes stretched to include a number of apparently unrelated virtues, such as dignity in one's leisure time, courage in battle, and dependability in friendship. However, the link between an official's loyalty to his ruler and a son's filiality to his parents was widely recognized and had a powerful impact on the culture. John Knoblock and Jeffrey Riegel, *The Annals of Lü Buwei* (Stanford, CA: Stanford University Press, 2000), 302–3 (book 14, chapter 1).

28. Chen Li, annotator, *Baihu tongyi* (1875; rpt. Taipei: Guangwen, 1987), 5:12B–13A (*zhufa*).

29. Ying Shao, *Fengsu tongyi* (Taipei: Zhonghua shuju, 1985), 4:2B.

30. Zang Zhifei, "Chunqiu Gongyangxue yu Handai Fuchou fengqi fazheng," *Xuzhou Shifan Xueyuan xuebao (zhexue shehui kexue ban)* (February 1996): 23–28; Chen Enlin, "Lun 'Gongyang zhuan' Fuchou sixiang de tedian yu jing jin, guwen fuchoushuo wenti," *Shehui kexue zhanxian* (February 1998): 137–45. For a discussion of vengeance in the ritual canon, see Makino Tatsumi, *Chūgoku kazuko kenkyū* (*shita*), (Tokyo: Ochanomizu, 1980), 4–6.

31. Schaberg, *A Patterned Past*, 170, 207–21, 310.

32. He Xiu and Xu Yan, annotators, *Chunqiu gongyanzhuan zhushu* (1815; rpt. Taipei: Yiwen, 1955), 6:76–77 (Zhuang 4).

33. Fan, *Hou Hanshu*, 83:2761.

34. Fan, *Hou Hanshu*, 77:2498.

35. Ban Gu, *Hanshu*, annotated by Yan Shigu (1962; rpt. Taipei: Dingwen, 1979), 90:3673; Fan, *Hou Hanshu*, 11:477.

36. Ban, *Hanshu*, 28B:1656.

37. Liu Liming, "Handai de xiezu fuchou yu 'Chunqiu' jueyu," *Xinan minzu xueyuan xuebao—zhexue shehui kexue ban* 23, no. 3 (2002): 73–74.

38. Jen-Der Lee, "Conflicts and Compromise between Legal Authority and Ethical Ideas: From the Perspective of Revenge in Han Times," *Renwen ji shehui kexue jikan* 1, no. 1 (1988): 359–408, explores this contradiction. The six tables in this article demonstrate the uncertain outcome for cases involving vengeful murder, highlighting the ambivalence of government officials.

39. Lin Sujuan, "Chunqiu Zhanguo shiqi wei junfu Fuchou suoshe zhi zhongxiao yiti ji xiangguan jingyi tanjiu," *Hanxue yanjiu* 24, no. 1 (2006): 43.

40. He and Xu, *Chunqiu gongyanzhuan zhushu*, 25:321 (Duke Ding, year 4).

41. For example, Ban, *Hanshu*, 47:2215.

42. Fan, *Hou Hanshu*, 44:1502.

43. Makino, *Chūgoku kazuko kenkyū (shita)*, 23.

44. Fan, *Hou Hanshu*, 52:1722.

45. Fan, *Hou Hanshu*, 67:2200–201.

46. Li Diaoyuan, ed., *Huayang guozhi* (Taipei: Hongye, 1972), 10C:6a (Chen Gang 陳剛).

47. For example, Ban, *Hanshu*, 31:1796.

48. Makino, *Chūgoku kazuko kenkyū (shita)*, 17.

49. Fan, *Hou Hanshu*, 42:1427.

50. Fan, *Hou Hanshu*, 28A:958.

51. A. F. P. Hulsewé, *Remnants of Ch'in Law: An Annotated Translation of the Ch'in Legal and Administrative Rules of the 3rd Century B.C., Discovered in Yün-meng Prefecture, Hu-pei Province, in 1975* (Leiden: Brill, 1985), 8.

52. Jia Gongyan, annotator, *Zhouli zhushu* (1815; rpt. Taipei: Yiwen, 1955), 14:215.

53. Lin Jiali et al., eds., *Xinyi shenjian duben* (Taipei: Sanmin, 1996), 2:55.

54. Fan, *Hou Hanshu*, 36:1236.

3

Jin Dynasty (265–420 CE)

Buddhism and Changing Masculinity

According to the *Biographies of Eminent Monks* (*Gaoseng zhuan*), the venerable Fotudeng (Buddhacinga) was blessed with amazing talents. After smearing sesame oil on his palm, he could gaze at the sticky blotch and observe distant events. The sounds of bells revealed hidden prophecies that always came true exactly as he foretold. Because he could infallibly predict a battle's outcome in advance, a murderous warlord appointed him as an adviser. He could also cure incurable diseases. Once he cast a spell to make rain, thereby ending a devastating drought. When Fotudeng passed away at the ripe age of 117, officials and common people mourned so grievously that their weeping shook the earth.[1]

How should readers today interpret this sort of fanciful life story presented as a factual account? Because interpretive contexts shift considerably with time, over the centuries this narrative has becomes increasingly difficult for readers to understand and appreciate.[2] As with every text, we must read it against the original horizon of cultural and literary expectations to recover its original meaning. The original audience found this fictionalized narrative reasonable and accepted it as a compelling and instructive story. But tastes change, and readers today bring a fresh set of expectations that elicit extremely different reactions. No matter how much the contemporary reader struggles to suspend disbelief, this style of writing now seems much closer to fantasy than reality.

Fotudeng's life story has come to seem so strange because the narrative's aims are now largely irrelevant. The author of this collection, the erudite cleric Huijiao (497–554), never intended to present an objective representation of his subject's life. Instead he employed hagiography as an expedient medium to

Fotudeng. *Source*: Shi Baocheng, *Fojia de chuanshuo* (Changsha: Yuelu, 2004), 30.

address a wide spectrum of pressing concerns, including religious life, society, politics—and gender identity. In imbuing the narrative with multivalent meanings and functions, Huijiao intended Fotudeng's biography to serve as far more than just the story of one highly exceptional individual. Instead he deployed his impressive rhetorical arsenal to address some of the most vexing problems confronting believers at a time when Buddhism still seemed exotic to many Chinese and its critics were both vocal and numerous. If one anachronistically assumes that every biography is intended as an objective representation, a fictionalized life story seems strange and even incomprehensible. But reading the "biography" of Fotudeng against the background of authorial intent and original context reveals it as an astute piece of ideological rhetoric.

The author of Fotudeng's fictionalized life story intended the account to inspire ordinary Buddhists to think more deeply about how they might successfully negotiate a spiritual life in a deeply flawed world. Although the intended readership may not have been able to imitate Fotudeng in predicting the future or controlling the weather, they could nevertheless reflect on this story to discover what sort of qualities might allow a pious man to flourish. Powerful and respected, Fotudeng presented Buddhists with a compelling example of the successful believer. Even men in humble circumstances might learn from this paragon and improve their own lives to some degree. Because readers understood the utility of this narrative, they willingly suspended disbelief so that they might gain some practical wisdom about how to live as a respected Buddhist man.

It is important to remember that the faithful did not isolate religious beliefs from other aspects of their lives. A man would interpret this story within the context of his own busy and complicated existence, trolling the text for templates of behavior that he might borrow to reaffirm his manhood in a hostile world. No matter how outlandish a narrative might appear, if it could make life seem a bit more comprehensible or provide insights on how to thrive, readers readily overlooked its absurdities.[3] Faith is often strongest when there is potential for gain.

CREATING THE CHINESE BUDDHIST MAN

Early Chinese Buddhists struggled to reconcile the deeply rooted traditions of their proud civilization with compelling Indian alternatives. Among the many epiphanies engendered by this clash of civilizations was the Chinese realization that there are extremely different ways to be a man. Previous norms had always centered on a man's place within the network of secular social ties. He had to act out an interlocking series of normative roles encompassed by the dense web of social obligations that bound him to ruler, parents, older brothers, teachers, patrons, and so on.[4] Success in carrying out these normative roles brought public approval and acceptance. In general, the ideal Chinese man married, fathered children, owned property, pursued a literary education, deferred to parents and other superiors, behaved righteously toward others, obtained an official position, and displayed moral courage.[5] Whatever role he undertook at a particular time, he could expect praise if he displayed these standard masculine qualities.

Judged by these standards, the ideal monk presented a disturbingly flawed picture of aberrant manliness. He abjured marriage, renounced fatherhood, was ill positioned to care for parents, did not own property, declined public office, deprecated secular learning, mutilated his body (a gift from his parents) by shaving his head, and rejected orthodox manners and rituals for an alien set of rites. According to the masculine standards of the time, how could such a person even be called a man?[6] To Buddhists, however, severing mundane ties and manipulating the body were crucial to personal transformation, as is the case in many religions.[7] Negotiating an individual space between the dictates of their faith and the contrary expectations of secular society presented devotees with daunting challenges.

In every culture, one of the easiest ways to criticize a foe is to impugn his manhood.[8] Buddhism's many critics thus found it effective to accuse monks of a wide range of alarming practices that violated conventional masculine ideals. They pointed out that monks did not cultivate land, marry, respect filial piety, fulfill military service or corvée duties, or conduct lay rites. A monk was not even allowed to use force to uphold his own honor or that of his family, a core value of secular manhood.[9] The initial blowback was fierce. Some critics condemned Buddhist clerics as immoral hypocrites who feigned otherworldly purity while living a life of greed and adultery. Others took a more straightforward approach, simply reproaching Buddhism for its foreignness. According to their xenophobic logic, nothing worthwhile could possibly originate beyond China's borders.[10] Although the complaints about Buddhism took many forms, they all tended to focus on a single disturbing problem: the religion's rejection of normative Chinese manhood. This unabashed challenge to their own views of what it meant to be a proper man visibly disturbed Buddhism's critics.

The religion's apologists had to somehow reconcile divergent Chinese and Indian conceptions of the ideal man. In synthesizing a new masculine ideal, they wanted to remain true to core Buddhist teachings while gaining a measure of respect from both Chinese believers and critics. Authors directed much of the early Buddhist literature written in Chinese, particularly hagiography, toward constructing an acceptable model of Chinese Buddhist manhood.[11] Literary critic Frederic Jameson has pointed out that we should understand the creation of narrative as an ideological act that seeks imaginary solutions to seemingly irresolvable social contradictions.[12] Hagiographies of ideal Buddhist practitioners functioned in precisely this manner, efficiently disseminating a revised set of masculine ideals intended to bridge the gap between Buddhist and native traditions.

Fortunately for Buddhist apologists, Chinese already faced a crisis of confidence in their culture. The chaotic interlude between Han and Sui was unquestionably a low point in the history of Chinese governance. A breakdown in order known as the Yongjia chaos (307–310) allowed nomadic peoples to conquer northern China, initiating an occupation that lasted for centuries and sent swarms of refugees fleeing southward. The ruin of their homeland humiliated men of letters, who even feared for their lives. Many of the finest minds perished. Death, disease, and terrible cruelty conditioned people's worldview during this era, known as the Northern and Southern dynasties (420–589).[13] China's first experience with prolonged foreign occupation came at the hands of far less sophisticated nomadic foes who reduced the lands under their dominion to ignorance and destitution. The disgrace of prolonged foreign rule over the northern heartland called the most fundamental Chinese values into question.[14]

As with virtually every major aspect of culture, masculinity became a highly contested topic during this era. Given China's collapse into anarchy and then subjugation, it seemed as if traditional manhood had become impotent. Alien occupiers despised bookish pursuits and elaborate manners as the effeminate decadence of the conquered. Instead they flaunted the rough martial customs of their nomadic forebears as a superior style of manhood. The resulting atmosphere of cultural crisis formed the anxious backdrop to Buddhism's confrontation with China's traditional masculine ideals.

BIOGRAPHY AND MANHOOD

The most influential statement of Chinese Buddhist masculinity is the *Biographies of Eminent Monks (Gaoseng zhuan)*, a collection presenting the life stories of exemplary Buddhist men. The author Huijiao brought together these 257 narratives from a wide variety of sources, ranging from commemorative inscriptions to oral literature.[15] Although he appears to have edited heavily or even rewritten many sections, the collection displays a notable diversity of style and content, suggesting that he preserved much of the original source material.[16] The *Biographies of Eminent Monks* is unquestionably the most important work of Chinese Buddhist prosopography. Widely read down through the centuries, this work also set the standard for Buddhist biography and provided a model for subsequent writers in the genre.

Although now lauded as an illustrious biographer and an important historian of early Chinese Buddhism, Huijiao aimed mainly to propagate Buddhism, not to write objective history or biography. To this end, he had to provide portraits

of monks that clerics and pious laypeople found acceptable but that also reso-
nated with the emperor, court, ordinary nonbelievers, and Buddhism's many
prominent critics.[17] In other words, he had to fashion an image of Buddhist
manhood acceptable to extremely disparate constituencies.

When Buddhism began to gain popularity in China, the new faith initially
met with fierce resistance, initiating a long process of critique and response.[18]
Buddhism advocated many novel practices considered odd or disturbing at the
time, including unfamiliar ideas about how men ought to conduct their lives.
Apologists such as Huijiao had to frame disorienting standards of Buddhist
manhood in ways acceptable to Chinese sensibilities. His ideological objective
helps explain the fantastic nature of so many of these supposed biographies.
Huijiao selected and manipulated pertinent narratives to express a relentlessly
positive image of ideal Buddhist manhood, even if this meant ornamenting the
truth or even creating fanciful stories from scratch.

Exemplars of masculinity do not have to be famous. In fact, it is much easier
for an ordinary man to imitate a humble monk than a monarch or hero. Nevertheless, Huijiao sometimes depicted extreme behaviors, such as magic or
suicide, far outside the range of ordinary experience. Blatantly unrealistic writing presented general points of reference and contemplation rather than literal
rules for masculine conduct. The average man was willing to comply tacitly
with lofty masculine ideals, even when personally unattainable.[19] The belief
that some monks were heroes or magicians raised the prestige of all Buddhists,
even if few were as successful as these paragons. To this end, Huijiao's collection presents a farrago of the real and imagined, feasible and impracticable,
lofty and humble, grand and subtle. An ordinary man could utilize the sundry
components of masculine narratives as the raw material for constructing an in-
dividualized male identity suitable to his particular circumstances. As he aged,
different stories and images from the collection would become useful at each
point along his life trajectory. The richness of this collection provided people
in different circumstances with aspirational masculine behaviors, making it an
invaluable compendium of ideas about how to thrive as a Buddhist man.

CHANGING MASCULINITY

The confrontation of Buddhist and native Chinese masculinities is merely one
example of a much larger theme in gender studies. The history of world masculinities features many instances of men who felt compelled to reject mainstream
views of manhood. Such was also the case with Chinese Buddhists. In response
to persecution, believers rejected many mainstream gender norms, replacing
them with a resourceful new vision of ideal masculinity that initially met with
incomprehension and hostility.

Contradictions between normative secular masculinity and a religious vocation were certainly not unique to China. To the contrary, as religious life is often very different from the ordinary male experience, reconciling it with mainstream masculinity often presents a challenge. To take a well-studied example from another part of the world, some scholars have argued that Christian monks in medieval Europe were widely perceived as nonmasculine or even feminized, as their tonsure, clerical garb, and behavior made them seem like quasi-transvestites.[20] Similarly, to outsiders the gentle rabbi might seem unmanly or even asexual, even though many of the pious regarded him as the quintessence of Jewish manhood.[21] Although these cases come from distant places, they highlight a problem common to all men of faith. A spiritual life demands departure from secular norms, threatening conventional masculine identity. In response, early Chinese Buddhists constructed a new image of religious manhood acceptable to lay society.

The Buddhist confrontation with Chinese masculinity exemplifies a central subject of gender studies: how and why mainstream perceptions of masculinity change over time. Because the Buddhists' reappraisal of male identity marks a seismic shift in the history of Chinese manhood, how they dealt with secular culture exemplifies the general strategies that men everywhere have used to challenge normative manhood. Although conflicts between different masculinities can be extremely nuanced, for heuristic purposes one can identify three major strategies for challenging prevailing gender norms. The first approach is most stark. Sometimes men reject masculine ideals outright. Although absolute rejection provides maximum room for individual agency, it attracts disapproval. The second method is appropriation. Sometimes men can deploy a standard attribute of manhood in a fresh way, maintaining some fidelity to normative masculine ideals while providing space for novelty. Finally, a third approach transforms norms into something new. Men past and present have regularly used all three techniques to confront normative manhood. Rejection, appropriation, and transformation are not only applicable to early medieval Buddhist masculinity but equally useful in accounting for how manhood has changed in every time and place.

REJECTION

The most blatant strategy that Buddhists employed was an outright rejection of prevailing ideas about manhood. For example, Buddhist teachings often challenged traditional manifestations of filial piety. Given the importance of the filial bond to traditional models of manhood, a monk who left home to live in a monastery opened himself up to accusations of gross immorality. To become fully integrated into the fabric of Chinese society, Buddhist clerics would have to assuage this concern. Of course Indian Buddhism did not lack a concept of filial devotion. In China the faithful disseminated Indian views of filial piety, which differed somewhat from Chinese customs, via translated Sanskrit literature.[22] Chinese monks employed Indian ideas of filiality to engage their secular counterparts on this issue, and this dialogue had a significant impact on ideas about this keystone value.

While it was sometimes possible to maintain a filial image through recourse to Indianized values, the gap between monasticism and filial piety was nevertheless difficult to bridge as many monks had distant relationships with their parents. When forced to choose between spiritual practice and secular duty toward parents, many rejected traditional filial obligations outright. According to one of Huijiao's narratives, after the monk Faxian's father died, his uncle tried to force him to return to lay life to care for his widowed mother. Faxian steadfastly resisted these entreaties. However, after the death of his mother, Faxian conducted proper mourning to make up for his previous inattention.[23] So although Faxian showed appropriate veneration toward his mother after her death, while she was still alive he would not have qualified as an exemplary son. Unable to harmonize opposite demands, he simply rejected conventional family duty.

Marriage constituted one of the most important expressions of filiality for men. To outsiders, the link between marriage and obedience to parents might seem tenuous, but in Chinese culture the two have become intimately linked. Because the family functioned as an economic unit that needed a member of each sex to carry out both sets of gendered work roles, properly caring for one's parents required a man to take a wife. Moreover, marriage allowed a man to produce the descendants who would carry on the family line and ensure the continuity of ancestral sacrifices. Given the importance of marriage, even today most Chinese men see taking a wife as a prerequisite for full masculine adulthood, and many people not only disparage an aging bachelor as a bad son but also regard him as somewhat unmanly.[24] Of course, this deeply rooted attitude posed considerable problems for monks.

Narratives about ideal Buddhist men not only describe many admirable celibates but sometimes even portray women and heterosexual relations in a negative light. Huijiao occasionally displays an attitude of ambivalence toward women, almost to the point of misogyny. Sometimes he expressed this negative attitude using fanciful images appropriated from anomaly literature, a genre of writing popular at the time.[25] One story describes how Zhufa Chong went off to live alone in a remote place to further his spiritual cultivation, and a mountain sprite (*shanjing*) turned into a beautiful woman and tempted him to renounce his vows.[26] This tale implies that the true nature of woman is both dissolute and demonic, so a man must resist the enticements of female beauty if he is to attain enlightenment. Rather than portraying woman as man's companion, this tale depicts the monk as a superior being who maintains masculine purity by avoiding polluting contact with women.

Although Chinese Buddhists eventually integrated filial rhetoric into their teachings, at this stage it seems that a monk had to choose between mundane obligations to family and a higher spiritual calling. The story of Zhixiu exemplifies these stark alternatives. Despite his determination to become a monk, his parents forbade him to pursue his calling. No doubt this was a common reaction, particularly in the early history of Chinese Buddhism. His parents even secretly arranged an engagement to tie their son to the secular world. Nevertheless, Zhixiu remained steadfast in his resolve to enter a monastery. When the wedding day approached, he simply ran away from home and took the tonsure in defiance of his parents' explicit commands.[27] Intriguingly, Huijiao considered this grossly unfilial monk a Buddhist paragon. Because Zhixiu rejected filial piety to pursue a higher goal, his unwillingness to submit to parental authority became a dramatic act of self-sacrifice. Despite the immorality of his behavior from a conventional point of view, the inescapable pain of his sacrifice elevated his actions to almost heroic proportions. Zhixiu embodied a novel view of manhood. Although readers of the time would have found his behavior deeply shocking, Huijiao nevertheless put him forward as a Buddhist exemplar worthy of emulation.

Filial piety extended to the body, demanding that a man keep his person intact, as he had received it from his parents. However, Buddhists expressed skepticism regarding the value of a perfect body. For example, hair was traditionally an important symbol of gender identity, and filial piety demanded that a man keep his hair fairly long. The society of the time associated hair on both the head and the face with ideal masculinity. For example, Prince Rencheng of Wei was famous for his valor and manliness, as well as for his magnificent beard.[28] And in a continuation of Han dynasty judicial practices, medieval officials shaved the heads of convicts as a humiliating punishment.[29] So for a monk to shave his head and face not only violated gender norms but also disfigured the body that he had received as a precious gift from his parents.[30] Accordingly, Buddhism's opponents pointed to the monk's cleanly shaven head and chin as proof of the religion's contempt for filial piety.[31]

Once freed from the filial prohibition against self-mutilation, monks occasionally took this practice to disturbing extremes. Although the Buddha's original teachings firmly reject harmful asceticism, radical reinterpretations of Buddhism inspired by the *Lotus Sutra* taught that extreme acts such as suicide could lead to positive self-transformation.[32] In Huijiao's concluding essay to the section titled "Death," which concerns exemplary monks who commit suicide, he justifies taking one's life in certain situations by noting that our existence is merely an illusion. Moreover, if a person has already become a bodhisattva, suicide is a way of casting off a useless body to attain greater spiritual heights.[33]

The *Biographies of Eminent Monks* includes a number of stories about clerics who killed themselves through immolation. For example, Huishao burned himself to death on a pile of firewood, with the resulting fire lasting for three days. Witnesses said that they saw stars come out to escort him to the heavenly palace.[34] There could be no more direct rejection of familial responsibilities than a voluntary death that annihilated the body so completely. By directly rejecting traditional norms, Buddhists opened the way for the creation of radically different images of successful manhood.

APPROPRIATION

The second major strategy early Buddhist faithful used to confront native masculine norms was appropriation. Although Chinese initially regarded Buddhism as extremely exotic, believers nevertheless discovered that this foreign faith had many things in common with their native culture. So instead of rejecting all local customs outright in favor of new practices, Buddhists often found it easier to gain acceptance by drawing links between their religion and Chinese culture. This strategy influenced the construction of the new Buddhist manhood.

This grafting of a new religion onto an established culture is far from unique in world history. In fact, regardless of the religion, whenever the faithful begin proselytizing in a new place, they appropriate useful indigenous traditions to win acceptance.[35] Anthropologists describe this cultural borrowing with the unflattering expression "identity piracy," a phenomenon present wherever cultures collide and members of one group adopt characteristics of the other.[36] When the strong appropriate the cultural traditions of the weak, arrogating their interpretation and use, they reinforce their hold over society. But selectively borrowing components from a stronger culture can empower a weaker group, though at the cost of watering down its identity.

Buddhist apologists understood that a controversial minority religion could gain power and prestige by prudently borrowing from the mainstream, and selective cultural appropriation was an important theme in the early history of Chinese Buddhism. At times Buddhists stretched and strained to draw tenuous links between their faith and Chinese culture. Theorists have pointed out how allegory and willful misreading can ease cultural appropriation.[37] Deliberately misconstruing native ideas and practices allowed apologists to present Chinese traditions as akin to Buddhist teachings and thereby to claim useful aspects of the mainstream culture as their own.

Conformity held out tangible advantages to a growing religion, allowing devotees to gain acceptance by adhering to prevailing social norms. Émile Durkheim emphasized that although new social practices continuously emerge through random contingency, only useful behaviors endure and become normative. This process was particularly visible in the shattered society of early medieval China. Creative people devised new practices and ideas to bring a degree of order to the enveloping chaos. However, too much innovation would itself be destabilizing. All levels of society recognized the utility of having a set of common values to foster stability.[38] It would not serve Buddhist interests to undermine the core values binding this fissile society together. If Buddhists were to avoid undermining the society they intended to convert, they would have to find ways to achieve their goals within the context of the prevailing culture. This middle path between two cultures led the faithful to integrate practices associated with respectable Chinese manhood.

The *Biographies of Eminent Monks* often appropriates standard tropes of Chinese masculinity and presents them as Buddhist male norms. For example, the education of the erudite Kumārajīva began in the womb, as his mother listened to expositions of wise teachings at a temple while pregnant. Not coincidentally, this sort of fetal education was also an ancient tradition in China.[39] Other paragons were said to have displayed remarkable intellectual precocity during their schooldays, a standard claim that secular biographers made for talented literati. The young Huichi could learn as much in one day as others learned in ten days, and he particularly enjoyed the secular fields of history and literature.[40] Not to be outdone, the youthful Juexian could learn in one day what it took his classmates a month to master.[41] Of course, since Buddhist views of wisdom differed from secular traditions, the new breed of child prodigies departed somewhat from traditional prototypes. Fasheng attained enlightenment at an early age, a transference of the standard child prodigy motif into an appropriate spiritual equivalent.[42]

Whether in youths or adults, filial piety was one of the prime virtues used to judge any man.[43] Medieval readers found narratives about extraordinary children who sacrificed themselves for their elders extremely touching. One typical secular story describes a man who loyally served his stepmother. Despite his model dedication, one night the evil woman entered his bedroom, intending to kill him while he slept. It so happened that he had gotten up to relieve himself, unwittingly foiling her scheme. When he recognized her violent intentions, instead of becoming angry, he blamed himself for failing to please her. The next morning he begged her to kill him as punishment for his inadequacy as a stepson. This shocking show of filial deference, in stark contrast to her own cruel behavior, stunned her into realizing the error of her ways.[44] Although readers today might find it hard to empathize with such exaggerated filial passions, the original audience would have found this sort of story both believable and touching.

Given the significance of these values to social relations, Buddhists somehow had to appropriate some of the basic conventions of filial piety from secular culture and reconcile them with the Buddhist way of life. However, this project was far from easy, as monasticism made it difficult for a monk to devote himself to his parents. Even so, Buddhist thinkers found many ways to stress filial teachings in both dogma and practice. For example, they reinterpreted sutras to stress latent filial elements. In addition to reassessing their inherited traditions, the Chinese faithful also absorbed certain secular ethics and recast filial piety as a religious duty. This merger resulted in the steady secularization of Chinese Buddhism. By the Tang dynasty (618–907), monks routinely maintained many connections with the lay world, family in particular. Most important, many monks returned home to mourn a deceased parent, thereby reaffirming family ties and acting out the role of dutiful son.[45] In the end, Chinese secular filial values overwhelmed the religion's Indian spiritual otherworldliness and radical individualism. To reach that point, however, Chinese Buddhists appropriated normative filial ideas and disseminated hagiographic narratives to publicize how filial virtue fit with spiritual practice.

Hagiography employed various means to depict monks as sincerely filial, hence respectable. Fayuan showed a bookish concern for the subject, discussing the secular *Classic of Filial Piety* (*Xiaojing*) and *Mourning Costume* (*Sangfu*) in addition to Buddhist texts.[46] Even so, most narratives focused on deed rather than word. For instance, the biography of Daowen describes how a man exhibited exemplary filiality prior to entering a monastery and thereby became a cleric with clear conscience.[47] In other words, he fulfilled his secular obligations to the letter as long as he was part of lay society, enabling him to cut those ties without disgrace. Similarly, while young Sengdu lived with his mother, he was a model of filiality. He had even originally planned to marry and continue leading a secular life, but after his parents' untimely death, he changed his plans and decided to become a monk.[48]

Many tales of filial monks describe them mourning for parents. As traditional mourning customs were long and arduous, few people ever fulfilled them entirely, so anyone who managed to carry out full mourning for a parent demonstrated unusual commitment to filial virtue. Given this mind-set, stories of monks who completed mourning rites to the letter illustrated a passionate devotion to parents among the Buddhist faithful. For example, Kang Senghui's parents died while he was in his teens. Although he planned to enter a monastery, he waited until he had completed full mourning before being tonsured.[49] Because Chinese culture held filial piety, and mourning in particular, in such high regard, these virtues were especially useful for elevating the prestige of foreigners with nebulous backgrounds. Although neither Tanwuchan nor Anqing was Chinese, both performed extensive mourning for their parents, thereby proving to xenophobes that they possessed exemplary virtue.[50]

Voluntarily extending one's devotion to a surrogate parent demonstrated consummate filial merit, and several stories in Huijiao's collection feature this

Kang Senghui. *Source:* Shi, *Fojia de chuanshuo,* 20.

Anqing. *Source:* Shi, *Fojia de chuanshuo,* 16.

unusually scrupulous regard for filial virtue. Orphaned at a young age and raised by an uncle, Yu Daosui in return treated his uncle as a surrogate parent and served him in an exemplary fashion.[51] Similarly, the parents of both Faguang and Daoheng died when the boys were young, and both treated the stepmothers who raised them with model filial devotion. When Daoheng's stepmother died, he waited until he had fully completed his mourning obligations before becoming a monk.[52] These narratives depict monks as not merely complying with secular morals but even outshining their lay peers in the performance of filial duties. In the realm of literature at least, Buddhists succeeded in appropriating a key secular virtue.

TRANSFORMATION

In addition to rejection and adoption, Buddhists sometimes dealt with native Chinese masculinity by transforming aspects of mainstream manly ideals to render them amenable to their own religious sensibilities. Most people find it difficult to accept absolutely novel gender identity. Any man who dares to present himself to the world in an entirely new manner takes an enormous risk, and others will likely perceive him as a failure. Popular opinion can more readily accept change when it is presented as a variation on mainstream manhood instead of outright transgression. Due to the conservatism inherent in mainstream gender values, revisions to masculinity usually constitute variations of existing images rather than an entirely new vision of the ideal man. These variants often emerge in response to evolving social, political, cultural, and economic conditions. The transformation of masculinities provides new templates for male behavior, expanding the scope of agency. When individuals play out novel possibilities, transformed ideals become new social and cultural practices. Transformation allows for some innovation in masculine behavior while preserving other aspects of conventional masculinity, thereby facilitating acceptance. The result is an innovative yet accessible new version of manhood.

Narratives embodying transformations of native masculinity can take several forms. Sometimes a story recounts familiar actions but reads them differently, thereby changing their overall significance. In other instances it preserves the externals of a particular practice while altering the contents somehow. Then there are transformations of language rather than form or content. Using new tropes to describe the masculine can imbue behavior with novel meaning. However the writer achieves this transformation, amending the narratives of idealized masculinity can legitimize unfamiliar behavior.

Masculine ideals transform most quickly as a society undergoes rapid change. Although Chinese historians have traditionally looked askance at the Northern and Southern dynasties as a dark age of chaos, heterodox ideas, and national division, these conditions can spur rapid change. As brilliant nineteenth-century historian François Guizot emphasized, crisis is a catalyst for social dynamism.[53] The Han dynasty's traumatic collapse discredited many customs, values, and ideologies closely associated with the state, making it necessary to adapt many aspects of life to radically new circumstances. Masculinity was no exception.

However necessary change may be, we rarely greet it with enthusiasm. Humanity is inherently conservative; most people cling to the familiar and resist the unknown. Particularly in an impoverished age when prospects are few and problems legion, innovation generates suspicion. Even when necessary to keep up with new conditions, adaptive change must often be coated with a familiar veneer to accord with conservative sensibilities. For this reason, new masculine archetypes frequently emerge as transformations of existing standards. Partial change is the subtlest and most flexible strategy for introducing men to new forms of acceptable male behavior.

The Buddhist confrontation with worldly secular values, and masculinity in particular, exemplifies how one group transformed masculine ideals to create a more amenable vision of manhood. For centuries, Chinese elite identity had been inextricably tied to the state. Since the beginning of the imperial system, because the gentry (*haozu*) lacked the security of hereditary titles, they could only maintain an elevated status over multiple generations by repeatedly placing family members in official posts. Service to the state came to define the group, along with landownership, intermarriage with other gentry families, and a distinctive culture and lifestyle. As the gentry were society's most respected members, people looked up to the ways they expressed masculinity.

Given the gentry's prestige, monks desiring acceptance as respectable men sought ways to imitate elite masculine conventions. Direct appropriation was not easy, however, as monks' lifestyles differed so greatly from those of the men they strove to emulate. So instead of blindly imitating them, monks usually had to transform the gentry's masculine archetypes to make them appropriate to their own way of life. The ways in they adjusted gentry values to suit religious goals went a long way toward shaping ideal Chinese Buddhist manhood.

Buddhist had to reconcile their vision of masculinity with the meticulously hierarchical network of Chinese social relations. Confronted with a social pyramid, Buddhist men of course wanted to establish a place for themselves as close to the top as possible. By imitating the conventions of elite social intercourse, particularly as it had existed during the Han dynasty before the violent disruption of social norms, monks could gain respect. For example, the Han dynasty social elite saw the ties between patron and client as a fundamental social bond.[54] Although this social model declined with the collapse of the Eastern Han, the hierarchy between monks of different ages, birth, and talents within the *sangha* replicated, to a degree, the idealized patron-client relations previously prevalent among elite laymen. At the same time, the horizontal ties between influential monks, or even between prominent monks and literati, mimicked the new sort of relationships between men of similar status that had risen in importance during this chaotic age. In many respects, Huijiao's grand biographical project aimed to encapsulate elite secular masculinity into models appropriate to monastic life.

Because relations with kin were also fundamental to a man's place in the social hierarchy, Buddhists also had to transform normative kinship practices as well. Upon entering a monastery or hermitage, monks deliberately removed themselves from frequent interaction with kin, risking social marginalization. One solution to this problem was to replicate the dynamics of kin relations within the temple. Monks did not interact with one another as strangers. Instead they created a community of brothers bound together by the orderly bonds of fictive kinship. Anthropologists have pointed out that we should not underestimate the pull of relations mimicking kinship. To the people involved, these relationships can seem just as real and important as blood ties.[55] Because faux blood bonds replicated real kinship, they were of course hierarchical, as well as motivated by some of the same feelings and values that held the kinship system together. Moreover, by excluding women from the ceremonial privileges of male temple life, monks institutionalized the gender distinctions at the heart of the patrilineal kinship system, as well as the androcentrism characterizing the male bureaucratic hierarchy of elite lay society.[56]

The emergence of fictive kinship bonds molded life within the temple community. For example, the interaction of monks of different ranks involved displays of authority and deference that mimicked secular filial piety. This key value had already undergone a major shift in society at large, as filial piety came to include deference to one's superiors in the bureaucratic hierarchy.[57] The Buddhist transformation of filial piety broadened this fundamental ideal further still, using it to bolster the clerical hierarchy between junior and senior monks. By transforming a key native Chinese virtue to suit their own purposes, monks replicated an aspect of normative social hierarchy among men, making their own homosocial relationships seem more familiar and comprehensible.

Monks further mimicked the social relations of laymen by turning the *sangha* into a simulacrum of the unequal social strata constituting society as a whole. As Buddhism developed, monasteries became foci of wealth, power, and cultural capital. However, access to these valuable resources by members of the clerical community was extremely unequal. A small minority of monks at the top of the system had almost full control over all temple property and other resources. Senior monks dominated both lower-ranking clerics and any lay tenants and hangers-on attached to the monastery. The unequal relationships among monks of different ranks constituted a striking imitation of secular social strata.[58] This transformation of religious hierarchy along the lines of lay society went further toward making the interactions of Buddhist men seem like a nonthreatening alternative form of conventional masculine relationships.

Service to the state marked another key secular masculine value, and some monks duly served as advisers and courtiers. As clerics gained roles in government, the monastic hierarchy became institutionalized. Some monks, such as Sengrou, enjoyed imperial favor, and these influential clerics gained sway over officialdom, court ladies, and even the ruler.[59] Monks provided invaluable services to the state. They conducted ceremonies for the protection of the realm, cursed the ruler's foes, performed magic to invoke rain, shared wise counsel, and provided the sovereign with access to a valuable trove of learning and scholarship. The state could not allow resources this beneficial, and potentially dangerous, to remain beyond its control. Inevitably, it organized the Buddhist hierarchy into stratified official ranks comparable to posts in the state bureaucracy.

As Buddhism rose in political importance, monks came to occupy a well-defined system of official monastic posts managed by the state, transforming secular bureaucracy to their benefit. A head monk with authority over the entire *sangha* presided over the abbots of monasteries, who also received official titles. At times this blend of religion and administration influenced the underlying ideology of the entire Chinese system of government. Instead of reigning according to Confucian principles, some emperors preferred to employ an overtly Buddhist ideology. The most famous example is Emperor Wu of Liang (502–549), a fanatical Buddhist who required the state to symbolically ransom him four times from the *sangha* as a way to provide huge cash infusions to Buddhist institutions. At times the government operated openly as a theocratic monarchy that proved its legitimacy through patronage of Buddhism and by receiving the blessings of monks.

These examples of transformation round out this survey of strategies that Buddhists employed to challenge

Emperor Wu of Liang.

native masculine ideals. When Buddhist missionaries first entered China, they met with withering criticism. Even during the Tang dynasty, the golden age of Chinese Buddhism, eloquent detractors such as Han Yu (768–824) continued to attack the religion as manifestly alien and incompatible with traditional Chinese values. Although critics interrogated many aspects of this imported foreign faith, they found the transgression of normative gender roles particularly disturbing. Buddhist clerics often failed to conform to conventional standards of male behavior, precipitating a backlash against all aspects of their religion. Buddhists soon realized that to flourish in China, they would have to construct an image of manhood that local laypeople found acceptable. For this reason, early apologists often went far beyond matters of thought and belief to focus on how model Buddhists ought to behave, portraying monks as exemplary men despite their divergence from traditional gender norms.

In the long run, this ambitious project to selectively reject, appropriate, and transform native masculinity was surprisingly successful. Although Chinese literature is replete with populist anticlericalism, the average person nonetheless came to view celibate life in a male community as an alternate but acceptable expression of masculinity. The fact that some parents even placed a son in a monastery to raise the family's collective prestige demonstrates the eventual acceptance of Buddhist manhood.[60] From being a liability, acting out the ideal Buddhist male role became a standard strategy for achieving upward social mobility, both for individual men and their families. Nor was this process limited to this particular case. In fact, the development of Chinese Buddhist manhood demonstrates the more general mechanism of how masculinity changes over time. These potent strategies of rejection, appropriation, and transformation exemplify the standard means that men everywhere employ to challenge prevailing masculine norms. The same techniques would reappear regularly for the remainder of Chinese history, as well as in societies across the globe, and indeed they persist today.

NOTES

1. His name can also be pronounced Fotucheng. For his biographies, see Zhu Hengfu, Wang Xuejun, and Zhao Yi, *Xinyi Gaoseng zhuan* (Taipei: Sanmin, 2005), 9:587–623; Arthur Frederick Wright, "Fo-t'u-teng: A Biography," *Harvard Journal of Asiatic Studies* 11, nos. 3–4 (1948): 321–71.

2. Sheldon Hsiao-peng Lu, *From Historicity to Fictionality: The Chinese Poetics of Narrative* (Stanford, CA: Stanford University Press, 1994), 7, 165. For a model of reading the rhetoric in narratives of masculinity, see Andrew Herman, *The "Better Angels" of Capitalism: Rhetoric, Narrative, and Moral Identity among Men of the American Upper Class* (Boulder, CO: Westview, 1999).

3. Paul Veyne, *Did the Greeks Believe in Their Myths?: An Essay on the Constitutive Imagination*, trans. Paula Wissing (Chicago: University of Chicago Press, 1988), 84, 87.

4. Connell, "The Big Picture," 603–4. For a current Chinese view of research into native masculinity, see Zhao Huijuan and Guo Yongyu, "Xingbie chayi yanjiu de sizhong quxiang," *Xinan Shifan Daxue xuebao (Renwen shehui kexue ban)* 29, no. 5 (September 2003): 32–36.

5. According to late imperial legal documents, a normative male was seen as an adult, married, commoner householder with a respectable family and occupation. Matthew H. Sommer, "Dangerous Males, Vulnerable Males, and Polluted Males: The Regulation of Masculinity in Qing Dynasty Law," in *Chinese Femininities, Chinese Masculinities: A Reader*, ed. Susan Brownell and Jeffrey N. Wasserstom (Berkeley: University of California Press, 2002), 83. For other discussions of some traditional ideas about normative masculinity, see James L. Watson, "Self-Defense Corps, Violence and the Bachelor Sub-culture in South China: Two Case Studies," *Proceedings of the Second International Conference on Sinology* (Taipei: Academia Sinica, 1989), 215; Gilmore, *Manhood in the Making*, 169–71; Ji Dejun, "Lishi yanyi xiaoshuozhong 'rujiang' xingxiang de wenhua jiedu," *Guangzhou Shiyuan xuebao (shehui kexue ban)* 21, no. 2 (2000): 13–15; Susan Mann, "The Male Bond in Chinese History and Culture," *American Historical Review* 105, no. 5 (2000): 1600–1614; Kam Louie, "Global Masculine Identities," in *Asian Masculinities: The Meaning and Practice of Manhood in China and Japan*, ed. Kam Louie and Morris Low (London: Routledge Curzon, 2003), 3–6.

6. In medieval Europe, Christian monks were often portrayed as demasculinized. In fact, in many cultures a religious identity is often expressed through the inversion of gender norms. Steven F. Kruger, "Becoming Christian, Becoming Male?" in *Becoming Male in the Middle Ages*, ed. Jeffrey Jerome Cohen and Bonnie Wheeler (New York: Garland, 1997), 27. New religions often have to reconcile their novel views toward gender with established masculine norms. For example, see Janet Moore Lindman, "Acting the Manly Christian: White Evangelical Masculinity in Revolutionary Virginia," *William and Mary Quarterly* 57, no. 2 (2000): 393–416.

7. Peter Van der Veer, "The Power of Detachment: Disciplines of Body and Mind in the Ramanandi Order," *American Ethnologist* 16, no. 3 (1989): 459.

8. There are countless examples of this practice. For example, English colonizers in India considered Indian men effeminate. Mrinalini Sinha, *Colonial Masculinity: The "Manly Englishman" and the "Effeminate Bengali" in the Late Nineteenth Century* (Manchester: Manchester University Press, 1995), 5.

9. Lewis, *Sanctioned Violence in Early China*, 36–43; Wang Li and Wu Haiyong, "Zhonggu Hanyi fojing Fuchou zhuti chutan," *Zhonggu bijiao wenxue* 3 (1999): 101–18.

10. In a memorial recorded in Zhu, Wang, and Zhao, *Xinyi Gaoseng zhuan*, 9:595, an official lambasts Buddhism for its foreignness.

11. Previous scholarship has demonstrated how biographical narrative has been used to construct a positive masculine image. For example, see Trev Lynn Broughton, *Men of Letters, Writing Lives: Masculinity and Literary Auto/Biography in the Late Victorian Period* (New York: Routledge, 1999), 39.

12. Frederic Jameson, *The Political Unconscious: Narrative as a Socially Symbolic Act* (Ithaca, NY: Cornell University Press, 1981), 79.

13. He Shanmeng, *Wei Jin qinglun* (Beijing: Guangming Ribao, 2007), 51, 53.

14. Mori Mikisaburō, *Rōsō to bukkyō* (Kyoto: Hōsōkan, 1986), 96–97, discusses the general impact of subjugation on Chinese culture.

15. For a comprehensive prolegomenon to the work, see Makita Tairyō, "Kōsōden no seiritsu (ue)," *(Kyōtō) tōhō gakuhō* 44 (1973): 101–25, and Makita Tairyō, "Kōsōden no seiritsu (shita)," *(Kyōtō) tōhō gakuhō* 48 (1975): 229–59. For a discussion of prior works of clerical biography, see Liu Yao, "'Gaoseng zhuan' xulu suolun siben shu kao," *Zhongguo wenhua yanjiu* (spring 2007): 87–92. For the relation of this collection to other works, see Lin Chuanfang, "Ryō Kōsōden no ikyō ni tsuite," *Indogaku butsukyōgaku kenkyū* 24, no. 2 (1976): 272–75.

16. John Kieschnick, *The Eminent Monk: Buddhist Ideals in Medieval Chinese Hagiography* (Honolulu: University of Hawaii Press, 1997), 13–14; Dong Zhiqiao, "'Gaoseng zhuan' de shiliao, yuliao jiazhi ji chongxin jiaoli yu yanjiu," *Dongnan Daxue xuebao (zhexue shehui kexue ban)* 6, no. 4 (2004): 111–16. For Huijiao's rivalry with Baochang, see Tom De Rauw, "Baochang: Sixth-Century Biographer of Monks . . . and Nuns?" *Journal of the American Oriental Society* 125, no. 2 (2005): 203, 208.

17. Robert Shih, trans., *Biographies des Moines Éminents (Kao Seng Tchouan) de Houei-Kiao* (Louvain: Institut Orientaliste, 1968), ix–x; Kieschnick, *The Eminent Monk*, 8, 60. Kiritani Seiichi, "Ryō Shaku Keikō ni okeru rekishi ishiki—toku ni kan kai ishiki no igi ni tsuite," *Indogaku butsukyōgaku kenkyū* 20, no. 2 (1972): 298–301, interprets this collection not as an objective set of biographies but as a calculated response to the author's environment. Yang Haiming, "Jianxi 'Gaoseng zhuan' yu 'Xu gaoseng zhuan' cheng shumu de ji zuo zhuan linian zhi yitong," *Xian Shiyou Daxue xuebao (shehui kexue ban)* 16, no. 4 (2007): 86–90, contrasts Huijiao's collection with later hagiography, showing his writing to be a response to his times.

18. Nakajima Ryūzō, *Rokychyō shisō no kenkyū: shidaibu to butsukyō shisō* (Kyoto: Heirakuji, 1985), 116–270, 515–61.

19. Connell, *Masculinities*, 77, 79.

20. Ruth Mazo Karras, *From Boys to Men: Formations of Masculinity in Late Medieval Europe* (Philadelphia: University of Pennsylvania Press, 2003), 161.

21. Daniel Boyarin, *Unholy Conduct: The Rise of Heterosexuality and the Invention of the Jewish Man* (Berkeley and Los Angeles: University of California Press, 1997), 1–2.

22. Di Yanchun and Zhang Yunhui, "Zhongguo fojiao jielü yu xiaodao guannian," *Wenshan Shifan Gaodeng Zhuanke Xuexiao xuebao* 19, no. 2 (2006): 59–60; Zeng Youhe, "Shixi fojiao xiaodaoguan yu rujia xiaodaoguan de chayi ji qi yinying zhi dao," *Shanxi Gaodeng Xuexiao shehui kexue xuebao* 19, no. 11 (2007): 30–32. Kenneth K. Ch'en, *The Chinese Transformation of Buddhism* (Princeton, NJ: Princeton University Press, 1973), 18, provides a general typology of the main responses of Buddhists to Chinese filial ethics.

23. Zhu, Wang, and Zhao, *Xinyi Gaoseng zhuan*, 3:133.

24. Rubie S. Watson, "The Nomad and the Nameless: Gender and Person in Chinese Society," *American Ethnologist* 13 (1986): 619–31.

25. Alan Sponberg, "Attitudes toward Women and the Feminine in Early Buddhism," in *Buddhism, Sexuality, and Gender*, ed. by Jose I. Cabezon (Albany: State University of New York Press, 1992), 3, 18.

26. Zhu, Wang, and Zhao, *Xinyi Gaoseng zhuan*, 4:241.

27. Zhu, Wang, and Zhao, *Xinyi Gaoseng zhuan*, 8:556.

28. Liu I-ching, *Shih-shuo Hsin-yü: A New Account of Tales of the Word*, trans. Richard B. Mather (Minneapolis: University of Minnesota Press, 1976), 470.

29. Liu, *Shih-shuo Hsin-yü*, 28; Yu Jiaxi, *Shishuo xinyu jianshu* (Taipei: Huazheng, 1991), 2:59.

30. Hairstyles often have important cultural significance. Alf Hiltebeitel et al., eds., *Hair: Its Power and Meaning in Asian Cultures* (Albany: State University of New York Press, 1998).

31. Kenneth K. S. Ch'en, "Filial Piety in Chinese Buddhism," *Harvard Journal of Asiatic Studies* 28 (1968): 82.

32. Kieschnick, *The Eminent Monk*, 42–44.

33. Zhu, Wang, and Zhao, *Xinyi Gaoseng zhuan*, 12:801–2.

34. Zhu, Wang, and Zhao, *Xinyi Gaoseng zhuan*, 12:791–92; for some other examples, see 12:798–800.

35. For example, Andrew Finlay Walls, *The Cross-Cultural Process in Christian History* (London: Continuum, 2002).

36. Simon Harrison, "Cultural Boundaries," *Anthropology Today* 15, no. 5 (1999): 11.

37. David Dawson, *Allegorical Readers and Cultural Revision in Ancient Alexandria* (Berkeley: University of California Press, 1991).

38. Charles Holcombe, "The Exemplar State: Ideology, Self-Cultivation, and Power in Fourth Century China," *Harvard Journal of Asiatic Studies* 49, no. 1 (1989): 98–101.

39. Wu Pinxian, "Cong Da Xiao Dai Liji kan funü renshen qijian de lisu guifan," *Kongmeng yuekan* 7 (2000): 36–45.

40. Zhu, Wang, and Zhao, *Xinyi Gaoseng zhuan*, 6:343; for some other examples of precocity, see 1:20, 2:120, 4:220, 4:245, 5:249, 6:367, and 8:537.

41. Zhu, Wang, and Zhao, *Xinyi Gaoseng zhuan*, 2:110.

42. Zhu, Wang, and Zhao, *Xinyi Gaoseng zhuan*, 4:213.

43. For views of filial piety in this era, see Tadao Yoshikawa, *Rokuchyō seishinshi kenkyū*, 2nd ed. (Kyoto: Dōhōsha, 1986), 548–67.

44. Liu, *Shih-shuo Hsin-yü*, 8.

45. Huang Qingfa, "Tangdai sengni de chujia fangshi yu shisuhua qingxiang," *Nantong Shifan Xueyuan xuebao (zhexue shehui kexue ban)* 18, no. 1 (March 2002): 91; Lu Tongyan, "Cong 'chujia wujia' dao chujia er you 'jia'—Tang dai sengni xiaodao lunli xianxiang luexi," *Linyi Shifan Xueyuan xuebao* 30, no. 4 (2008): 77–81.

46. Zhu, Wang, and Zhao, *Xinyi Gaoseng zhuan*, 8:512.

47. Zhu, Wang, and Zhao, *Xinyi Gaoseng zhuan*, 7:473.

48. Zhu, Wang, and Zhao, *Xinyi Gaoseng zhuan*, 4:245.

49. Zhu, Wang, and Zhao, *Xinyi Gaoseng zhuan*, 1:23.

50. Zhu, Wang, and Zhao, *Xinyi Gaoseng zhuan*, 1:6, 2:122.

51. Zhu, Wang, and Zhao, *Xinyi Gaoseng zhuan*, 4:239.

52. Zhu, Wang, and Zhao, *Xinyi Gaoseng zhuan*, 5:287, 6:378.

53. François Guizot, *The History of Civilization in Europe*, trans. William Hazlitt, ed. Larry Siedentop (1846; rpt. London: Penguin, 1997), 28–31.

54. Patricia Ebrey, "Patron-Client Relations in the Later Han," *Journal of the American Oriental Society* 103, no. 3 (1983): 541–42.

55. Julian Pitt-Rivers, "The Kith and the Kin," in *The Character of Kinship*, ed. Jack Goody (Cambridge: Cambridge University Press, 1973), 89–106.

56. Sponberg, "Attitudes toward Women and the Feminine in Early Buddhism," 13.

57. Michael Nylan, "Confucian Piety and Individualism in Han China," *Journal of the American Oriental Society* 116, no. 1 (1996): 2–5, 8–11.

58. You Biao, *Songdai siyuan jingjishi gao* (Baoan: Hebei Daxue Chubanshe, 2003), 236–48.

59. Zhu, Wang, and Zhao, *Xinyi Gaoseng zhuan*, 8:534.

60. Walter Liebenthal, "Chinese Buddhism during the 4th and 5th Centuries," *Monumental Nipponica* 11, no. 1 (1995): 54, 57–58.

4

⁂

Tang Dynasty (618–907 CE)
Masculine Honor and Women

Scholars have sometimes approached the study of gender with the mistaken assumption that the masculine and feminine occupy discrete realms. To the contrary, however much the experiences of men and women may diverge, they are never completely dichotomous.[1] Because masculine norms affect every aspect of social endeavor, cutting across politics, commerce, ritual, warfare, and culture, they invariably affect women as well. In addition, women influence how men think about themselves. The construction of masculinity and femininity is dialectical, with changes in expectations regarding each side provoking responses from the other. Given the interactive nature of gender, discussions of historic Chinese manhood should remain conscious of the ways in which masculine ideals influenced women's lives and vice versa.

Chinese masculinity evolved within the context of an honor culture, making the safeguarding of reputation a key goal of men's relations with the opposite sex. Unlike their counterparts in modern Western societies, which view reputation as an individual quality, Chinese men traditionally received praise or criticism not just on their own behalf but also for the behavior of those in their social circle. When a culture conceives honor so broadly, a misbehaving woman can easily destroy the carefully nurtured reputations of the men around her. From the man's perspective, a woman was above all a tool for elevating and preserving his reputation. Because a woman had the power to destroy a man's good name, men had to organize relations between the sexes in such a way as to neutralize this threat. Masculine honor thus gave rise to patriarchal values and even outright misogyny.[2]

As is typical of an honor culture, codes of ideal female behavior in imperial China tended to emphasize loyalty and obedience to male kin, particularly fathers, husbands, and fathers-in-law. Ethical discourse regarding women also stressed sexual fidelity.[3] These rules regulating female behavior were usually justified as virtues or simple norms. Although rules mandating fidelity targeted women, these behavioral restrictions clearly emerged to benefit male kin. Once restrictive codes of female conduct were in place, the community could criticize and shame any woman who failed to uphold these standards.[4] Men thus gained a powerful tool to control their womenfolk and thereby protect their own reputations.

Anthropologists emphasize the importance of women to the construction of male identity. Even if women are physically absent when men are working together or socializing, their immaterial "presence" in men's minds still influences male subjectivity. In some respects, men understand themselves vis-à-vis women, whether in contrast or complementarity.[5] However, female influence on masculinity did not translate into power over men. While women had certain forms of agency and privilege, the social system benefited men more than women overall.

The role of women in the construction of masculinity can be quite complex, as honor cultures harbor contradictory views of female sexuality. Claude Lévi-Strauss famously conceptualized marriage as a system for exchanging women among families, often as a strategy for obtaining material gain or social status.[6] According to this model, a woman is analogous to scarce property owned by her patrilineal group. Chastity represents ownership by male kinsmen, making the female body a symbolic token of male honor.[7] A woman's premarital virginity and subsequent wifely fidelity bring prestige to all her male kin. However, in many honor cultures, men seek premarital or extramarital sexual conquests to prove their virility. If a man has sexual relations with a woman outside marriage, his own reputation increases while that of her kinsmen declines. Honor thus becomes a zero-sum game: one man's victory is another man's loss. This contradiction exemplifies the two forms of masculine power. Men seek to exercise "external hegemony" over women while struggling for "internal hegemony" over other men.[8]

ORIGINS OF CHASTITY

In early China, female behavioral norms emerged that reduced the potential for social conflict, stabilized an unequal gender system, and maintained male honor and privilege. Society expected absolute fidelity to their spouses from married women, and ideally the unmarried and widowed would practice abstinence. Other key female virtues included self-sacrifice for the sake of family harmony, obedience to kinsmen, fidelity, and devoted service to senior in-laws. The early Chinese referred to this constellation of related virtues as chastity (*zhenjie*).[9]

The physical partition of women from men safeguarded male honor by making it difficult for women to have sexual relations outside marriage. Separating "inner" feminine space from "outer" masculine space had a significant impact on the movements of each sex. While society expected men to venture forth and participate in the outside world of affairs, the virtuous woman preserved her modesty by remaining inside the home as much as possible.[10] Significantly, inner and outer did not just denote different spaces but also took on moral connotations as well. By remaining hidden in the inner quarters of the home, the good woman shielded herself from the gaze of strange men and possible sexual temptation. Limiting female movement thus helped safeguard the honor of a woman's husband and kinsmen.

The priorities of honor culture channeled the development of gender norms to ensure that men could effectively control female kin. By the Tang dynasty (618–907), both the law and custom institutionalized gender inequality. For

Even a high wall could not guarantee chastity. *Source:* Yang Yi, *Zhongguo gudian xiaoshuo shier jiang* (Shanghai: Shanghai sanlian, 2007), 114.

example, a woman was legally obligated to demonstrate filial piety toward her elders and to obey senior men in the household.[11] The penalty for a wife who beat her husband was heavier than that for a husband who beat his wife. And a wife who killed her husband faced a heavier punishment than a husband who murdered his wife. The courts meted out similarly unequal penalties for adultery, abandonment, and other crimes.[12] Moreover, the senior man in the household controlled almost all property, with a wife's belongings theoretically limited to her personal effects and dowry.[13]

Some people compared the perfect marriage to musical harmony, and it was up to the wife to do whatever necessary to maintain an air of concord.[14] By the Tang era, popular opinion held that marriages were fixed by heaven, hence sacred and immutable.[15] This idea permeated popular consciousness, becoming a common theme in literature. For example, in the late imperial era belief was widespread that an evil wife risked being struck dead by lightning as divine retribution for her wickedness.[16]

The ideal of wifely fidelity even stretched to include commitment to a deceased husband. Beginning in the Eastern Zhou, it was standard practice to inter spouses together in a common grave or tomb, signifying that the marital bond endured even after death.[17] By the Tang, these spousal burials were justified as an expression of the righteous (*yi*) bond that unites a couple.[18] Eventually the idea of wifely fidelity toward a deceased spouse expanded much further. Some widows refused remarriage out of a sense of permanent loyalty to a dead husband.

Widow chastity was certainly not customary in antiquity. In the Zhou era, female remarriage was not yet an important topic of moral discourse.[19] Ideas on the matter exhibited a noticeable shift during the late Western Han dynasty when the erudite Liu Xiang (79–8 BCE) compiled his influential *Biographies of Women* (*Lienü zhuan*). A collection of this sort, narrating significant events in the lives of exemplary women, was absolutely unprecedented. The general sense of moral decay and rising female influence at court seems to have concerned Liu.[20] Although he composed *Biographies of Women* to address specific political machinations, which it failed to resolve, the work's long-term impact on gender discourse was nevertheless profound. It initiated a literary genre that allowed male authors to write systematically and at length about ideal female behavior. Writers composed many similar works down to the end of dynastic history. By the Tang, Liu Xiang's belief that wives should remain eternally faithful to their husbands had become so commonsensical that families sometimes conducted posthumous weddings to unite two deceased people in matrimony.[21] As people believed the marital bond extended into the afterlife, marrying the dead seemed perfectly reasonable.

Although most of the stories in Liu's collection emphasize female wisdom and moral competence, a few exalt wifely fidelity and even widow chastity.

Even if chastity narratives were initially rare, the influence of these early narratives was considerable nonetheless. The ideal of the wife or widow sacrificing herself as proof of fidelity would strengthen through the centuries, while tales about wise women declined in popularity.[22] Anthropologists who study chastity

The widow Gaoxing cuts off her nose. *Source:* Lai Xinxia, ed., *Mingke lidai lienü zhuan* (Tianjin: Renmin meishu, 2004), 2:35.

in other regions have noted that when social mobility increases, heredity can no longer form the basis for family honor as position is no longer fixed from birth.[23] Accordingly, as Chinese society became more dynamic, chastity became increasingly important as a mark of reputation.

Maintaining a commitment to permanent widowhood was in fact extremely difficult for the average woman, as it usually doomed her to a life of penury.[24] Nevertheless, the ideal chaste widow willingly went to extremes to prove her commitment to marital fidelity. Perhaps the most famous example of the model chaste widow from *Biographies of Women* is Gaoxing of Liang. Her husband died while she was still young, and her beauty and outstanding conduct attracted noble suitors, including the ruler of Liang himself. Faced with unbearable pressure to forsake her deceased husband, she declared, "I have learned that the principle of the wife is that once having gone forth to marry, she will not change over, that she may keep all the rules of chaste loyalty." Then she held a mirror in front of her face, took up a knife, and cut off her nose. Gaoxing knew that her mutilated appearance would repel all suitors, allowing her to maintain a pure state of chaste widowhood permanently. The ruler's reaction reveals the moral to the story. Rather than condemning this grotesque self-mutilation, he praised Gaoxing for her righteous conduct.[25]

Significantly, this ideal chaste widow justified self-destructive violence as an expression of righteousness (*yi*). Although closely associated with normative manhood and masculine honor, this virtue also frequently appears in didactic literature as the moral principle underpinning widow chastity and wifely fidelity. It is not surprising that the culture associated male honor so closely with female chastity, as the two concepts are readily intertwined. In fact, the conduct of female kin was crucial to men, as it redounded on their own reputation. Anthropologists have observed that in many cultures, a man can inherit honor from his father, but the mother can pass down only shame.[26] The need to discourage female behavior that might shame kinsmen accounts for many of the gendered values of Chinese honor culture.

Liu Xiang's story of the wife of Duke Zhuang of Li reveals the implications of this link between male and female righteousness. This woman forthrightly declares righteousness to be the key to a good marriage. "The principle of the husband and wife is that there is righteousness and then they are united."[27] Although righteousness was originally a moral quality associated with male honor, as a wife belonged to her husband's inner circle she had an important role in fostering his reputation. Because a wife's actions redounded on her husband's honor, it seemed reasonable to judge her according to the standards of righteousness. Assessing female virtue according to the fundamental value underpinning male honor implied that a woman should behave well not just for her own sake but, more important, to preserve her kinsmen's reputations, particularly her husband's.

Righteous suicide for the sake of chastity. *Source:* Lai, *Mingke lidai lienü zhuan,*
1:211.

This intimate connection between male honor and female righteousness
explains why behavioral restrictions so often expressed female virtue.[28] Ritual
experts sought to protect male honor by propounding numerous rules designed
to separate the sexes, thereby minimizing opportunities for female sexual
malfeasance. Far more was expected from women than men in this regard.
In *Biographies of Women*, the widow Bo Ji explains to bystanders why being
incinerated alive was preferable to leaving a burning building unescorted and
shamefully exposing herself to the gaze of strange men. "To transgress a rule of
righteousness in order to save one's life is not as good as to keep the rule of righteousness and to die in doing so."[29] These stories assume that a woman's body
constitutes her fundamental essence; her sexuality synecdochically represents

Preferring to burn to death rather than be exposed to the male gaze. *Source:* Lai, *Mingke lidai lienü zhuan*, 1:218.

the woman herself.[30] Overall, her impact on male honor reflects a woman's worth. If her sexual integrity becomes compromised, disgracing the men in her circle, a woman's existence is worthless.

Although chastity narratives coalesced as a distinct genre in the late Western Han dynasty, they burgeoned further into a major medium of gender discourse. These stories steadily increased in popularity and influence, and many thousands of imitations appeared up until the end of the imperial era. Even Ouyang Xiu (1007–1072), respected as a skeptical and rational commentator on past events, cast aside his usual high standards of evidence to embrace this factually dubious genre.[31] Apparently the propagandistic value of these stories, which served as potent didactic tools for propagating masculinist ideology, compensated for any shortcomings in literal veracity.

As chastity ethics grew in importance, these values intensified, and the acceptable degree of female self-sacrifice for the sake of male honor increased. Narratives about virtuous female martyrs gradually mutated, becoming increasingly violent over the centuries.[32] By the Ming dynasty (1368–1644), chastity stories routinely culminated in self-mutilation or suicide. For example, in *Ming History* (*Mingshi*), the standard account of that dynasty, 78.5 percent of narratives about chaste women end with the heroine's death.[33] Maintaining male honor required increasingly costly sacrifices from women.

TANG DYNASTY CHASTITY

Although society in every era of imperial history lauded female chastity, academics have studied the expression of this practice during the Tang dynasty particularly well. Years of vigorous scholarly debate have teased out many of the subtleties, complexities, and contradictions inherent in chastity rhetoric, shedding light on how female ethics related to masculine norms. The mechanics of Tang chastity provide many clues for understanding how male and female gender constituted a unitary system, with each influencing the other.

Tang dynasty widow chastity is richly attested. Given the violence and chaos that plagued the era and the fact that the average husband was almost a decade older than his wife, widowhood was a common condition.[34] In addition to documentation provided by transmitted texts, numerous stone commemoratory inscriptions describe specific widows from elite families who deliberately refused to remarry, a state known as *shuangju*. Whereas only a handful of stone inscriptions document a woman's remarriage, one scholar has collected 264 specific examples of chaste widows, making the records of remarried widows just 3.8 percent as numerous as those for chaste widows.[35]

Some have argued that the chastity ideal strengthened during the late Tang, a period initiated by the momentous An Lushan Rebellion (755–763).[36]

During this unruly era, factionalism, eunuch rule, the rise of independent local warlords, and periodic foreign invasions together condemned the dynasty to steady decline. Interestingly, as the state decayed, emperors and their officials promoted widow chastity more enthusiastically. The patronage of female virtue in fact demonstrated a concern for masculine honor, thereby raising the ruler's prestige among powerful men to help sustain a crumbling political system. The popularity of this strategy attests to its utility, as rulers employed it throughout imperial history.[37] In addition, the great lineages of the northeast became increasingly prominent as the imperial center declined, and these old families also boosted their reputation for honor by adhering to particularly strict interpretations of the rites governing marriage and gender roles. In this manner, prominent groups and institutions strengthened themselves through deliberate association with the ideals underpinning masculine honor, including the affiliated virtue of wifely fidelity.

The politicization of masculine honor highlights a contradiction regarding the standard interpretation of Tang dynasty relations between the sexes. Academic stereotypes depict the Tang as a relatively "open" society as compared to those of later, allegedly more conservative periods. Not only did nomadic cultures to the north and west exert considerable influence on Tang customs, calling restrictive traditional gender norms into question, but the general atmosphere seems to have been fairly relaxed in some respects. Polychrome ceramic statues of ladies on horseback and a painting of gregarious beauties relaxing at a picnic depict elite women enjoying far more freedom of movement than in later eras, when prosperous families often confined their womenfolk to the home. The evidence regarding Tang gender relations thus presents the historian with two quite different impressions.[38] On the one hand, women seem to have enjoyed a high degree of autonomy in many ways. And literature depicts men treating their spouses with respect, with strong women advising their husbands or even berating them. But at the same time, law, ritual, and philosophy hardened steadily on questions regarding female virtue. As time progressed, masculine honor increasingly became a fundamental guiding principle of social relations.

MUTILATION TALES

The rising popularity of stories about women who cut out their own flesh to feed their in-laws dramatically illustrated the ideal of female submission to a patriarchal kinship order. The earliest narratives about self-mutilation and cannibalism described loyal male retainers or filial sons who cut off their own flesh to feed a hungry lord or sick parent. Even though these tales were factually dubious, mutilating oneself to feed a father or mother became a stock expression of painful self-sacrifice for the sake of filial devotion.[39] By the Tang dynasty, apocryphal stories about this practice were common. The *New Records of the Tang* (*Xin Tangshu*) provides a typical example of the genre. "Zhang Quanyi was a man of Fucheng in Zizhou. When he was young his father passed away and he was raised by his older brother Quanqi. Their mother became sick. Quanqi cut flesh from his thigh to feed her and she recovered."[40] According to prevailing medical theory, human flesh contained powerful curative properties.[41] However, as buying human meat was impossible, one could only acquire this exotic healing agent by cutting off some of one's own flesh. Self-mutilation was known as *gegu* (cutting flesh from the thigh), although narratives described the harvesting of meat from other parts of the body as well.

Although self-mutilation for the sake of medicinal cannibalism was originally the purview of filial sons, during the Tang this practice became associated with exemplary women. The link with women intensified over time so that by the late imperial era, most self-mutilation tales featured female protagonists.[42] In fact, the tone of women's biographies became increasingly violent in every respect. Suicide, self-mutilation, cannibalism, and murder became standard themes in narratives about exemplary women. The Tang histories feature several violent stories of the sort that would later become extremely common. For example, one Ms. Wang drank poison rather than betray her natal family. Then there was the seven-year-old Gao Meimei, who chose to die, along with her family, at the hands of her father's enemy rather than survive and live in disgrace. The Dou sisters jumped off a cliff to avoid rape.[43] Overall, of the fifty-three biographies of exemplary women in the two Tang official histories, twelve involve mutilation while others end in death.[44] Although female biographies began as a fairly pacific genre, by the Tang dynasty violence had already become a hallmark feature.

Many of these stories feature a woman who mutilates herself to provide nourishing flesh that might heal one of her husband's kin, a literary trend that increased in popularity over time. By glorifying female sacrifice for the sake of the male-oriented kinship group, this influential genre taught readers that the virtuous woman is willing to give up anything, including her own flesh, to benefit her husband's family. By teaching women to surrender their bodies to the androcentric group, the culture of male honor extended even greater control over women. Even if very few women actually mutilated themselves, stories celebrating the act propagated the message that the good woman should dedicate herself to furthering the interests of her husband and parents-in-law.

SHREW STORIES

Of course not all women submitted quietly to the harsh dictates of masculinist honor culture. Strong and wily women would always strive for greater autonomy. Some rebelled outright, while others manipulated the system to their own benefit. Accounts of high-profile jealous wives, such as Emperor Han Gaozu's vengeful consort Empress Lü (d. 180 BCE), provided the kernel of this compelling theme in historiography and literature.[45] Over time, plots and characters became standardized, resulting in the emergence of so-called shrew stories as a distinct genre. These tales initially evolved during the early rise of narrative fiction, matured during the Tang, and remained extremely popular until the end of imperial history. Because the shrew dominated her husband by bullying him, she represented a direct inversion of the normative gender order.[46] By rejecting the core values underpinning honor culture, the shrew threatened her male kin with emasculation. As the Chinese literary canon often focuses on issues of masculine identity, it is not surprising that stories of women who menaced the foundations of masculine power fascinated readers.

The shrew was the product of unequal expectations regarding gender.[47] While the virtuous woman maintained her virginity before the wedding, stayed faithful within marriage, and if possible took a vow of permanent chastity when widowed, her husband could take concubines, have assignations with serving girls and slaves, and patronize prostitutes. From the standpoint of honor culture, these inequitable standards seemed perfectly reasonable. While a woman's promiscuity dishonored the men in her kinship circle, demonstrations of sexual prowess bolstered a man's reputation. Masculinist thought, literature, and ritual all taught that female virtue required acquiescence to these unequal rules.

While most women seem to have tacitly accepted this imbalanced state of affairs, some did not, giving rise to stories about violent and abusive wives. The shrew is a standard archetype in Tang literature.[48] Usually this character enjoys an exalted social station, empowering her to cause major headaches for her wayward spouse. While her husband usually bears the brunt of her anger, others can suffer as well. She often chooses easy targets, such as her husband's low-status sexual partners (concubines, slaves, and prostitutes), who have few means to resist her attacks. She not only makes her husband miserable but often torments herself as well by obsessing about her victimhood. One reason for the perennial Chinese fascination with the virago is her ambiguous status as both bully and victim.

The shrew is both the promiscuous husband's worst nightmare and also an extreme manifestation of the model wife. Chinese society expected a wife to value fidelity above all else. However, the virago is fanatical in this regard. Whereas the original intent of female fidelity was to safeguard male honor, by demanding reciprocity from her husband, the shrew compromises his masculine image. The problems arising from demands for marital fidelity from men as well as women highlighted the contradictions in the value system underpinning masculine honor. Men in shrew stories are often pathetically comic figures, to the point where a man who stays out too late feasting with friends is afraid to go home and face his wife's jealous rage.[49] Men could even suffer a termagant's wrath for no particular reason.

> Shen Cunzhong [Shen Gua, 1030–1094] married Madame Zhang at a ripe old age and was often flogged by her. She would pull out his hair and beard until he was running with blood. Upon Madame Zhang's death, everybody rejoiced for him.[50]

Authors sometimes made the shrew even more extreme by depicting her as irrationally moody, treacherous, violent, or lazy, emphasizing her faults to bring out the full satirical or comic potential of this stock character.[51] Although exaggerated to comic proportions, the shrew was a symptom of the highly unequal rules regulating gender relations, which safeguarded male honor at the expense of female dignity and autonomy.

We can understand some shrews as rebels contesting a gender system based on masculine honor and privilege. However, in many cases the virago's terrifying rages expressed an odd kind of affection. As it was her duty to remain faithful to her husband and ideally develop an exclusive emotional bond with him, she fought against his extramarital dalliances. Some shrews were just trying to make the marriage system work better by enforcing monogamy for both partners.

ESCAPES FROM MASCULINE HONOR

The shrieking termagant may have been a stock character in fiction, but this stereotype had a basis in the underlying social context. Not all Tang dynasty women acquiesced to male domination. In fact, the law allowed women to sever their bonds with undesirable men. Divorce was the most obvious option. Either husbands or wives could initiate noncontested divorce, known as *heli*, which was not uncommon.[52] It seems that women generally sought divorce for economic reasons, such as a husband's poverty or debilitating chronic illness.

A legal process known as righteous separation (*yijue*) empowered a government functionary to declare a couple divorced without the instigation or even consent of either party.[53] This arrangement had a humane intent, providing local officials with the means to protect abused wives who did not dare initiate divorce proceedings themselves. More rarely, authorities invoked righteous separation to free a man from marriage to a dangerous woman. The *Old Tang History* (*Jiu Tangshu*) records an unusual incident in which a man named Fang Rufu married the daughter of an important official surnamed Cui.[54] The marriage was unhappy, as Fang's jealous wife constantly terrorized him. She even beat two of Fang's serving girls to death and had them buried in the snow. A local prefect ordered the marriage dissolved, extricating Fang Rufu from this nightmarish union with a well-connected but violent spouse.

To appreciate the realities of Tang dynasty divorce, it is important to remember that couples did not generally understand marriage in romantic terms or see it as a path to personal fulfillment. For most, marriage was above all an economic necessity. Households apportioned mundane tasks by sex and thus required both an adult man and an adult woman to function properly. Moreover, as children represented the only means of support for the elderly, the main goal of marriage was reproduction. Divorce thrust a woman outside this economic institution, condemning her to an uncertain future. Given the hardships of unmarried life, a woman didn't take the idea of leaving her husband lightly, however much she might long for freedom. Some women increased their autonomy by building close relationships with one another, even establishing formal self-help organizations to provide material aid in times of need.[55] But while female coalitions might provide temporary help during emergencies, they could not offer an unmarried woman permanent security.

A more drastic way for women to escape from the constraints of marriage and masculine honor was to simply withdraw from secular society. Both Buddhism and Daoism flourished amid the famously effervescent culture of the Tang, allowing some women the chance to leave home and sever formal ties with male kin to become nuns. Scholars in China have described a "Daoist nun craze" during the Tang, when large numbers of women left behind the dust of the world to enter Daoist temples. These female clerics, known as *nüguan*, had very different lives from their austere Buddhist counterparts.[56] A Daoist nun severed regular social ties, but under the rubric of a relatively worldly religion that condoned sensuality. Some elegantly appointed Daoist temples even boasted luxurious touches to attract women from the upper stations of society. Daoism granted nuns considerable emotional and sexual autonomy, and they were often the equals of men in temple life. Some of the greatest Tang poems describe the romantic life of Daoist nuns.

Not surprisingly, this lifestyle attracted widows in particular. By renouncing worldly ties, a woman removed herself from the suffocating constraints of male honor. Her behavior now redounded on herself alone. Some women sought to become nuns as an alternative to marriage; others entered a temple upon becoming widowed. Considering the self-sacrifice expected of the chaste widow and the practical rigors of life without a husband, Daoist institutions offered an appealing refuge. Even some widowed imperial princesses became nuns, signifying the respectability of a Daoist vocation.

Tang literature presents an exaggerated fantasy of the Daoist nun in the persona of the female immortal (*xiannü*).[57] Stories about these angelic deities descending to earth to present surprised mortal men with gifts, and perhaps seduce them, were highly popular, often portraying these idealized women as sexually desirable yet unfailingly kind and selfless. The female immortal and the jealous shrew presented readers with opposite female stereotypes, one representing man's romantic fantasy and the other his marital nightmare.

The female immortal genre presented male readers with a daydream about a romantic relationship with a strong, beautiful woman outside the restrictive gender system grounded in honor culture. These gauzy visions of a flawless woman, autonomous and desirable, hint at male discontent with the state of gender relations. Although women bore the brunt of patriarchy's hardships, some men also resented the limitations of intransigent gender roles. Neither an arranged marriage with a resentful wife nor forcing oneself on a purchased concubine or prostitute could provide a man with a fulfilling emotional life. Even though the marriage system bolstered male privilege, men nevertheless sometimes chafed under its constraints. However, the prevailing social order would condemn as unfilial and unrestrained the discontented man who dared to rebel.[58] With escape forbidden, lonely men sought refuge in their imaginations. Romantic tales of desirable female immortals provided a psychological sanctuary from the emptiness of unfulfilling conventional relationships with the opposite sex.

Although less than respectable than conventional marriage, high-class prostitution also provided a measure of personal autonomy, allowing courtesans to mingle with men outside marriage and possibly establish close emotional connections.[59] There were many kinds of prostitutes during this era, and the line between slaves, concubines, and household prostitutes was often vague. In addition to regular prostitutes, who simply satisfied carnal appetites, a small group of exceptional women served as entertainers and companions for elite men. Often intelligent and highly talented, these women had studied poetry, music, dance, and conversation so that they could entertain groups of men at feasts.

Courtesans and their admirers exchanged numerous poems, many of which connoisseurs preserved in recognition of their literary quality, allowing scholars to chart the changing relations between these women and their clients. When the dynasty began, relations between courtesans and elite men were fairly distant. Early Tang poems about these women dwell on their physical and sensual aspects, emphasizing their appearance, as though the poet is observing them objectively from a distance. In this era, men usually only encountered courtesans at feasts and did not have many opportunities to become familiar with the women their poems described. As a result, poets resorted to symbolism to convey their general impressions of these detached entertainers.

As China degenerated into chaos after the An Lushan Rebellion, the nature of relationships between courtesans and their patrons changed. Prominent men grew less concerned with propriety and began to nurture close bonds with courtesans, whose company provided a refuge from society's intractable problems.

A courtesan might serve as an emotional companion, providing a man with the friendship and understanding absent from the unglamorous atmosphere of his own home. Finally, as the dynasty slid into terminal decline, educated men began to see these women in explicitly sexual terms. Disappointed with their careers, they turned to sex and drink to escape reality.

Gentlemen and courtesans. *Source:* Yang, *Zhongguo gudian xiaoshuo shier jiang*, 120.

Across this trajectory, the relationships between men at the apex of society and elite courtesans became increasingly intimate and intense. The openness of these relationships and the satisfactions they provided men were possible because courtesans were not members of their clients' kinship networks. Even if a privileged man formed a close bond with one of these women, her behavior did not affect his reputation. Men could enjoy refined companionship or even a sexual relationship without worrying about the possible impact on their masculine pride.

Historical records present conflicting images of Tang dynasty women that encompassed courtesans, shrews, chaste widows, nuns, divorcees, and even fictional female immortals. Given this diversity, gender roles were far from unitary or deterministic. Sometimes women and men could choose from among a broad range of options presented by society. Not only did the gender identity of each sex influence the other, but individuals also exercised agency to make the best of social constraints and opportunities. In many cases, they managed to thrive despite considerable limitations on normative gendered behavior. And as the conditions of society changed, ideas about gender responded. Over the centuries, chastity rhetoric became increasingly common, as well as extreme, with suicide and mutilation as standard themes. This intensification of chastity rhetoric arose in response to a number of factors, from the increasing politicization of gender norms to rising pressures on men in a more competitive society.[60] As the sexes interacted amid dynamic social conditions, this complex dialectic drove expressions of manhood and womanhood in new directions.

NOTES

1. Harry Brod, "Some Thoughts on Some Histories of Some Masculinities: Jews and Other Others," in *Theorizing Masculinities*, ed. Harry Brod and Michael Kaufman (Thousand Oaks, CA: Sage, 1994), 82–96.

2. Campbell, *Honour, Family, and Patronage*, 275–76.

3. For an example of how male honor can lead to control over the sexuality of female kin, see Peter C. Dodd, "Family Honor and the Forces of Change in Arab Society," *International Journal of Middle East Studies* 4, no. 1 (1973): 40–54. A more general analysis appears in Patricia M. Rodriguez Mosquera, Anthony S. R. Manstead, and Agneta H. Fischer, "The Role of Honour Concerns in Emotional Reactions to Offenses," *Cognition and Emotion* 16, no. 1 (2002): 144.

4. Louise Edwards, "Women in Honglou Meng: Prescriptions of Purity in the Femininity of Qing Dynasty China," *Modern China* 16, no. 4 (1990): 411–12.

5. Matthew C. Guttman, "Trafficking in Men: The Anthropology of Masculinity," *Annual Review of Anthropology* 26 (1997): 386.

6. For an influential interpretation of this concept, see Pierre Bourdieu, *Masculine Domination*, trans. Richard Nice (Cambridge, UK: Polity Press, 2001), 43–45.

7. Schneider, "Of Vigilance and Virgins," 18.

8. Demetrakis Z. Demetriou, "Connell's Concept of Hegemonic Masculinity: A Critique," *Theory and Society* 30, no. 3 (2001): 341.

9. Wei-hung Lin, "Chastity in Chinese Eyes: *Nan-Nü Yu-Pieh*," *Hanxue yanjiu* 12 (1991): 26. Lin's article explains how the concepts of *zhen* and *jie*, initially quite vague, acquired specific connotations over time. For a critique of the early concept of harmony as applied to women, see Bret Hinsch, "Harmony (*He*) and Gender in Early Chinese Thought," *Journal of Chinese Philosophy* 22 (1996): 109–28.

10. Lisa Raphals, *Sharing the Light: Representations of Women and Virtue in Early China* (Albany: State University of New York Press, 1998), 195–206, traces the early development of gendered inner and outer space.

11. Duan Tali, "Tangdai nüxing jiating jiaose ji qita diwei," *Zhongguo wenhua yanjiu* (2002): 141–49.

12. Duan Tali, "Cong fuqi guanxi kan Tangdai funü jiating diwei bianhua," *Lanzhou Daxue xuebao* 6 (2001): 53.

13. Wang Houxiang, "Tangdai jiating caichan ye jicheng zhidu shulun," *Wenshi zazhi* 4 (2003): 66–68.

14. Yao Ping, *Tangdai funü de shengming licheng* (Shanghai: Shanghai Guji, 2004), 108.

15. Niu Zhiping, "Tangdai hunyin de tianmingguan," *Hainan Shiyuan xuebao* 2 (1995): 59–61; Yao, *Tangdai funü de shengming licheng*, 111.

16. Charles E. Hammond, "Waiting for a Thunderbolt," *Asian Folklore Studies* 51, no. 1 (1992): 38–44.

17. Yao, *Tangdai funü de shengming licheng*, 118–22.

18. Chen Ruoshui, *Tangdai de funü wenhua yu jiating shenghuo* (Taipei: Yunchen, 2007), 285.

19. Chen Xiaoang, "Chunqiu shiqi de zhenjieguan," *Xinan minzuxue xuebao (zhexue shehui kexue ban)* 21, no. 19 (2000): 105–9.

20. Raphals, *Sharing the Light*, 78–86.

21. Yao, *Tangdai funü de shengming licheng*, 173–98.

22. Raphals, *Sharing the Light*, 249, describes the decline of the so-called learned instructress motif.

23. Pitt-Rivers, "Honour and Social Status," 65.

24. Jennifer Holmgren, "The Economic Foundations of Virtue: Widow-Remarriage in Early and Modern China," *Australian Journal of Chinese Affairs* 12 (1985): 1–27.

25. Albert Richard O'Hara, *The Position of Woman in Early China: According to the Lieh Nü Chuan "The Biographies of Chinese Women"* (Washington, DC: Catholic University of America Press, 1945), 122–24; Shinomi Takao, *Ryū Kō Retsujoten no kenkyū* (Tokyo: Tōkai Daigaku, 1989), 515 (4.14).

26. Pitt-Rivers, "Honour and Social Status," 42, 53, 61–62.

27. Shinomi, *Ryū Kō Retsujoten no kenkyū*, 474 (4.5); O'Hara, *The Position of Woman in Early China*, 109.

28. A link between male honor and female chastity occurs in many cultures, particularly those espousing Mediterranean-style manhood. Campbell, *Honour, Family, and Patronage*, 269–70, 286–88.

29. Shinomi, *Ryū Kō Retsujoten no kenkyū*, 454 (4.2); O'Hara, *The Position of Woman in Early China*, 105.

30. Sherry J. Mou, *Gentlemen's Prescriptions for Women's Lives: A Thousand Years of Biographies of Chinese Women* (Armonk, NY: M. E. Sharpe, 2004), 139.

31. Richard L. Davis, "Chaste and Filial Women in Chinese Historical Writings of the Eleventh Century," *Journal of the American Oriental Society* 121, no. 2 (2001): 204–18.

32. Matthew H. Sommer, "The Uses of Chastity: Sex, Law, and the Property of Widows in Qing China," *Late Imperial China* 17, no. 2 (1996): 77–130, explores in detail the implications of the fact that female chastity benefited the husband and his family, as well as the legal mechanisms used to safeguard the husband's interests under Qing law.

33. Du Fangqin, "Ming Qing zhenjie de tedian ji qi yuanyin," *Shanxi Shida xuebao* 10 (1997): 43. Paul S. Ropp, Paola Zamperini, and Harriet T. Zurndorfer, *Passionate Women: Female Suicide in Late Imperial China* (Leiden: Brill, 2001), explores various aspects of the issue.

34. Yao, *Tangdai funü de shengming licheng*, 92, calculates that wives were on average 8.5 years younger than their husbands.

35. Mao Yangguang, "Cong muzhi kan Tang dai funü de zhenjieguan," *Baoji Wenli Xueyuan xuebao (shehui kexue ban)* 20, no. 2 (2000): 68.

36. Jin Xia, "Qianlun Tangdai houqi hunyin de tedian," *Shandong Jiaoyu Xueyuan xuebao* 91 (2002): 46–48, 51.

37. Mark Elvin, "Female Virtue and the State in China," *Past & Present* 104 (1984): 111–52.

38. Duan, "Cong fufu guanxi kan Tangdai funü jiating diwei bianhua," 53–58, explores this contradiction in detail.

39. For the origins of this practice and the evolution of the term *gegu* (cutting flesh from the thigh), see Fang Jinhua, "'Gegu' ciyi kaoshi," *Taizhou Shizhuan xuebao* 20, no. 4 (1998): 41–43; Liu Guangming, "'Gegu' ciyi de yanbian," *Chizhou Shizhuan xuebao* 16, no. 4 (2002): 60–61.

40. Ouyang Xiu, *Xin Tangshu*, annotated by Song Qi et al. (Beijing: Zhonghua Shuju, 1975), 195:5591.

41. For a detailed description of the myriad curative properties attributed to consuming human flesh, see Qiu Zhonglin, "Renyao, xieqi yu xiaogan—gegu liaoqi xianxiang zhong de yiliao guannian yu minsu xinyang" (paper presented at *Medicine and Society: A Symposium*, Institute of History and Philology, Academia Sinica, Taipei, Taiwan, 1997), 3–16.

42. Fang Yan, "Songdai nüxing gegu liaoqin wenti shixi," *Qiusuo* 11 (2007): 210–12, explores why women embraced this practice.

43. Mou, *Gentlemen's Prescriptions*, 148.

44. Mou, *Gentlemen's Prescriptions*, 160–61.

45. Hans van Ess, "Praise and Slander: The Evocation of Empress Lü in the *Shiji* and *Hanshu*," *Nannü* 8, no. 2 (2006): 221–54.

46. Keith McMahon, *Misers, Shrews, and Polygamists: Sexuality and Male-Female Relations in Eighteenth-Century Chinese Fiction* (Durham, NC: Duke University Press, 1995), 57.

47. Ōsawa Masaasa, *Tō Sō jidai no kazoku, kekkon, josei: tsuma wa tsuyoku* (Tokyo: Akashi, 2005), 110–12, discusses the theory that the shrew motif in Chinese literature arose out of contradictory gender expectations in the cultures of Han and northern nomadic peoples.

48. Niu Zhiping, "Tangdai dufu shulun," in *Zhongguo funüshilunji xuji*, ed. Bao Jialin (Taipei: Daoxiang, 1991), 55–65.

49. Niu Zhiping, "Shuo Tangdai junei zhi feng," *Shixue yuekan* 2 (1988): 38.

50. Yenna Wu, *The Chinese Virago: A Literary Theme* (Cambridge, MA: Council on East Asian Studies, Harvard University, 1995), 31.

51. Wu, *The Chinese Virago*, 7.

52. Jia Yanhong, "Tangdai funü lihun leixing qianxi," *Qining Shizhuan xuebao* 4 (2002): 63–65; Yao, *Tangdai funü de shengming licheng*, 125–33.

53. Yao, *Tangdai funü de shengming licheng*, 124.

54. Liu Xu et al., *Jiu Tangshu*, annotated by Liu Jie and Chen Naiqian (Beijing: Zhonghua, 1975), 111:3325.

55. Lin Yanzhi, "Tangdai shiqi Dunhuang diqu de nüren jieshe," *Zhongguo wenhua yuekan* 6 (2000): 32–50.

56. Qiu Guihua, "Tangdai nüxing rezhong rudao yuanyin chutan," *Anhui Daxue xuebao (Zhexue shehui kexue ban)* 24, no. 3 (2000): 55–58.

57. Jiao Jie, "Xiannü xiafan—jituo Tangdai nanzi lixiang de wenhua xianxiang," *Lishi yuekan* 4 (1999): 122–26.

58. Ōsawa, *Tō Sō jidai no kazoku, kekkon, josei*, 81–83.

59. Zheng Zhimin, "Tang dai shiren yu jinü guanxi de yanbian—yi 'Quan Tang shi' wei zhongxin," *Zhongxing shixue* 12 (1994): 65–85.

60. Guo Songyi, "Qingdai funü de shoujie he zaijia," *Zhejiang shehui kexue* 1 (2001): 124–32, provides statistics clearly documenting the intensification of chastity rhetoric in the Qing dynasty. For the increasing pressures on men in the late imperial era, see Matthew Sommer, *Sex, Law and Society in Late Imperial China* (Stanford, CA: Stanford University Press, 2000), 10. For an example of the politicization of chastity, see Janet M. Theiss, *Disgraceful Matters: The Politics of Chastity in Eighteenth Century China* (Berkeley: University of California Press, 2004), 25–54.

5

-涅槃-

Song Dynasty (960–1279 CE)
Cultural Capital and Manhood

Convention singles out the Song dynasty (960–1279) as a decisive turning point in Chinese history. Prior to this era, an aristocratic culture put more value on bloodline than ability; economic activity was modest and government institutions limited. During the Song, however, society came to value men largely for their own accomplishments and refinement. Hereditary privilege declined, to be replaced with an increasingly sophisticated bureaucratic system run by officials chosen for their education and talent. In addition, rapid economic expansion transformed society. Unprecedented prosperity and urban growth opened up a wide range of new possibilities for the ambitious. These changes expanded and transformed the social elite. The apex of society no longer embraced only a small number of old families. A much larger group of educated gentry staffed the bureaucracy, thereby achieving prominence and affluence. At the same time, nouveau riche merchants used their wealth to challenge the prestige of landed gentlemen. All of these changes affected the ways in which men manifested masculinity, as the norms of manhood adjusted to suit changing circumstances.

During the Song, literati culture came of age. Although men could previously gain respect by demonstrating cultural literacy, for the first time cultured accomplishments became recognized as the supreme social distinction. Education and refinement consequently signified ideal elite masculinity. Kam Louie has argued that we can understand ideal Chinese manhood through the bipartite model of *wen* (civil) versus *wu* (martial), with the warrior personifying *wu* manhood, whereas the literatus exemplified the values of *wen*.[1]

Of course this typology had limited relevance to the lives of ordinary men, as peasants were unconnected to either professional warfare or high culture. Despite its limitations, however, this model remains useful for conceptualizing hegemonic masculinity. People respected some masculinities more than others, and both scholar and warrior, while poles apart in terms of personality and behavior, represented two archetypes of hegemonic masculinity. Although most men only strove to achieve normative manhood, society deemed these two masculine identities superior. Nor were civil and marital masculinity mutually exclusive. A soldier might display his erudition by circulating poetry, while some literati showed a conversance with military matters.[2] But of these two masculine ideals, the man of civil culture, educated and tasteful, was overall the most highly regarded paragon of manhood. The Song witnessed a fundamental transformation of Chinese masculinity—the emergence of the literatus, a paragon of *wen*, as the exemplar of hegemonic elite manhood.

CULTURAL CAPITAL

To achieve literatus status, one had to be able to deploy high culture in an orthodox manner. In consequence, cultural capital became inextricably linked to the most highly respected expressions of manhood. Sociologist Pierre Bourdieu stressed the importance of culture to the achievement and maintenance of social position, an observation that fits squarely with the nature of hegemonic masculinity in Song China.[3] Whereas social theorists have traditionally interpreted social class and status in economic terms, Bourdieu pointed out how the social elite of every era use cultural performance to construct a superior identity. In other words, one attains high status not just by flaunting wealth but also by demonstrating a familiarity with prestigious cultural practices. To gain true acceptance as a full member of the elite, even the wealthy must behave with propriety and show an appreciation for the right cultural productions. The vulgar parvenu lacks this ability, making him a perennial target of ridicule.

Because a man can teach his sons the cultural practices he has acquired, he has the opportunity to bequeath a measure of his own cultural supremacy to his heirs. Reproduction of the family is not just a biological process. To perpetuate the family in its current form, members strive to pass down their privileges to the next generation, including not just wealth but also cultural capital. Elite families in particular hope that their heirs will be able to continue employing the prestigious objects and practices that mark superior status.[4]

Bourdieu's powerful insight into the relation between culture and social station is particularly relevant for understanding precapitalistic societies such as imperial China, in which prestige did not always directly correlate with wealth. According to prevailing opinion, a literatus of modest means was superior to a wealthy merchant, at least in theory. Bourdieu found that educated people tend to be much more adept at assimilating high taste than the ignorant, as education teaches students how to acquire cultural capital and also trains them in the language, customs, and content of high culture. Besides education, family background also plays a vital role in elevating taste, as children absorb numerous cultural cues from their home environment. As Song literati tended to have both education and high family background, they were far more likely to inherit prestigious taste than those raised in merchant families. Not surprisingly, the attributes of hegemonic masculinity, as personified by the *wen* literatus, often ran in families.

Bourdieu takes his analysis even further by specifically linking the accumulation of symbolic capital to masculine honor.[5] In early times, the circulation of women through the kinship system via marital alliances acted as a primary vehicle for conferring honor on men. Women had value not just as human beings but also as prestigious symbolic objects exchanged through the formal rites of marriage. If a man received a wife from a high-status family, she represented her entire kinship group, imbuing her with a symbolic value far beyond her individual identity. Even accumulating concubines could symbolize masculine power, hence honor. The symbolic value of women helps account for the rise of widow chastity, as a woman's remarriage removed her symbolic prestige from the reputation of the deceased and thereby decreased his honor. By the Song, various symbolic tokens of high culture had become central to male honor. Accumulating a repository of cultural capital and passing it down to one's sons became a prime strategy for maintaining hegemonic masculinity down through the generations.

Masculinity is often agonistic. However, the shift away from vengeful violence toward the skillful deployment of cultural symbols transformed competitive hegemonic masculinity. In antiquity, elite men were ready to defend their honor through violence. Early sources attest to the frequency of vengeful fights, murder, vendettas, and even large-scale warfare undertaken to demonstrate manliness. Over time, however, violent quarrels between elite men declined, such that by the Song people would have thought it bizarre and even shameful for one literatus to attack another physically. An increasingly strong state asserted the rule of law and strove to prohibit private vengeance. Moreover, newer interpretations of Confucian ethics taught the importance of moderation and self-control. Elaborate codes of manners increasingly emphasized the need to treat other members of the elite with elaborate politesse to avoid causing them to lose face in public. Due to a series of complex social and political changes, violent revenge took on negative connotations at the higher end of society.

The decline of violence among the elite did not mark the end of competitive masculinity. Reputation still mattered as much as before but was constructed in extremely different ways. This transformation correlated with the emergence of the *haozu*, a social stratum often referred to in English as the gentry. The Qin dynasty (221–207 BCE) swept away the feudal aristocracy, thereby detaching social status from hereditary title and allowing wealthy landlord families to emerge as the new elite. However, wealth alone did not distinguish the gentry; they also cultivated common cultural practices to symbolize their lofty status. A dedication to learning, archaic rituals, literary composition, and patronage all became closely related to gentry status. This transformation in the markers of elite social status had a huge impact on hegemonic masculinity. The most admirable man increasingly became one able to demonstrate publicly a mastery of high culture.[6]

The connection between taste and manhood grew more intimate over time. In particular, the institutionalization of a sophisticated examination system during the Song, which remained in place for the remainder of imperial history, solidified this link. State service was not only lucrative but also an invaluable source of prestige. Previously, recruitment into the bureaucracy had often been ad hoc, and the well connected might obtain a post despite lacking a proper education. From the Song onward, however, most members of the civil service had undergone a grueling series of tests.[7] To remain competitive, elite men had no choice but to undergo a rigorous education in the classical canon. This redirection of manhood toward the correct deployment of high culture went far beyond the examination system. Cultural refinement became intimately connected with ideal manhood. The educated and tasteful connoisseur, conversant in classical learning and adept at polite aesthetic pursuits such as tea connoisseurship and calligraphy, became the new icon of hegemonic masculinity.

FLOWERS AS CULTURAL CAPITAL

The popularity of flower appreciation during the Song dynasty, as well as the association of flowers with the most prestigious form of manhood, exemplifies the intimate link between symbolic capital and elite masculinity. Flowers are a particularly intriguing case study because they have feminine associations in many cultures. But Chinese masculinity did not rest on absolute opposition to the feminine, leaving room for both sexes to exhibit some similar feelings and inclinations.[8] During the Song, a gentleman could buttress his masculine image by becoming intimately familiar with the culture of flowers, conversant in their metaphors and symbolism, and adept at manipulating flower imagery. Literati deemed ordinary peasants and merchants too vulgar to understand the profound beauty of the natural world. Hence an excruciatingly refined appreciation of flowers became a mark of literati hegemonic masculinity.

Given the prestige of floral culture, people referred to gardeners and connoisseurs in elevated terms as "famous gentlemen" (*mingshi*), "gentleman friends" (*shiyou*), "distinguished gentlemen" (*jiashi*), or just plain gentlemen (*shi*). They also referred to flower cognoscenti as "high-ranking men" (*gaoren*), "high-ranking famous men" (*gaomingren*), "famous notables" (*minggong*), "gentlemen" (*junzi*), "scholars" (*ru*), and "worthies" (*xian*).[9] This rhetoric of exclusivity raised the status of flower experts, identifying them as superior to the hoi polloi, who lacked this civilized talent.

Gardening and high status became so closely linked that men known for their outstanding taste in this field were called "gentlemen who study gardening."[10] These were not necessarily the wealthiest flower lovers. Others might have far larger or more lavish gardens. Instead, certain gentlemen earned respect for their gardens' notable tastefulness rather than their size. A family closely associated with the fame of its garden became distinguished as a flower household (*huahu*) or garden household (*yuanhu*).[11] Men from these select families nurtured a common identity grounded in shared cultural practices such as horticulture and garden construction. In the absence of social supremacy based on aristocratic title or pure wealth, elite identity lacked an objective foundation. Recognition as a member of one of the handful of local flower households thus became a practical means for a man to confirm his social superiority. And if they banded together, the prestige of individual flower connoisseurs could rub off on one another, and all would benefit from the resulting elevation in status.

In earlier ages, when social position was largely hereditary, flowers, though perhaps appreciated for their beauty, were certainly not a key to ideal manhood. With increasing mobility and social complexity, however, the symbolic dimension of material culture became an important component of a man's identity, leading connoisseurs to imbue flowers with layers of complex symbolism. Because literati had relatively homogeneous educations, experiences, and goals, they used flowers to symbolize aspects of their common worldview, constructing a subtle system of elite masculine discourse.

Outsiders who lacked the same cultural and social background found literati flower discourse difficult to fathom. This enigmatic air lent horticulture prestige as a profound art associated with the upper echelons of society, and demonstrating a familiarity with the language and values of orthodox flower connoisseurship became a way for elite men to compete for honor. Whereas men of the Zhou and Han dynasties might have struggled for supremacy by waging a violent vendetta, during the Song mastery of the proper manner of discussing, collecting, growing, and displaying flowers became a far more appropriate way to prove oneself as a successful man. Together with the numerous other accomplishments of the ideal literatus, from landscape painting to poetry composition, flower culture served as a competitive arena for displaying masculine prowess. If a man showed an aptitude for appreciating flowers in the approved fashion, he won praise and honor. In this way horticulture became an important component of the cultural capital underpinning hegemonic masculinity.

PEONIES AND HEGEMONIC MANHOOD

According to the painstakingly refined conventions of Song culture, flowers could convey a surprising range of connotations. Particular flowers became closely associated with ideological and philosophical positions, lifestyles, and even political factions. The lotus symbolized Buddhist otherworldliness, chrysanthemums recalled principled recluses, the long-leaf Chinese orchid was a favorite of scholars, and so on. Among these symbolic flowers, peonies were perhaps most popular with the Song elite, who associated them closely with worldliness, wealth, power, luxury, and pedigree—all attributes conveying elite manhood. The different ways men appreciated the peony and manipulated its symbolism serve as a vivid case study in how they employed material culture to express and contest hegemonic masculinity.

Song dynasty vase with peony decor. *Source:* Zhang Daoyi, *Zhongguo tuan daxi* (Qingdao: Shandong meishu, 1993), 4:68.

In fact people at all levels of society admired the peony. During the late Tang, it was already common for residents of the capital to travel to scenic spots near the city to view peonies in a beautiful natural setting, a custom even more popular during the Song. Some towns hosted large peony festivals completely unrelated to high culture and featuring lively events such as outdoor feasting beneath peony-covered scaffolding.[12] While the wealthy could appreciate peonies in their own gardens, men of lesser means admired these flowers in public spaces. Large crowds thronged the famous gardens of urban temples and ruined homes to sing and play musical instruments in tribute to these luxuriant blooms.[13] These raucous popular celebrations were far removed from the dignified fetes of self-consciously refined gentlemen, who disdained these coarse activities as unworthy of the true connoisseur.

Originally the peony was nothing more than an unusually large and vivid wildflower native to northern China. Even during the Song, when gentleman gardeners bred magnificent hybrids, they were still actively collecting rare specimens from the wild. As gardening became a standard leisure activity for the elite, some officials sought out unusual varieties of wild peonies when they traveled to remote areas on government business. Once introduced into the gardens of the elite, wild peonies proved popular largely because they are so easy to hybridize, allowing clever gardeners to produce new varieties exhibiting extravagant shapes, colors, and scents.[14] By the Song, the peony garden had become a standard accoutrement of worldly success.

The painstaking effort that high-placed growers put into peony cultivation attests to the importance accorded these flowers. As connoisseurs began reading meaning into the peony, they transformed it from a mere pretty object into a significant cultural symbol that could serve as a mark of superior manhood. Among the various significations ascribed to this flower, perhaps most important is that it symbolized wealth. Gentry families made peonies the centerpiece of their gardens as the flower most appropriate to their station. Some privileged families even gained fame for their intimate connection with a rare hybrid. For example, the "Zuo Purple" peony's association with the wealthy and powerful Zuo family became a kind of trademark that brought its members fame and honor.[15]

As gentry families embraced peony cultivation with enthusiasm, this flower became a stock symbol of worldly success, a quality referred to as nobility (*fugui*). The Confucian canon repeatedly mentions this ideal as an acceptable goal in life. By the Song, *fugui* had become a standard term applied to the prosperous and respected official. Important ideals demand representative symbols, so gentry officials appropriated the peony to embody their worldly success. In this way the peony became a standard symbol of the cultured, educated, landed elite whose status was tied to government service, as opposed to the rising group of rich merchants who may have had wealth (*fu*) but lacked high rank (*gui*).

The reception accorded these flowers at court demonstrates the prestige of peony culture. The peony became a standard gift from the tasteful official to the emperor. The gift of a rare peony solved a difficult problem: what sort of present could one possibly give the emperor of China? Since the monarch lacked for nothing, a gift reflecting good taste and appropriate symbolism proved the ideal solution to this quandary. For example, one official presented a hundred peonies to the palace every year.[16] Conversely, the emperor might present a potted peony as a particularly prestigious gift to a favored courtier.[17] Although inexpensive in material terms, these gifts were redolent with symbolic meaning.

As flowers gained symbolic significance, connoisseurs classified people and plants into analogous hierarchies under the assumption that the garden served as a metaphor for the human world. Just as people fell into different ranks, so

Peony design on Song dynasty silk fabric. *Source:* Zhang, *Zhongguo tuan daxi,* 4:244.

too could their floral counterparts be exalted or base. To this way of thinking, the yellow peony was as handsome as a king, the red peony as lofty as a queen; lesser breeds of the plant were analogous to royal concubines, teachers, officials, imperial clansmen, gentlemen, sycophants, and the vulgar. With peonies at the apex of the garden world, enthusiasts extended the parallels with human society to encompass other plants, insects, and even weather conditions, all arranged into a strictly defined hierarchy.[18]

The peony became infused with additional profundity when connoisseurs asserted that it exemplified moral virtue, thereby turning this flower into an even more potent form of cultural capital. While the connection between plants and virtue might not seem very logical those outside this cultural milieu, Song garden experts considered this linkage entirely reasonable. Thus, in contrast to ordinary flowers, they believed the peony exhibited lofty moral purity (*gaojie*) and described it as "lustrous and pure as jade," another object thought to embody virtuous qualities.[19] Some flower lovers even argued that the peony possessed mysterious metaphysical attributes that manifested the deepest workings of the cosmos.[20] The connoisseur who understood this flower had therefore mastered profound esoteric wisdom as well as beauty.

PEONY WARS

Song gentlemen faced daunting competition from ambitious merchants who aggressively used their wealth to attain respectability. An explosion in economic activity had made Chinese society far more prosperous and mobile than ever before. As a result, individuals could no longer simply inherit status generation after generation. A man had to prove himself worthy of honor or else decline in station. The need to compete with others for reputation and achievement elicited intense insecurity among the educated gentry.

Because the dynamic commercial economy had commoditized almost everything, the nouveau riche could simply purchase the trappings of respectability, making them formidable foes. A typically droll couplet by Ouyang Xiu highlights the contradictions between the values of literati and merchants.[21]

> Pure breeze and a radiant moon are priceless.
> Too bad they only cost forty thousand cash!

Although natural beauty was theoretically free, it brought the most prestige when enjoyed with the confines of a refined (and very expensive) garden. This meant that a merchant could simply purchase a lavish garden full of rare flowers and stake a claim to the same masculine honor accorded the refined literatus.

Peonies. *Source:* Liu Qiulin and Liu Jian, eds., *Zhonghua jixiangwu datudian* (Beijing: Guoji wenhua, 1994), 439.

A standard sign of elite status was a tasteful garden devoted to peonies. In this commercialized milieu, families with a long history of cultural accomplishment might have labored for generations to mold their gardens according to the most discerning standards of good taste, only to have prodigal descendants sell off their prized status symbols to arrivistes. For example, at the height of their fortunes, men of the Wei family of Loyang collected an unusual variety of rare wild peony that symbolized their prominence. Eventually the fortunes of the Wei failed, and they sold off their garden, including the "Wei peony," which had brought them fame and admiration.[22] But disaster for the seller was a precious windfall for the buyer. The purchaser not only gained an outstanding garden but, far more important, could publicly flaunt his owner-ship of a supremely prestigious cultured space representing indisputably good taste. Famous gardens regularly traded hands as established families decayed and ambitious parvenus sought out the material tokens of literati honor.[23]

Masculine peony culture gave rise to an endless tug-of-war between elitism and commercialization. First, refined literati would define a particular cultural practice as prestigious. Then clever entrepreneurs would market it for easy con-sumption by prosperous merchants. In response, literati would concoct even more complex forms of appreciation. However, all too often merchants com-mercialized these newer cultural practices as well to further bolster their own prestige. The endless competition for honor between men of the mercantile and landed elites was akin to a cultural arms race.

Commoditization of the privileged symbols of elite masculine culture threatened the superior status of the educated gentleman. In effect, good taste was now for sale to the highest bidder. Merchants eagerly bought up the ac-coutrements of masculine prestige to legitimize their new fortunes in the eyes of the world. Literati might smirk behind their elegant painted fans, but when a merchant purchased a garden equal to their own, condescension became far more difficult.

Enterprising entrepreneurs even made the symbols of elite masculinity avail-able to people of relatively modest means. Elegantly decorated restaurants, taverns, teahouses, and brothels appeared in towns and cities. Some establish-ments provided access to the tokens of elite masculinity as a cultural bait to lure social climbers, allowing customers to spend their leisure hours in refined environments decorated in literati taste. High-end tavern keepers modeled their establishments on the homes of government officials, in some cases even converting actual official residences.[24] The owners of teahouses and restaurants decorated their venues with antiques, curios, paintings, gardens, and arrange-ments of cut flowers.[25] While relaxing in these elevated surroundings, patrons could imagine themselves temporarily elevated to the same heights of elegance as the literati in nearby private gardens. Men who lacked a family tradition of high taste, formal education, or inherited wealth could now imitate some of the trappings of literati culture. The rampant commercialization of elite cultural symbols threatened the exclusivity of literati identity. If hegemonic manhood lacked exclusivity, in what way were the gentry superior? This troubling ques-tion haunted Song literati.

A cultured gentleman might distinguish himself from the vulgar crowd through the kinds of flowers in his garden. A merchant might easily grow or-dinary peonies purchased in the marketplace, but the gentleman collected rare varieties. Because there existed so many peony hybrids, a man of taste could set himself apart by seeking out exotic new types not readily available on the open market. The dense network of connections among the gentry allowed them to circulate rare flowers among themselves, thereby enabling a closed social group to monopolize the most prestigious peonies. By deliberately excluding outsiders, they cooperated to maintain their collective claim to hegemonic manhood.

The best way to make a name in the world of horticulture was to become associated with a specific unique cultivar. As a result, prominent families had close links to certain peonies. The Yao, Wei, Zuo, Niu, Jin, Li, Zhang, Min, Liu, Ou, and Yuan families, among others, all named unusual peonies after themselves. They became eligible for this honor by discovering an unknown variety in the wild and transplanting it to their garden, hybridizing a new kind of flower from existing domestic stock, or publicizing a lesser-known type of peony by making it the focal point of an outstanding garden.

One example shows how the elite could translate a unique type of peony into public honor. The Niu family bred a beautiful new variety in a striking shade of yellow that became known as the "Niu Family Yellow." Eventually this flower came to the attention of Emperor Zhenzong. At one imperial feast dedicated to flower appreciation, members of the Niu family presented him with one of their namesake flowers, thereby earning public renown.[26] The fact that a rare peony could draw imperial notice illustrates the utility of these flowers in raising social status. In contrast, a merchant who assembled a peony collection through commercial channels would never be able to attract such attention. Given the prestige derived from success at hybridization, the creation of new peonies was an extremely competitive pursuit. Wealthy gardeners strove to produce the most unique and beautiful new strains. Even the name of a hybrid could display this spirit of one-upmanship. The Yao family dazzled the floral world with its new variety of yellow flower, but when a Mr. Jin created a superior variation, he proudly called it "Jin Yellow Beats Yao Yellow."

One wealthy garden enthusiast summed up the importance of rare plants to a family's prestige in a poem.[27]

> Varied books and ancient classics fill the halls.
> The Floral Pavilion has visiting immortals at the base of a misty mount.
> In years to come, if you do not sell these flowers,
> our family will have worthy descendants.

These verses emphasize how important the symbolic capital of flowers was to men of the elite, both for themselves and their progeny. As long as a man's descendants preserved these tokens of refinement, they could maintain an honorable facade of high culture that set them above wealthy parvenus.

Commercial forces made an increasing number of peony cultivars available on the open market, rendering the garden filled with myriad varieties practicable to anyone with enough money. Song authors mention a flourishing market in these plants. Farmers took up horticulture as a lucrative cash crop, flooding the market with ordinary but affordable peonies. Some flower households even used commercial forces to their advantage, turning their family gardens into commercial operations, growing large numbers of flowers for sale.[28]

A few gardeners sought renown by cultivating peonies on a gigantic scale. One family grew an estimated fifty to sixty thousand peonies in its extensive gardens.[29] However, as peonies became commonplace, a man could no longer distinguish himself simply by owning a large number of flowers. He had to procure increasingly rare hybrids to impress visitors with his high status. Of course families committed to horticulture for generations were much likelier than social arrivistes to have accumulated unusual hybrids. When someone created a unique cultivar, he and his descendants usually tried to keep it prestigious by maintaining a monopoly, denying the flower to outsiders. Arrivistes had to content themselves with the mundane varieties available in the marketplace.[30] So while the peony symbolized status, exotic hybrids served as double confirmation of elite identity.

This demand for unusual flowers created a speculative market in rare plants. New hybrids could be outrageously expensive, such that a single cutting of the "Elegant Yellow Peony" demanded an astronomical sum that only the wealthiest gardener could possibly afford.[31] With prices of exotic hybrids so high, theft became a problem. Guards had to be posted to watch the most valuable peonies round the clock to protect them from thieves.[32]

Even though they could earn huge sums from rare flowers, many people still refused to sell, a resistance to economic self-interest rooted in the values of the age. To wealthy gardeners, these expensive plants represented something far more precious than money. As gentlemen strove to distinguish themselves from wealthy merchants, rare flowers became an invaluable source of prestige. Unable to procure the best flowers on the open market, powerful officials sometimes even bullied the owners of famed gardens into handing over their most treasured blooms.[33]

REFINING THE MANLY PEONY

Because literati were often inferior to merchants in terms of wealth, they redefined male honor by associating it more closely with cultural activities than tangible objects. According to this new standard of ideal manhood, men who could perform exclusive cultural activities with fluency and taste earned the greatest prestige. Threatened by an army of cultural epigones, Song literati became obsessive about demonstrating elegance (*ya*) and condemning vulgarity (*su*). The elite flower connoisseur went to enormous lengths to set himself above uncouth commercialized taste, making sure that his own garden was completely devoid of any trace of vulgarity.[34]

As peonies were a symbol of wealth and privilege, the rich but unrefined often appreciated them during sensual celebrations involving eating, drinking, and perhaps even sex. An evening of peony appreciation might begin with guests entering a hall perfumed with the intoxicating fragrance of countless blooms. Servants would bring in alcohol and snacks, and the revelry would begin. Courtesans might appear, their hair and clothing decorated with brilliant red cut peonies. As one woman sang, the rest plied the guests with drink as the evening degenerated into raucous, drunken revelry.[35] Though able to buy the right kind of peony and a cultured setting, a merchant would still likely appreciate the flowers in a patently crass manner. When a wealthy parvenu's concubines tossed peonies at a target to decide who would get to sleep with him that night, flower culture devolved into mere crudity. The merchant tendency to associate prize flowers with expensive baubles also revealed a deficiency of refinement. Only the tasteless would arrange cut flowers together with jewels and pearls.[36]

Of course this sort of loutishness was absolutely incompatible with literati masculine honor, which flaunted painstaking aesthetic and moral refinement as a source of prestige. To maintain the peony as a source of cultural capital, literati rejected the popular view of beautiful flowers as accoutrements to empty luxury and sensuality. To the contrary, they fashioned an elaborate culture of connoisseurship that associated peony appreciation with lofty, subtle aesthetics and sophisticated artistic pursuits. Whereas anyone could get drunk while seated at a table adorned with a potted peony, few could appreciate the elaborate literati conventions associated with the highest forms of connoisseurship. Appreciating the flower in an elaborate or arcane manner became a new way to prove one's superiority over other men. Peony appreciation thus became refined, standardized, and formalized into elaborate, set conventions that most people found inaccessible. The elaborate activities of connoisseurship could then serve as rites of hegemonic manhood.

Proper appreciation began with placing peonies in the appropriate garden. It was not enough simply to enclose a piece of fertile land, erect some garden architecture, and plant a few hundred peonies. Any arriviste could do as much. The addition of subtle elements beyond the range of the average person's aesthetic sensibility distinguished the refined garden. In Song paintings, peonies are almost always portrayed among other symbols of refinement.[37] For example, Song gentlemen appreciated oddly shaped rocks, known today as "scholar's rocks," and carefully integrated them into their gardens.[38] Rock appreciation was extremely useful for literati who wanted to prove their good taste. Although not beautiful in the conventional sense, a misshapen rock nevertheless recalled concepts integral to literati aesthetics: the tortuous crags of the landscape painting, the weirdly twisting lines of an ancient mountain-shaped incense burner, and the unearthly alpine landscape of the wise hermit's cave. A rich merchant might appreciate the high cost, delicacy, and glittering surfaces of artificial craftsmanship, but the educated gentleman displayed far subtler taste. He could recognize the beauty of a simple rock, free for the taking on a mountain crag. By deliberately pairing the peony with carefully chosen rocks rather than vulgar luxuries, the connoisseur displayed cultured discrimination, raising himself above other men in terms of masculine image.

Literati often undertook multiple activities in conjunction with flower viewing, deliberately making peony connoisseurship dauntingly complex. They might compose poetry, perform elegant music, or play *weiqi* while appreciating their favorite flowers.[39] Combining various cultured pastimes with flower viewing made elite flower culture extremely difficult to master. A busy merchant might possibly have become adept at one or two cultured pursuits, but mastering the entire constellation of literati pastimes was out of the question. In contrast, the gentleman landlord could devote his copious leisure to the challenging pursuits that brought him acclaim as a paragon of manhood.

In contrast to raucous gatherings of ordinary revelers, literati peony parties took on a highly aestheticized air. The ideal assembly of gentleman connoisseurs would involve feasting and drinking, but in gentle moderation. Instead of winsome courtesans, the flowers themselves were the star attraction. Celebrants would languidly appreciate the flowers bathed in candlelit sfumato, declaring themselves deeply moved by the beauty of the scene.[40]

Another strategy for displaying elevated appreciation was the creation of artistic arrangements of cut blooms. People commonly arranged flowers in vases for indoor viewing, giving rise to an elaborate connoisseurship of cut peonies.[41] The average person lacked the training necessary to create a sophisticated flower arrangement, giving the literatus another way to distinguish his superior taste. By carefully positioning peonies in an orthodox arrangement within the appropriate vessel, he transformed the flowers into an art object worthy of quiet contemplation.

Choosing the right beverage to accompany peony appreciation also displayed good taste. Originally alcohol was the drink of choice, but by the Song, tea had become the more refined option, so tasteful peony lovers began drinking tea while appreciating their favorite flower.[42] This switch in beverages lent a new tone to peony parties. While alcohol tends to make guests loud and boisterous, tea drinkers favor quiet conversation. The peaceful atmosphere of the peony-garlanded tea party helped bring this flower further into the embrace of high culture. When merchants appreciated peonies with loud, drunken revels, the gentleman who admired the flowers while sipping tea and composing poetry could feel smugly superior.

Perhaps the most important characteristic of literati identity was mastery of the written word. Associating peony appreciation with literature not only elevated it even further in prestige but also excluded those who lacked extensive

Flower arrangement. *Source:* Yang Yi, *Zhongguo gudian xiaoshuo shier jiang* (Shanghai: Shanghai sanlian, 2007), 8.

education. The desire for exclusivity helps account for the obsession with writing about peonies. Literati considered skill at poetry composition the height of literary cultivation. A poem was also an orthodox medium for expressing one's appreciation for something important. By attributing meanings and moods to the peony through poetry, educated gentlemen flaunted their sophisticated connoisseurship. And because they could share a poem with friends, family, colleagues, and even strangers, it was also a way to publicly demonstrate their good taste.

Despite the prestige accorded poetic composition, few wealthy merchants with a garden full of peonies would be able to compose a good poem about their flowers. Crafting acceptable verses was difficult, as a good poem alluded to images and tropes from China's long poetic tradition. Only someone with both education and leisure could possibly hope to master such a complex mode of expression. Due to this inherent difficulty, literati seized upon the ability to write suitable poetry about flowers as a mark of the true peony connoisseur.

Peonies are just one example of the way elite men manipulated material culture to confirm their superior masculine status. The same was true of tea drinking, collecting ancient bronzes, studying and writing calligraphy, and many other elite cultural pursuits. As fathers could pass the correct deployment of peonies down to their sons, alongside other prestigious cultural practices, this sort of knowledge constituted an important repository of a family's cultural capital. The symbolism central to hegemonic masculinity would not necessarily vanish after just one generation. If correctly maintained, this masculine capital could descend from one generation to the next, easing the passage of one's sons and grandsons into the symbolic network of elite manhood.

NOTES

1. Louie, *Theorizing Chinese Masculinity*, 10.
2. Kathleen Ryor, "Wen and Wu in Elite Cultural Practices during the Late Ming," in *Military Culture in Imperial China*, ed. Nicola di Cosmo (Cambridge, MA: Harvard University Press, 2009), 219–42; Liu Qing, "'Wenren lun bing' yu Songdai bingxue de fazhan," *Shehui kexue jia* 49, no. 5 (1994): 56–60.
3. Pierre Bourdieu, *Distinction: A Social Critique of the Judgement of Taste*, trans. Richard Nice (London: Routledge, 1984).
4. Pierre Bourdieu, "Marriage Strategies as Strategies of Social Reproduction," in *Family and Society: Selections from the Annales Economies, Sociétés, Civilisations*, ed. Robert Forster and Orest Ranum, trans. Elborg Forster and Patricia M. Ranum (Baltimore: Johns Hopkins University Press, 1976), 117–44.
5. Bourdieu, *Masculine Domination*, 44.
6. Appiah, *The Honor Code*, 187–90, discusses these sorts of mechanisms encouraging the shift from violence toward more pacific manifestations of honor.
7. For a discussion of how a parallel examination system became linked to hegemonic masculine identity, see Paul R. Deslandes, "Competitive Examinations and the Culture of Masculinity in Oxbridge Undergraduate Life, 1850–1920," *History of Education Quarterly* 42, no. 4 (2002): 544–78.
8. Furth, "Androgynous Males and Deficient Females," 1–3; Barlow, "Theorizing Women," 259.
9. Chen Si, *Haitangpu* (Taipei: Xinxing, 1988), 1757, 1759; Fan Chengda, "Fancun meipu," in *Yingyin Wenyuange siku quanshu* (Taipei: Taiwan Shangwu, 1983) 845, 1a; Liu Meng, "Liushi jupu," in *Yingyin Wenyuange siku quanshu* (Taipei: Taiwan Shangwu,

1983), 845, 4a–4b; Shi Zhu, "Baiju jipu," in *Yingyin Wenyuange siku quanshu* (Taipei: Taiwan Shangwu, 1983), 845, introduction, 1a, 2:ia, 2:10a, 2:17a; Shi Zhengzhi, "Shishi jupu," in *Yingyin Wenyuange siku quanshu* (Taipei: Taiwan Shangwu, 1983), 845, 1b; Zhou Shihou, *Luoyang mudanji* (Taipei: Xinxing, 1980), 1737; Wang Guixue, *Wangshi lanpu* (Taipei: Xinxing, 1980), 1709.

10. Fan, "Fancun meipu," 1727.

11. Lu You, *Tianpeng mudanpu* (Taipei: Xinxing, 1988), 1749, 1751, 1752; Zhang Bangji, *Chenzhou mudanji* (Taipei: Xinxing, 1988), 1747.

12. Zhang Bangji, *Mozhuang manlu* (Beijing: Zhonghua, 1985), 9:98.

13. Ouyang Xiu, *Luoyang mudanji* (Taipei: Xinxing, 1988), 1689–90. Ouyang noted the most popular sites in Luoyang for peony appreciation. For popular festivals centered on peonies, see Zhang, *Mozhuang manlu*, 9:98; Lu, *Tianpeng mudanpu*, 1754; Wang Guan, "Yangzhou shaoyaopu," in *Yingyin Wenyuange siku quanshu* (Taipei: Taiwan Shangwu, 1983), 845, 10b.

14. Two different species from the same genus are both called peony in English. The largest and most famous, *Paeonia moutan*, was known to Song gardeners as the *mudan* (牡丹). A closely related flower is the *shaoyao* (芍藥; *Paeonia albiflora*), which has fewer petals. During the Song, peony hybrids were already numerous. For example, sixty-five varieties were grown in Tianpeng, Sichuan, during the Southern Song. Lu, *Tianpeng mudanpu*, 1750–51.

15. Zhou, *Luoyang mudanji*, 1744.

16. Zhang, *Mozhuang manlu*, 6:73.

17. Zhang, *Mozhuang manlu*, 2:15.

18. Qiu Xuan, *Mudan rongruzhi* (Taipei: Xinxing, 1988), 1623–29. Also see Zhou, *Luoyang mudanji*, 1737, 1739; Tang Guizhang, ed., *Quansongci* (Beijing: Zhonghua, 1965), 2:678.

19. Zhou, *Luoyang mudanji*, 1737, 1745.

20. Wang, "Yangzhou shaoyaopu," 1a–1b, emphasizes the peony's ethereal *qi*, imbued by nature. Qiu, *Mudan rongruzhi*, 1623, asserts a close connection between the peony and the basic cosmological triad of Heaven, Earth, and Human Being central to classical Confucian metaphysics.

21. Fan Chengda, *Wujunzhi* (Shanghai: Shangwu, 1939), 14:124.

22. Ouyang, *Luoyang mudanji*, 1686.

23. References to sales of gardens are numerous. For some examples, see Zhou Mi, *Guixin zazhi* (Beijing: Zhonghua, 1985), *qian* 21; Zhang Gongfu, *Meipin* (Taipei: Xinxing, 1988), 1733.

24. Anonymous, "Ducheng jisheng," in *Yingyin Wenyuange siku quanshu* (Taipei: Taiwan Shangwu, 1983), 590, 3b.

25. Wu Zimu, *Mengliangu* (Beijing: Zhonghua, 1985), 16:139; anonymous, "Ducheng jisheng," 3b, 7b; Fan, "Fancun meipu," 3a.

26. Zhou, *Luoyang mudanji*, 1738.

27. Chen Shijiao, *Hualihuo*, ed. Congshu jicheng (Changsha: Shangwu, 1939), C:34.

28. Lu, *Tianpeng mudanpu*, 1754.

29. Wang, "Yangzhou shaoyaopu," 2b.

30. Lu, *Tianpeng mudanpu*, 1752.

31. Ouyang, *Luoyang mudanji*, 1690.

32. Ouyang, *Loyang mudanji*, 1686; Lu, *Tianpeng mudanpu*, 1751, 1754; Zhang, *Chenzhou mudanji*, 1747; Zhang, *Mozhuang manlu*, 9:104; Lu, *Tianpeng mudanpu*, 3a; Chen, *Haitangpu*, 1758; Wang, "Yangzhou shaoyaopu," 3a.

33. Ouyang, *Luoyang mudanji*, 1690.

34. Chen, *Haitangpu*, 1775.

35. Chen, *Hualihuo*, C:37.

36. Wu, *Menglianglu*, 19:175.

37. For example, see Guoli Gugong Bowuyuan Bianji Weiyuanhui, *Gugong shuhua tulu* (Taipei: Guoli Gugong Bowuyuan, 1989), 3:57 (*Shiba xueshitu*), 3:163 (*Huawangtu*).

38. For an excellent introduction to rock connoisseurship, see Robert D. Mowry et al., *Worlds within Worlds: The Richard Rosenblum Collection of Chinese Scholars' Rocks* (Cambridge, MA: Harvard University Art Museums, 1997).

39. Zhang, *Meipin*, 1733; Wu, *Menglianglu*, 19:175; Zhao Shigeng, *Jinzhang lanpu* (Taipei: Xinxing, 1988), 1693.

40. Lu, *Tianpeng mudanpu*, 1755.

41. Zhou, *Luoyang mudanji*, 1737. For a painting depicting a Song flower arrangement featuring peonies, see Guoli Gugong Bowuyuan Bianji Weiyuanhui, *Gugong shuhua tulu*, 2:239 (*Siji pingan*).

42. Chen, *Hualihuo*, C:33.

6

⚌⚍

Ming Dynasty (1368–1644 CE)

Marginal Heroes

Although convention tied manhood to markers of social status evoking class, wealth, and political power, marginal men could also sometimes attain honor. The *haohan* (loosely translated as "good fellow") exemplified ideal plebeian masculinity. The stereotypical *haohan* valued loyalty to a tight group of male comrades and celebrated vengeance, valor, and toughness. Its close association with ruffians and bandits notwithstanding, lowborn men esteemed and widely emulated this masculine archetype. Despite occupying the bottom rungs of society, *haohan* nevertheless put forth an alternate form of hegemonic masculinity that rivaled elite literati manhood in prestige.

Men of late imperial China faced two prestigious forms of manhood, *wen* and *wu*, which were both hegemonic though largely contradictory. While the cultured refinement embodying *wen* enjoyed greatest respect overall, it was accessible only to a small elite. For a rough peasant to ape gentlemanly manners would have seemed comic. As *wen* masculinity was too remote to be relevant to the lives of most men, martial *wu* manhood idealizing confrontation and violence presented a far more realistic alternative. Most men did not act out either archetype in its entirety but instead borrowed elements from each to construct a masculine image appropriate to their particular circumstances.

Although low-status hegemonic masculinity might seem like an oxymoron, in fact it is not unusual for ordinary or even marginalized men to adopt alternate codes of masculinity that allow others to see them as laudable or even exemplary. A classic example is the development of "cool" among African American men.[1] Because African Americans have traditionally faced severe economic and social marginalization, until recently they had little hope of living up to the gender norms of the white majority. But while masculine norms embody power, they also tend to generate systematic resistance.[2] Rather than passively accept imposed inferiority, African American men empowered themselves by constructing alternative standards of masculinity, allowing them to garner admiration within their own communities. For example, if a man had a high degree of emotional self-control and maintained an insouciant attitude in the face of danger, in other words if he was "cool," he could win the respect of his peers.

Unexpectedly, some whites found this alternative masculinity so appealing that they imitated it, despite its not having evolved to suit their own situation. In this way, a masculine model that began as a strategy for the disadvantaged to gain esteem became an alternative hegemonic masculinity copied by privileged members of society. Decades ago, sociologists derided alternative masculinities as nothing more than deviance caused by inadequate socialization, criticizing them as threats to social order. According to the more inclusive theoretical model of hegemonic masculinity, however, manhood encompasses a broad spectrum of possible expressions, a number of which can simultaneously earn respect.[3] In consequence, "marginal" masculinities can become compelling behavioral archetypes that influence even men of higher social strata.

In much the same way that cool emerged as a way for marginalized American men to gain respect, low-status Chinese also created codes of masculine behavior suited to their humble condition. Popular literature, music, storytelling, opera, puppetry, and folk art diffused this *haohan* archetype, presenting it as a type of hegemonic masculinity accessible to the average man.[4] Men could employ *haohan* conventions to belittle those embodying subordinated masculinities and also to maintain the patriarchal system of male dominance over women.[5] By imitating the *haohan*, a man with limited possibilities, however poor or powerless, might possibly achieve a measure of masculine honor. In fact Chinese so admired *haohan* manhood that even members of the elite sometimes found it expedient abide by its norms.

Because mainstream society excluded real *haohan*, their actual numbers at any time were probably quite small. Nevertheless, we can still consider this masculine image normative, not because *haohan* were numerous but because society honored the masculinity they represented so highly. Hegemonic masculinity does not refer to the fixed values or behavior of a group of men. Instead it encompasses a discursive locus that men can adopt permanently or borrow temporarily as circumstances dictate.[6] Even ordinary men could raise their status in the eyes of others by imitating *haohan* as the opportunity arose, occasionally deploying an appropriate flourish or phrase, thereby gaining the benefits of this masculine role without having to make the considerable commitments and sacrifices expected of a genuine *haohan*.[7]

Qin Ming, a *haohan* famed for his bad temper. *Source:* Lao Tan,
Shuihu—yizhi bei wudu (Chongqing: Chongqing daxue, 2010), 4.

PRECURSORS TO THE *HAOHAN*

The tough bandit hero celebrated in late imperial popular fiction descended from a long line of masculine archetypes stretching back to antiquity. The earliest predecessors of the *haohan* were *xiake*, virtuous outlaws who initially rose to prominence during the chaos of the Eastern Zhou dynasty prior to the Qin unification. Although English lacks a precise equivalent, some scholars have rendered *xiake* as "knight errant," even though these men usually lacked noble origins and in fact sometimes came from the bottom rungs of society. This popular hero was willing to break the law for the sake of grassroots justice, such as vengeance ethics. In times of turmoil when the state apparatus broke down, the *xiake* could sometimes help bring a modicum of order to society by penalizing those who had transgressed popular custom. But by operating outside the law, he risked punishment.[8]

Some *xiake* were little more than petty thugs who justified illegal activities by feigning a higher calling. Others were relatives of local landlords or minor officials who connived with the local elite to terrorize their rivals. Wealthy landowners not only tried to co-opt the local administration but also manipulated ethical norms to control local affairs. Sons and relatives of the powerful might present themselves to the world as *xiake*, a potentially respectable social role that conveniently justified violence. This ideal persisted into the medieval era. During the Tang dynasty, the *xiake* was sometimes an important fixture in the local community, participating in the era's internecine political struggles.[9] Whatever his goals, allegiance to vengeance ethics and the informal righting of wrongs could sometimes earn a *xiake* honor, marking him as a paragon of successful manhood.

Jing Ke unsuccessfully tries to assassinate Qin Shihuang. *Source:* Wang Jianzhong, *Handai huaxiangshi tonglun* (Beijing: Zijincheng, 2001), 429.

The assassin (*cike*) was another ancient precursor to the *haohan*. Like the *xiake*, the assassin operated outside the law, often pursuing vengeance on behalf of a patron. However, assassins differed from *xiake* in some fundamental ways. They usually came from the bottom rungs of society and lacked pedigree, wealth, or talent. Having little to lose, they were willing to undertake dangerous missions and even commit cold-blooded murder. Killing a prominent figure could gain a powerful patron's gratitude and earn material rewards.

People often admired assassins for their bravery and skill. However, unlike the supposedly conscience-driven *xiake*, the assassin did not act on his own behalf. He was the hireling of someone more important, voluntarily making himself a pawn in the intrigues of the powerful.[10] The assassin was not a psychopathic monster who enjoyed killing for its own sake; he undertook murder as a paid service. Because he worked at a patron's behest, he did not act according to his inner moral sense, and so he was not necessarily just. In consequence, early historiography portrays assassins as morally dubious figures.

THE CHINESE HERO

Historical accounts of assassins and *xiake* had enormous influence on the development of Chinese ideas about heroism. During the decay of the Eastern Han dynasty and throughout the subsequent age of chaos, the collapse of formal institutions made individual valor and initiative particularly valuable. As the man of action became more useful, the characteristics of the ideal hero accordingly became an important topic of discussion.

A close association always existed between the cult of heroism and political disorder in China.[11] During times of chaos, not only did society esteem heroism highly, but the opportunities for heroic action also increased in tandem with rising oppression and anarchy. The chaos engendered by the collapse of the Han and invasions by northern nomads brought terrible suffering, and literature accordingly turned to exploring relevant themes such as the anguish of self-sacrifice and deus ex machina salvation by a valiant hero.[12] Guan Yu, a valiant soldier so highly admired that he came to be worshipped as a god, epitomizes the medieval hero cult. Since his deification, he has become one of the most important folk gods and an icon of martial masculinity.[13]

Traditionally the Chinese hero is a tragic figure.[14] As with heroes from many times and places, from Achilles to Roland, the Chinese hero finds himself wedged between lofty personal principles and the grubby demands of an unfair world. Because society and government are so flawed, he must either compromise his high ideals or else defend them at great cost.[15] Choosing to adhere to his principles forces him down a difficult path toward suffering and even death.[16]

Confucianism, grounded in the depressing fact that life poses insolvable conundrums, has an inherently tragic worldview.[17] Confucian meditations on the contradictions between moral ideals and real circumstances informed discourse about heroism. The hero is someone who acts according to principle, even at great personal cost. Of course, most men would not dare take this path, and the hero's personality reflects his unusual integrity. Authors often depict him as a brooding loner who suffers from oversized pride, isolated from others by his uncompromising attitude.[18] Even if his stubborn adherence to impossibly high standards does not ruin him, in the long run his sense of commitment does not make him happy or provide an easy life.

If the hero's path is so difficult, what motivates him to follow it? Of course the hero's life is not entirely grim. The Chinese word for hero (*yingxiong*) literally means "outstanding male," implying that others admire him as a paragon of ideal masculinity.[19] More than just strong, the classic Chinese hero combines physical prowess with other ideal qualities, such as talent, wisdom, and devotion to honor, making him the personification of a range of manly traits.[20]

Even though the hero excels in both mind and body, he nevertheless stands apart from normative society in his willingness to break the law and defy quotidian custom. Chinese didactic biography explores the fascinating contradiction of how transgressive individuals create and maintain moral order. Society considered the widow who commits suicide, the filial son who feeds his mother with his own flesh, and the brave official who criticizes an evil monarch to be moral paragons despite (and because of) behavior that violates conventional propriety. Heroes tend to be people whose actions place them beyond the bounds of mainstream society. Exceptional behavior and values that differ considerably from those of ordinary people make their oversized achievements possible. For this reason, Chinese tended both to admire and to fear heroes.

Success ended in punishment for some of the greatest heroes of Chinese history, highlighting the danger of standing outside the herd. Stories of men destroyed for their heroism formed a staple topos of imperial historiography. For example, although Han Xin played a crucial role in helping Emperor Han Gaozu found the Han dynasty, the jealous ruler feared his outstanding ability and had him imprisoned. Similarly, realists executed the Song hero Yue Fei, objecting to his steadfast commitment to waging war against China's enemies regardless of danger or cost. The hero's inherently nonconformist behavior threatens the state, which must either coopt, constrain, or destroy him.

HAOHAN: THE MARGINAL HERO

During the Ming dynasty (1368–1644), the subversive low-status hero known as the *haohan* was a stock protagonist in oral and written literature. It is important to distinguish between countercultural and subcultural discourse in traditional Chinese writing. Authors produced works of subcultural discourse (such as vernacular fiction) to entertain the less-educated portion of society. Although sometimes ironic and critical, these works usually avoided challenging the basic premises underlying the status quo. In contrast, more serious countercultural discourse aimed at the educated included thoughtful social and political critiques.[21] According to this typology, the most influential *haohan* literature was subcultural. People of higher status may have enjoyed it, but it targeted the lower orders of society. Although intended for ordinary people and lacking in critical depth, this discourse nevertheless exerted enormous influence on perceptions of manhood.

The most famous and influential Ming work about *haohan* was the popular novel *Water Margin* (*Shuihu zhuan*). Whereas earlier narratives of heroism such as *Romance of the Three Kingdoms* (*Sanguo yanyi*) focused on highborn men, *Water Margin* injected the heroic archetype into a mundane setting, setting forth a model of masculinity appropriate for those of lower status. Because this novel developed out of a long tradition of oral storytelling, the epic never became standardized.[22] *Water Margin* circulated in editions of extremely different lengths with varied content, all dealing with the same group of 108 bandit heroes and utilizing similar repetitive narrative patterns.[23] Woodblock prints often illustrated popular novels, increasing their impact, broadening their appeal, and making them more accessible to people with limited literacy.[24]

Haohan genre fiction had an immense impact on popular Chinese views of manhood. A passage from *Water Margin* sums up this masculine ideal.

> They are three brothers, and they live in the village of Stone Tablet near Liang-shan Marsh in Jizhou Prefecture. They are fishermen, though they've also done a bit of smuggling in the marsh. Their family name is Ruan. Second Brother is known as Ferocious Giant. Fifth Brother is called Recklessly Rash. Seventh Brother is nicknamed the Devil Incarnate. I once lived in their village a number of years and I got to know them. Although they haven't had any education, they're very loyal to their friends, and are good bold fellows, so we became quite close.[25]

The authors of these works may not have been the finest minds or the greatest literary talents, but their ideas about the successful man reached an infinitely greater audience than anything written in refined academic prose.[26] In fact, officials worried that popular literature was affecting the values of ordinary people in potentially disruptive ways, a testament to the tangible social impact of lowbrow fiction.[27]

As depicted in *Water Margin* and similar late imperial popular literature, the *haohan* exemplifies an emotional quality known as *qing* (sentiment). Opening oneself up to *qing* was controversial because doing so ran against traditional teachings. Classical Chinese ethics stress self-control. One becomes good by conforming to specific rules embodied by the rites (*li*) and the general ethical principles constituting righteousness (*yi*). To be a good person, a man must obey these restrictive social codes regardless of his actual feelings. However, although previous philosophers had traditionally disparaged *qing* as a potentially dangerous quality that individuals must keep carefully in check, some Ming thinkers began to see it more positively as an expression of personal authenticity (*zhen*). A man who follows his gut feelings seems far more authentic than someone who lives by an externally imposed moral code. So when judged by the standard of authenticity, the unruly *haohan*, quick to anger and obsessed with revenge, appears far more authentic than a literatus obsessed with propriety. The authenticity of fictional *haohan* was one key to their popularity. Even literati enjoyed this sort of literature, as it provided an escape from the pretense and affectation of upper-class life. To the reader who spent his life abiding by the myriad constraints of polite society, the *haohan* who dared to act on his feelings seemed especially manly. Sometimes heroism consists of simply daring to be oneself.[28]

More specifically, the *haohan* of legend was a specific kind of hero. Whereas most protagonists in early fiction were important generals and statesmen, *haohan* tended to come from the bottom rungs of society, and their behavior and values reflected their origins. Of the bandits portrayed in *Water Margin*, only the character Song Jiang has conventional aspirations and considers rejoining mainstream society. His fellow bandits lack conformist ambitions. Not only were most of these men born at the bottom of the social pyramid, but they were content to stay there.

These lowly origins are apparent in the behavior of fictional *haohan*. Whereas the literatus prides himself on Confucian or Buddhist moderation, the *haohan* feels no compunction about embracing sensual pleasure when the occasion arises. Readers of *Water Margin* encounter repetitive scenes of outrageous gluttony and drunkenness in which these indecorous heroes abandon themselves to base amusements.[29] Such uncouth behavior would be completely unsuitable in the gentleman who sought to prove superior manhood by demonstrating refinement and self-control, despising intemperance as a symptom of moral decadence. In contrast, the *haohan* demonstrates his manliness by outdoing his peers in consuming grotesque quantities of meat and alcohol. Not only does giving way to abandon demonstrate vigor, itself a manly quality, but flouting conventional moderation also demonstrates authenticity. By giving in to his desires and overindulging, he proves that he is brave enough to be himself.

In contrast to the refined literatus, who presents himself as a paragon of good taste, the archetypal *haohan* takes pride in his crudity. He wears his roughness as a badge of honor, because transgressing polite conventions marks him as brave and authentic. For example, some famous *haohan* in literature sported

A tattooed *haohan*. *Source*: Zhang Guofeng, *Huashuo shuihu* (Guilin: Guangxi shifan daxue, 2009), 174.

tattoos, markings traditionally considered utterly disgraceful, as violations of the filial injunction against mutilating the body also associated with punishments, slavery, and foreign barbarism. Nevertheless, five of the major characters in *Water Margin* have tattoos and display them unabashedly to the world.[30] Once again, ignoring polite conventions symbolizes the true man's moral courage. His deliberately transgressive behavior shows contempt for affectation and restraint; he subverts mundane values in pursuit of a higher path.

The archetypal *haohan* is not just true to himself but also strong in body and spirit. *Water Margin* and other works of late imperial literature describe bandits and warriors capable of amazing feats of physical strength. The hero Wu Song famously fought and killed a ferocious tiger that had slaughtered thirty people, demonstrating raw power combined with remarkable courage. Unlike ordinary men, when faced with danger the *haohan* shows no fear. Also, because the fictional *haohan* belongs to a gang, selflessness is another important trait. He willingly sacrifices himself for the sake of his sworn brothers, maintaining the cohesion of the group in the face of any hardship. Because self-sacrifice is so difficult, it demonstrates the moral discipline and strength of will that mark the true man. Finally, although the *haohan* sometimes temporarily abandons himself to sensual pleasure, in general he leads an extremely ascetic life. His disregard for luxuries and comforts expresses manly resolve.[31]

The *haohan* Wu Song killing a tiger. *Source:* Yang Yi, *Zhongguo gudian xiaoshuo shier jiang* (Shanghai: Shanghai sanlian, 2007), 56.

Authors of late imperial fiction often treat the *haohan* hero with a degree of irony, sometimes adopting an ironic tone to deflate him a bit instead of describing him solely through superlatives in the naive manner of epic prose. For example, a hero might lack appropriate physical prowess or behave in an awkward or bumbling manner. Or his companions might call him by a silly nickname.[32] Were he presented as absolutely perfect, the *haohan* would seem so distant that ordinary men could not hope to emulate him. By introducing some flaws into his persona, writers not only made the hero more interesting but also made *haohan* values seem potentially achievable. As the hero comes closer to ordinary men, he becomes a more realistic role model.

FICTIONAL *HAOHAN* AND REAL BANDITS

While legends presented bandits as heroes, Chinese generally despised real outlaws.[33] The masculine archetype of the *haohan* seems to have been more romantic fiction than reality. Men learned about *haohan* values by watching plays and hearing storytellers rather than observing the behavior of actual bandits. And while officials might have enjoyed reading novels such as *Water Margin* in their spare time, they detested criminals. The authorities tended to regard outlaws as stupid misfits lacking the fundamentals of civilized behavior and looked down on them as arrogant, undisciplined, shameless outcasts beyond the pale of respectable society.[34] In general, the elite held contradictory views toward outlaws. When appreciating literature about fictional bandits, educated men cast aside their regular value system and understood these characters according to the standards of lowbrow *haohan* masculinity. But when confronted with flesh-and-blood criminals, officials assessed them by the standards of literati masculinity as dangerous failures who threatened social order.

Nor do modern scholarly studies tend to depict real bandits as heroic. In Chinese academia, ideology has heavily influenced research on bandits. Because Marxist scholars regard defiance of government authority as potentially revolutionary, they exhibit a fascination with outlaws. Even so, historians have found no trace of any progressive ideology among historic bandit gangs. In fact, because bands of outlaws made their living from violent criminal activity such as robbery, kidnapping, and extortion, it is difficult to see them as representing anything positive. To the contrary, scholars generally portray bandits as a politically apathetic and socially destructive force.[35]

Despite the poor reputation of actual outlaws, low-status men often joined a bandit gang at least temporarily. Brigandage was the norm in some areas, particularly in poor, marginal, and remote places. Gang members were not necessarily permanent outlaws, as bandits might enter and leave a particular gang. As new recruits arrived, older men left to marry and settle down to farming.

In some places a young man commonly spent a few years in a bandit gang, as it offered the lowliest members of society a degree of opportunity unavailable elsewhere. Others joined outlaw bands for personal reasons, such as a desire for vengeance against a particular enemy or righteous anger at society's many injustices.[36]

Because banditry was so widespread, and sometimes even constituted a normative phase in the life cycle of the low-status man, the audience listening to a storyteller recount the *Water Margin* legend might easily have included some men with actual experience at banditry. Of course they would be eager to cast their own youthful activities in a positive light, using *haohan* masculinity as a way of legitimizing their time spent living outside the law. The porous boundary between village life and banditry, in tandem with the popularity of heroic legends, served to propagate *haohan* values as an alternative form of hegemonic masculinity accessible to ordinary men.

The core values of the late imperial *haohan* descended from those of ancient *xiake*, as they ideally adhered to a moral code that included not just loyalty and righteousness (*yi*) but also benevolence (*ren*), fidelity (*xin*), and of course bravery.[37] In name, these values overlapped considerably with Confucian ethics. In practice, however, the *haohan* was far removed from the model Confucian gentleman. Even so, appropriating the vocabulary of elite ethics helped low-status men legitimize their alternate masculine image.

Ideally, the *haohan* derived his primary motivation from righteousness, often referred to as *yiqi*.[38] As in Confucianism, righteousness in *haohan* ethics consists not of a specific set of rules but rather represents a general moral framework that is broad and flexible enough to apply to the myriad situations one encounters in real life. Righteousness provides a man with the standards to judge right from wrong, while bravery gives him the moral courage to abide by his principles. To the *haohan*, the fundamental motivation for righteous behavior is honor. Unlike lesser men motivated by a desire for money, luxuries, power, or other trappings of worldly success, legendary heroes such as the masculine paragon Guan Yu, immortalized in the novel *Romance of the Three Kingdoms*, garnered admiration for their scrupulous devotion to righteousness and honor.

Although they considered righteousness the key to honor, plebeian men interpreted this nebulous value differently from scholars. *Haohan* understood righteousness as absolute devotion to one's sworn brothers, in contrast to loyalty (*zhong*) directed toward one's social superiors and the state. *Haohan* borrowed from the language of elite ethics but reinterpreted loyalty to transform this conservative doctrine into a potentially subversive force.[39] Rather than directing loyalty upward toward the powerful, *haohan* focused it inward, toward a tight group of lawless outsiders. Righteousness strengthened the bonds between sworn brothers by emphasizing their reciprocal obligations to one another. Ming dynasty fiction exploited inevitable contradictions and conflicts between two types of loyalty, to the state and to one's male peers, as a major source of dramatic tension.[40] A hero often had choose between them, knowing that no matter what he decided, the outcome would ultimately be unsatisfying.

Most fundamentally, *haohan* righteousness involved self-sacrifice for the sake of the group. The gang ethos required a member to stick with his comrades, putting himself in danger to protect them from harm. In practice, righteousness also required the *haohan* to share his money and any other material goods with his peers. He did not make such self-sacrifice in vain, as it could win him a reputation for honor. In effect, the *haohan* often used his money to buy honor, making righteousness yield practical advantages in the form of elevated status.[41]

Haohan values emphasized reciprocity. Although Chinese ethics long stressed recompense (*bao*) as a foundation of just social intercourse, Confucian and Buddhist teachings on moderation and prudent self-restraint restrained this way of thinking among the elite.[42] Among the lower strata of society, however, reciprocity remained a paramount moral imperative. The struggles of fictional *haohan* to fulfill reciprocal obligations toward friends and vengeance toward enemies, a staple theme of late imperial fiction, illustrate this sense of urgency.[43] In practice, besides readiness to provide assistance and material support for one's sworn brothers, reciprocity also implied a willingness to avenge any taint of shame for oneself or one's group. Men at the bottom of society continued to see revenge as a way of publicly affirming masculine honor.

Of course the specter of unruly bandits spouting Confucian-sounding platitudes about righteousness while killing and stealing disconcerted the elite. Although the educated might feel just as disappointed with the state of society, they rarely resorted to violence. To express implicit criticism of the current state of affairs, they usually just quietly withdrew from public life.[44] But popular fiction ridicules the passivity of the elite in the face of injustice. Late imperial fiction often portrays literati characters as pretentious bookworms who squander their time discussing philology and metaphysics instead of addressing the injustices around them. They are more likely to cause problems than to solve them.[45]

Lawlessness threatened the rich and powerful, leading the educated to write about *haohan* in caustic tones. To literati, the true heroes were the men who established and maintained the normative rules underpinning society, not the lowly outsiders who challenged the prevailing order. The elite prized the smooth functioning of orderly administrative institutions, whatever their flaws, while *haohan* threatened the edifice of civilization by putting themselves and their comrades outside the purview of the state.[46] Even though both sides used similar moral language, literati critiques of *haohan* values reveal a rift in perceptions of heroic manhood that divided social strata.

Literati readers clearly enjoyed the primitivism and authenticity of *haohan* literature, which served as fantasy material for those hemmed in by respectability.[47] Nevertheless, when elite writers took a serious look at this alternative vision of manhood, they condemned these disruptive outsiders on a number of grounds.[48] Most fundamentally, literati placed enormous stress on ritual propriety (*li*). They believed it to be a man's duty to master his ego and force himself to conform to social norms. However, *haohan* refused to submit to the rules regulating ordinary behavior and in fact often rebelled against polite conventions. Although they claimed to be motivated by righteousness (*yi*), from the Confucian perspective they were merely "inferior men" (*xiaoren*).[49]

To educated gentlemen, failure to respect the rites revealed intolerable egotism. Because literati stressed self-mastery through unceasing cultivation of one's mind and taste, they regarded the egotism of the archetypal *haohan* as a major character flaw. A gentleman should not allow himself to follow his base emotions. In succumbing to arbitrary likes, hates, and grudges, he risked harming others. According to Confucian ethics, this sort of egotism revealed a lack of benevolence (*ren*). The base pleasures enjoyed by stereotypical *haohan*, famed for crazed bouts of feasting and drinking, seemed to confirm their fundamental egotism. To those trained to judge ethics from a Confucian perspective, hedonism betrayed not just bad taste but also a serious lack of moral cultivation.[50]

The competing hegemonic masculinities embodied by literati and *haohan* may have differed in fundamental ways, but they also shared traits common to normative views of Chinese manhood. Like the literatus who sought a good reputation among his peers and shared social and cultural activities with men of the same group, *haohan* also saw their bonds with other men as crucial to honorable manhood. In this respect, they differed from the average man who sought honor primarily by fulfilling mundane family obligations. Conforming to the stringent expectations of filial piety and living up to the roles of ideal father and husband brought a degree of approbation from the community. However, the path of the hero took a man beyond his family in search of a more exalted status. In fact, heroic honor was often antithetical to family life. While being a successful father or son usually demanded that a man avoid risks, the Chinese hero willingly took on dangerous challenges, either leaving his family behind or else bringing danger to their doorstep.

THE HOMOSOCIAL HERO

When the *haohan* turned his back on conformist family life, he was not alone. The archetypal Chinese hero surrounds himself with like-minded companions. Instead of spending his life in the company of women and children, he inhabits a masculine world where women tend to be absent or unimportant. According to the influential theory of masculinity posited by Eve Sedgwick, homosociality constitutes an integral component of manhood in every culture.[51] A man must interact with other men and integrate himself into male society in order for others to consider him a successful man. This was also the standard perspective in every era of China's history. Since antiquity, Chinese have seen sociability as a hallmark of humanity. Although inferior to kinship ties in their view, friendship is nevertheless vital to male identity in that it provides the appropriate audience to judge a man's masculine performance.[52]

The communities of heroic men immortalized in Chinese fiction usually exclude women, thereby intensifying bonds among their members. In this way, the hero lays claim to a special kind of particularly intense manhood. From the standpoint of homosociality, a hero living in an all-male community might seem far more virile than the family man surrounded by women and children. The *haohan* of fiction revel in the manly atmosphere of their world. Membership in a band of sworn brothers provides them with a common identity as exemplary men.[53]

This mind-set influenced the attitudes of Chinese men in the real world. As male reputation rested on the opinion of comrades, each man had to calculate what to do and say to attract the male gaze. This desire for attention manifested itself in an obsession with fame, virtually synonymous with honor. Winning the notice of other men would also often attract their loyalty, confirming one's social worth.[54] But attracting the male gaze was not always easy. As men continuously competed for attention, being part of a close-knit male group made it easier to gain the notice of male peers.

Fictive kinship bonds often held male groups together, the relationship between members loosely modeled on that between brothers. However, brotherhood was the most contentious and ambiguous Chinese kinship bond. Although theoretically hierarchical, with younger siblings under filial obligation to defer to elder ones, this sort of relationship in fact tended to be egalitarian. As each brother traditionally received an equal share of family property, they often found themselves in heated competition for scarce family resources. Sibling rivalry could easily lead to acrimony and occasionally even violence. Despite the fragility of this bond, unrelated men frequently imitated brotherhood to organize their relations with one another. Because fictive brotherhood was a way of attracting the attention of other men, it could also bolster a man's status, making faux fraternal ties an extremely useful means of constructing a positive masculine image.[55]

Not only did the group of brothers exclude women, but female attention could even reflect negatively on a man. Heterosexual love weakened men's bonds with one another, driving sworn brothers apart.[56] Late imperial literature differs somewhat from some antecedents to *haohan* manhood in the portrayal of female companionship. Tang dynasty *xiake*, for example, are sometimes romantic figures with strong emotional ties to women.[57] But because fictional *haohan* were so uninhibited, giving in to drunkenness, gluttony, and violent impulses, sexual abstinence became a way to prove that a man could still exercise considerable self-mastery. Whether Confucian, Buddhist, or Daoist, all schools of Chinese ethics esteemed certain forms of self-restraint as virtuous.[58] By the Ming dynasty, male chastity and even misogyny had become acceptable means for a man to exhibit his inner strength.

Nor was the celibate *haohan* a purely fictional invention. Real-life bandits were often involuntary bachelors, victimized by the shortage of marriageable women. Female infanticide and the low status of daughters meant that fewer women than men reached marriageable age. Compounding the problem, wealthy men took multiple concubines, removing women from the marriage market. And poverty made it impossible for many men to afford a spouse. Untethered from the kinship system, rootless men had little to lose and easily turned to a life of crime and random violence. Needless to say, mainstream society despised bandits, who were so lowly that they could not even attract a wife.[59] Portraying involuntary celibacy as a high-minded ideal transformed unfortunate necessity into a virtue, helping low-status men retain a modicum of respectability.

To justify male celibacy as virtuous in the face of all the rhetoric about the value of marriage, family, and procreation, popular fiction about *haohan* portrayed women as evil temptresses. Under the conventions of Western chivalry, a hero would have to win a woman's heart to prove his manhood. In contrast, the Chinese masculine paragon proved his strength by avoiding the clutches of the siren trying to woo him away from his band of brothers.[60] Conventional wisdom has long considered male loyalty (*zhong*) the counterpart to female chastity, giving rise to the assumption that a man's sexual abstinence implied loyalty to comrades in his group, turning avoidance of female company into a virtue confirming true manhood.

We can also view the portrayal of women in *haohan* legends as a reaction to the conventions of historiography, the most orthodox form of prose discourse. Because women usually played bit parts in the standard histories, readers found the detailed descriptions of women in prose fiction highly titillating in comparison. Authors found that they could use women as "narrative bait" to pique the reader's interest.[61] However, *haohan* fiction shows female characters in a negative light. Relationships with unfaithful women trouble six of the bandits in *Water Margin*, a development that the original audience would have found fascinating. The disloyalty of these women contrasts sharply with the fidelity the men show toward one another, implicitly critiquing female morals. And as writers had long portrayed female chastity as akin to the subject's loyalty to the ruler, these women's rampant infidelity symbolizes the political decadence driving these heroes to rebellion.[62]

The most striking female character in *Water Margin* is undoubtedly the wicked Pan Jinlian (Golden Lotus), wife of Wu Dalang (Elder Brother Wu). She initially demonstrates her unfaithfulness by trying to seduce her brother-in-law, the hero Wu Song, who roughly rejects her advances, lectures her on wifely propriety, and warns his hapless brother about her iniquity. Later Pan Jinlian has an affair with a rich merchant, and the two of them conspire to murder her husband. When Wu Song returns and discovers her treachery, he cuts off her head and delivers it to his dead brother's memorial tablet as a gruesome offering. The detailed description of her execution is lavishly violent, heightening the sense of requital.[63] More than mere punishment for murder, this calculated cruelty is retribution for her treachery and infidelity, which brought posthumous shame to her deceased husband. She not only killed him but, just as important, destroyed his reputation for honor by failing to practice proper wifely chastity. This murder dramatically symbolizes the rejection of women as a focal point for male attention. If women are so unworthy of the hero's trust, he has no choice but to turn to the homosocial world of male companionship in search of honor and dignity.

NOTES

1. Marlene Kim Conner, *What Is Cool?: Understanding Black Manhood in America* (New York: Crown, 1995), 3–13.
2. Demetriou, "Connell's Concept of Hegemonic Masculinity," 342.
3. Demetriou, "Connell's Concept of Hegemonic Masculinity," 340.
4. Jenner, *A Knife in the Ribs for a Mate*, 13.
5. Some scholars term the use of masculinity by a group of men to dominate other men "internal hegemony" and domination of women by men through the deployment of masculine norms "external hegemony." Connell and Messerschmidt, "Hegemonic Masculinity," 832, 844.
6. Margaret Wetherell and Nigel Edley, "Negotiating Hegemonic Masculinity: Imaginary Positions and Psycho-discursive Practices," *Feminism & Psychology* 9, no. 3 (1999): 335–56.
7. Connell and Messerschmidt, "Hegemonic Masculinity," 832.
8. Zhu Yi, "Han Tang jian xia de geren xingxiang he shehui neihan," *Zhongguo shehui lishi pinglun* 6 (2006): 165–68; Jenner, *A Knife in the Ribs for a Mate*, 11–12.
9. Zhu, "Han Tang jian xia de geren xingxiang he shehui neihan," 168, 171–72; Jenner, *A Knife in the Ribs for a Mate*, 24–25.
10. Cao Wei, "Shiji zhong cike xingxiang suo zaixian de rujia wenhua jingshen qizhi," *Xijiangyue* 1 (2010): 23–24.
11. Huang, *Negotiating Masculinities in Late Imperial China*, 90.
12. Jing Shuhui, *Wei Jin shiren yu zhengzhi* (Beijing: Zhonghua, 2007), 120–21.
13. Louie, *Theorizing Chinese Masculinity*, 79.
14. Kong Lingguang, "Zhongguo shenhua zhong de beiju yingxiong xinjie," *Qiqihaer Shifan Gaodeng Zhuanke Xuexiao xuebao* 104 (2008): 44–45.

15. Ji, "Lishi yanyi xiaoshuozhong 'rujiang' xingxiang," 14.

16. Ji, "Lishi yanyi xiaoshuozhong 'rujiang' xingxiang," 19. The contradiction between real and ideal was a major theme in early medieval literature that went far beyond heroic behavior. Jing, *Wei Jin shiren yu zhengzhi*, 129.

17. Yuan Jixi, *Renhai guzhou: Han Wei Liuchao shi de gudu yishi* (Zhengzhou: Henan Renmin, 1995), 7.

18. Andrew H. Plaks, "*Shui-hu Chuan* and the Sixteenth-Century Novel Form: An Interpretive Reappraisal," *Chinese Literature: Essays, Articles, Reviews* 2, no. 1 (1980): 43.

19. Huang, *Negotiating Masculinities in Late Imperial China*, 89–91. Third-century thinker Liu Shao explained it more specifically as referring to two qualities of outstanding men: sagacity and strength. Luo Yinghuan and Fu Junlian, trans., *The Classified Characters and Political Abilities* (Beijing: Zhonghua, 2007), 122–23.

20. Huang, *Negotiating Masculinities in Late Imperial China*, 89–91.

21. Henry Y. H. Zhao, *The Uneasy Narrator: Chinese Fiction from the Traditional to the Modern* (Oxford: Oxford University Press, 1995), 177.

22. Plaks, "*Shui-hu Chuan* and the Sixteenth-Century Novel Form," 16–19, discusses variations among different versions of *Shuihu zhuan* and the general relation of the text to oral traditions. More elements of orthodoxy, such as Confucian rhetoric, were injected into the narrative when it was written down. John Fitzgerald, "Continuity within Discontinuity: The Case of *Water Margin* Mythology," *Modern China* 12, no. 3 (1986): 372–75.

23. Fitzgerald, "Continuity within Discontinuity," 370–71.

24. Robert E. Hegel, *Reading Illustrated Fiction in Late Imperial China* (Stanford, CA: Stanford University Press, 1998).

25. Shi Nai'an and Luo Guangzhong, *Outlaws of the Marsh*, trans. Sidney Shapiro (Beijing and Changsha: Foreign Languages Press and Hunan People's Publishing House, 1999), 1:413.

26. Shelly Hsueh-lun Chang, *History and Legend: Ideas and Images in the Ming Historical Novels* (Ann Arbor: University of Michigan Press, 1990).

27. David Ownby, "Approximations of Chinese Bandits: Perverse Rebels, Romantic Heroes, or Frustrated Bachelors," in *Chinese Femininities, Chinese Masculinities: A Reader*, ed. Susan Brownell and Jeffrey N. Wasserstrom (Berkeley: University of California Press, 2002), 233–34.

28. Martin W. Huang, "Sentiments of Desire: Thoughts on the Cult of Qing in Ming-Qing Literature," *Chinese Literature: Essays, Articles, Reviews* 20 (1998): 163.

29. Scholars have written a great deal about this gluttony and drunkenness; for example, Louie, *Theorizing Chinese Masculinity*, 81.

30. Carrie E. Reed, "Tattoo in Early China," *Journal of the American Oriental Society* 120, no. 3 (2000): 370.

31. For a coherent summary of the main characteristics of "good" warriors in Ming popular fiction, see Song Geng, *The Fragile Scholar: Power and Masculinity in China* (Hong Kong: Hong Kong University Press, 2004), 163–64.

32. Plaks, "*Shui-hu Chuan* and the Sixteenth-Century Novel Form," 29–36, 47.

33. For an overview of Chinese research on outlaws, see Zhu Dake, *Liumang de shengyan: dangdai Zhongguo de liumang xushi* (Beijing: Xinxing, 2006), 1–27.

34. Ownby, "Approximations of Chinese Bandits," 228.

35. Xu Youwei and Philip Billingsley, "Out of the Closet: China's Historians 'Discover' Republican-Period Bandits," *Modern China* 28, no. 4 (2002): 477–78.

36. Xu and Billingsley, "Out of the Closet," 482.

37. Qiu Jian, "Qian qiu xia gu xiang—cong 'Shiji' hua xiake," *Yuwen xuekan* 5 (2005): 41–42. Cao, "Shiji zhong cike xingxiang suo zaixian de rujia wenhua jingshen qizhi," 24–25.

38. Jenner, *A Knife in the Ribs for a Mate*, 16.

39. Ownby, "Approximations of Chinese Bandits," 232.

40. Fitzgerald, "Continuity within Discontinuity," 375–76.

41. Huang, *Negotiating Masculinities in Late Imperial China*, 104–5.

42. L. S. Yang, "The Concept of *Pao* as a Basis for Social Relations in China," in *Chinese Thought and Institutions*, ed. John King Fairbank (Chicago: University of Chicago Press, 1957), 291–309.

43. Karl S. Y. Kao, "Bao and Baoying: Narrative Causality and External Motivations in Chinese Fiction," *Chinese Literature: Essays, Articles, Reviews* 11 (1989): 120.

44. Fitzgerald, "Continuity within Discontinuity," 375–76.

45. Stephen J. Roddy, *Literati Identity and Its Fictional Representations in Late Imperial China* (Stanford, CA: Stanford University Press, 1998).

46. This antipathy between the elite and rebels stretches back to antiquity. Liu Chaoqian, "Xiake yu ru wenhua de yizhi duikangxing," *Kongzi yanjiu jikan* 1 (1995): 42–44.

47. Huang, *Negotiating Masculinities in Late Imperial China*, 111.

48. For examples, see Liu, "Xiake yu ru wenhua de yizhi duikangxing," 44–45.

49. Liu, "Xiake yu ru wenhua de yizhi duikangxing," 40–41.

50. Liu, "Xiake yu ru wenhua de yizhi duikangxing," 38.

51. Eve Kosofsky Sedgwick, *Between Men: English Literature and Male Homosocial Desire* (New York: Columbia University Press, 1985), 1–2; Sharon R. Bird, "Welcome to the Men's Club: Homosociality and the Maintenance of Hegemonic Masculinity," *Gender and Society* 10, no. 2 (1996): 120–32.

52. Zhou, *Festivals, Feasts, and Gender Relations in Ancient China and Greece*, 137, 152–57. For some of the types of homosocial bonds in the late imperial era, see Mann, *Gender and Sexuality in Modern Chinese History*, 13. Joseph P. McDermott, "Friendship and Its Friends in the Late Ming," in *Jinshi jiazu yu zhengzhi bijiao lishi lunwenji* (Taipei: Zhongyang Yanjiuyuan Jindaishi Yanjiusuo and Department of History, University of California, Davis, 1992), 67–96, discusses Ming debates over the nature and value of friendship.

53. Louie, *Theorizing Chinese Masculinity*, 79. For an anthropological perspective on how these sorts of "brotherhood" networks can benefit working-class men, see Lee McIsaac, "'Righteous Fraternities' and Honorable Men: Sworn Brotherhoods in Wartime Chongqing," *American Historical Review* 105, no. 5 (2000): 1641–55; Andrew Walsh, "'Hot Money' and Daring Consumption in a Northern Malagasy Sapphire-Mining Town," *American Ethnologist* 30, no. 2 (2003): 283. Fei Xiaotong, *From the Soil: The Foundations of Chinese Society* (Berkeley: University of California Press, 1992), 92, sees intense male friendships as an outgrowth of separation of the sexes.

54. Song, *The Fragile Scholar*, 161, 173.

55. Adrian Davis, "Fraternity and Fratricide in Late Imperial China," *American Historical Review* 105, no. 5 (2000): 1630–31; Nye, "Kinship, Male Bonds, and Masculinity in Comparative Perspective," 1160–63.

56. Song, *The Fragile Scholar*, 175, 178–79.

57. Cheng Xiaolin and Zhu Jingxia, "Shilun Tang chuanqi xiaoshuo zhong de xiake xingxiang," *Mudanjiang Daxue xuebao* 19, no. 4 (2010): 40–41.

58. C. T. Hsia, *The Classic Chinese Novel* (New York: Columbia University Press, 1968), 75–114; Louie, *Theorizing Chinese Masculinity*, 91–92.

59. Ownby, "Approximations of Chinese Bandits," 240–45.

60. Song, *The Fragile Scholar*, 166, 168.

61. Hu Ying, "Angling with Beauty: Two Stories of Women as Narrative Bait in *Sanguozhi yanyi*," *Chinese Literature: Essays, Articles, Reviews* 15 (1993): 99–112.

62. Fitzgerald, "Continuity within Discontinuity," 377–78.

63. Huang, *Negotiating Masculinities in Late Imperial China*, 109–10.

7

╌╫╌

Late Qing and Republican Eras
Modernizing Masculinity

At the culmination of the Second Opium War, in 1860 a combined expeditionary force of British and French troops marched into Beijing. Faced with the hopeless prospect of fighting a modern army, the emperor and court simply fled. The invaders then went on a rampage. Infuriated by the imprisonment and torture of two British envoys, they burned and looted the magnificent Old Summer Palace on the outskirts of the capital. This complex of buildings, set among extensive gardens of otherworldly beauty, was home to an unparalleled collection of art amassed by China's emperors over the centuries. As looters ransacked the palace, the quintessence of the nation's patrimony scattered in every direction. Thousands of soldiers plundered then incinerated the massive palace complex, which remained alight for three days. In the wake of this catastrophe, China's demoralized government had no choice but to sue for peace on disgraceful terms.

Humiliations suffered during the Opium Wars traumatized China's collective psyche and remain a potent source of anger and shame to this day. This mortifying defeat not only dealt a blow to the Qing empire but also called into question the viability of Chinese manhood as well. In earlier eras when nomads overran their country, Chinese comforted themselves with a smug sense of cultural superiority. Although militarily weak, they remained confident in the peerless magnificence of their heritage. However, Great Britain and France were not nomadic hordes. Their soldiers represented the vanguard of an alien civilization that outshone China in technology, science, and productive power. Crushing defeat at the hands of such formidable foes shocked Chinese into reassessing every aspect of their society and culture, including gender norms. A memorial to the throne by the reformer Kang Youwei summed up the prevailing mood: "Now China is narrow and crowded, has opium addicts and streets lined with beggars. Foreigners have been taking pictures and laughing at us for these things and criticizing us for being barbarians. There is nothing which makes us objects of ridicule so much as footbinding. I, your humble servant, feel deeply ashamed at heart."[1]

Even in the absence of imperialist incursions, nineteenth-century China would still have faced a severe crisis due to unbearable demographic pressures. A long period of peace and unity, together with the introduction of New World foods easily cultivated on marginal land, such as corn and sweet potatoes, triggered an unprecedented population explosion. According to the best estimates, China's population tripled during the eighteenth century; by 1800 it had reached 300 million. Just feeding so many hungry mouths was an immense challenge. Moreover, a shortage of arable land meant that many families found themselves trapped in a spiral of downward mobility. And to make matters even worse, about a third of the population was under the age of eighteen.[2] Myriad restless youths found themselves locked into an inflexible system offering dwindling opportunities. Institutions and ideas developed to administer a much smaller state proved inadequate to meet these new challenges. When European soldiers marched into Beijing, they dealt the tottering imperial system a fatal blow.

This overarching sense of crisis extended to Chinese masculinity as well. The outsiders who bullied China with impunity, fortified by the powers of capitalism and science, judged a man's worth by completely unfamiliar criteria. Mastery of China's ancient classics and expertise in polite accomplishments such as peony appreciation were completely irrelevant to Western ideals of manhood. Confrontation with foreign ideas about masculinity, emanating from foes who had dramatically demonstrated their superior power, forced a sweeping reexamination of what it meant to be a man. Complicating the problem, Chinese had traditionally associated the most prestigious forms of manhood with service to the state; yet the government was clearly in decay. Society would have to revitalize masculinity as a prerequisite for rescuing the nation. China's survival required the creation of new expressions of masculinity that could allow Chinese men to compete against foreigners in the modern world.

NATIONALIZING MANHOOD

The imperialists threatening China did not see this conflict as merely a struggle between armies. Influenced by social Darwinism, many Europeans supported imperialism because they considered themselves racially superior, hence entitled by the birthright of biology to dominate lesser peoples. Racist ideology led the leaders of the imperial powers to stress the physical, mental, and moral strengthening of men as necessary to staying on top in this Darwinian struggle. The male body thus became a locus for expressing both individual and national pride.[3] For example, when a physical culture craze swept Britain in the late nineteenth and early twentieth centuries, men commonly expressed open admiration for strong, handsome male bodies and use group exercise as a form of homosocial bonding. The British public celebrated robust bodies as symbols of national strength, often justified by reference to popular ideas emanating from social Darwinism.[4] Imperialism became the ultimate expression of this hyper-aggressive masculine ethos. Men identified their own masculine pride with the strength of the nation, their sense of manliness bolstered by the conquest and domination of distant peoples.[5]

Conversely, Chinese saw their repeated defeats at the hands of foreign powers as a failure of indigenous masculinity. Discussions of social Darwinism, newly imported from the West, sent a shock wave through the intelligentsia. Reformers and revolutionaries embraced this alarming new theory and began to envision their country as locked in a fierce struggle for survival with other nations and races. The pathetic rout of China's armies during the Opium Wars and subsequent conflicts made talk about survival of the fittest seem particularly ominous. Panic at the threat of being swamped by foreigners armed with superior ideas and institutions led pragmatic thinkers to reassess every aspect of society.

Although the main focus of reform was political and economic, there were also urgent calls to modernize both manhood and womanhood in response to the challenges posed by a hostile world. During the late nineteenth century some forward-looking thinkers began to demand an outright sexual revolution. Liberating women from onerous traditional restrictions became a central theme of social renovation. Reformers reasoned that it was impossible for the nation to become strong if half the population remained trapped indoors, unable to attend school or work outside the home, and hobbled by deformed bound feet.[6] More generally, there was a growing sense that China's decline was partly attributable to an enervating sexual decadence. Nationalists advocated strengthening China by banning foot binding, outlawing prostitution and concubinage, suppressing pornography, and remaking sexual ethics and gender relations along westernized lines.[7]

The renovation of gender was a key component of a larger nationalist project to construct a new China that would be viable in the modern world. Nationalism serves as an extremely self-conscious expression of ethnicity, which takes form as a kind of public performance.[8] People perform their ethnicity in their daily lives and also through exceptional activities such as political events. The gendering of nationalism allowed men to express nationalist sentiments by adopting a masculine persona considered beneficial to the nation. In this respect China was far from unique. Men across the globe saw the predations of imperialism not just as a military or political assault but, more profoundly, as a blow to their manhood. Because Chinese had long associated masculine honor with a man's in-group, men easily identified with the condition of the nation as a whole.[9] As nationalism rose to become the premier ideology, Chinese had to reexamine every aspect of men's lives from this politically charged standpoint.[10]

Male pride expanded to encompass the strength and well-being of the entire nation. Many colonized peoples often come to conceive of the nation in feminine terms as a vulnerable motherland violated by outsiders.[11] Such was the case with China. As a sign of the times, influential writer Lu Xun (1881–1936) was fascinated by the popular Buddhist tale of the filial Mulian who rescues his mother from the depths of hell. When given a nationalist reading, this old story became an exhortation for the sons of China to save their helpless motherland.[12]

Scholarship has recognized nationalism as one of the most overtly masculine forms of political expression, and China was no exception.[13] The feeling that repeated defeats at the hands of foreign powers had neutered or feminized China's men fostered nationalist sentiments.[14] To defend the nation, men collectively asserted stereotypically masculine characteristics, sometimes to a highly exaggerated degree. Building a successful modern nation would require manly strength and self-sacrifice. Nationalism thus became a consciously masculinist project carried out through homosocial activities that strengthened individual men.[15]

ASSESSING TRADITION

Starting in the late nineteenth century, it became increasingly common to judge a man's conduct by his usefulness to the nation, making normative male identity into a tool of national renovation.[16] Reformers deliberately asserted new models of masculinity that they hoped would strengthen China. Sometimes the new style of manhood drew on traditional archetypes of manliness. Maintaining time-tested masculine attributes in the face of imperialism is a strategy seen in many societies. The dominated often assert native standards of ideal manhood within the indigenous community, even when overrun by foreign men who proudly flaunt their alien masculinity as a source of prestige.[17]

Chinese rebels employed the conventions of traditional manly behavior to resist the sense of disorientation caused by rapid change. Rebels often legitimized their band of brothers through reference to the ideal of righteousness (*yiqi*) that had inspired the *Water Margin* heroes.[18] For example, the Boxer rebels consciously modeled themselves on traditional portrayals of *haohan*. They appropriated a hodgepodge of images from grassroots culture, including popular religion, drama, and shamanism, to put themselves forward as virtuous *haohan*.

According to their own value system, they were not bloodthirsty rabble but heroes valiantly fighting against the evil forces threatening their homeland.[19]

China's repeated defeats and failures inspired a reassessment of manhood at the lower end of the social spectrum. During the late Qing era, stories about bandits inspired by *Water Margin* remained popular, even as changing circumstances led authors to adopt a different tone. For example, the novel *Quell the Bandits* (*Dangkouzhi*) by Yu Wanchun (1794–1849), published posthumously in 1853, depicts bandits as petty criminals, not heroes. Even when the rebels in *Water Margin* commit wrongs, the narrative still shows them in a basically positive light. In contrast, the plot of *Quell the Bandits* revolves around how authorities hunt down and exterminate each brigand, often killing them in deliberately gruesome ways as punishment for their misdeeds. The popular imagination increasingly viewed bandits as villains, and readers sympathized with their destruction. The changing treatment of bandits in literature reflects the sense of crisis brought on by increasing disorder.[20] As society spiraled downward into chronic chaos, bandits seemed like threatening thugs instead of romantic heroes. This reevaluation of stock narratives in the face of crisis called into question an important archetype of martial manhood that had long informed plebeian masculinity.

The critique of tradition in all its forms was in fact a major inspiration for Chinese nationalism. To modernizers, whether reformists or revolutionaries, love of the nation provided a refuge for those alienated by the failures of traditional culture. Because the Manchus had closely identified themselves with China's time-honored customs and values to gain the support of the Han elite, rejection of Manchu rule often became a de facto attack on tradition in general.[21] Critics derided the shaved forehead and braided queue that the Manchus had forced upon Chinese men as a humiliating symbol of submission.[22] Liang Qichao (1873–1929) famously repudiated the legacy of China's long history, dismissing past beliefs as retrograde superstitions impeding progress. He summed up his attitude with the shocking exhortation, "Wash out the poison of thousands of years!"[23]

As society rapidly transformed, wealthy families realized that a classical education had become irrelevant. Pragmatic landlords and merchants now sought a Western-style education for their children, replacing memorization of the *Analects* with training in science and foreign languages. To those with a modern education, the affected man of letters, steeped in the Confucian classics and stubbornly adhering to old-fashioned manners, became a source of amusement. Lu Xun lampooned the antiquated pedant in his story about a fictional literatus named Kong Yiji.[24] Kong has wasted years mastering arcane ancient knowledge, only to find himself pathetically out of place in the modern world and the butt of mockery. Similarly, author Lao She (1899–1966) portrayed literati not as exemplars of Confucian virtue but as lazy and dishonest

Westernized learning, Tsinghua University Library, 1934. *Source:* Feng Keli, ed., *Gushi fengwu* (Jinan: Shandong huabao, 2008), 153.

daydreamers.[25] Not only was literatus masculinity no longer hegemonic, but society increasingly came to see it as symptomatic of the enfeebling decadence responsible for many of China's ills.

Lu Xun's landmark novella, *The True Story of Ah Q (A Q zhengzhuan)*, which first appeared in serialized form in 1921–1922, transfixed readers with a withering indictment of contemporary Chinese manhood. The protagonist, Ah Q, repeatedly deceives himself into thinking that his defeats are in fact victories. He bullies anyone unfortunate enough to come under his control, yet cravenly toadies to his own oppressors. All the while, he consoles himself with the idea that he somehow possesses spiritual superiority over more successful men. His empty megalomania serves as pathetic consolation for his incompetence. In putting forward this critical allegory of contemporary manhood, Lu swept aside any pretentions of innate Chinese superiority and informed his readers that men would have to transform themselves if the nation were to survive in the modern world.[26] The new Chinese man would have to embody foreign middle-class virtues such as individualism, thrift, industriousness, tenacity, pragmatism, self-discipline, and a rational scientific mind-set.

CAPITALIST MAN

In tandem with nationalism, capitalism also reshaped modern Chinese masculinity. Between the Nationalist Xinhai Revolution in 1911 and the Communist Revolution in 1949, China's economy grew at a startling pace, even as the country suffered invasion and civil war. For example, from 1912 to 1920 the production of consumer goods increased at a stunning average annual rate of 21.6 percent.[27] The same trend held true for more basic commodities, such as steel and coal. In spite of weak governance and even outright chaos, China's economy roared ahead. The impact of industrial development on people's lives was obvious. Whereas the average person still lived close to subsistence level, a new middle class began to flourish. Material prosperity, however unequally distributed, opened up unprecedented new possibilities for many men. In the past, masculinity had to suit the conditions, mind-set, and customs of a poor rural agrarian society. But as manufacturing and commerce transformed urban life, new forms of manhood arose in response.

Capitalism puts a financial value on everything, even the symbols of manhood. Along with everything else, people came increasingly to understand masculinity in material terms. In the eyes of many, the paragon of manhood was now the rich businessman, regardless of the source of his fortune. This bluntly materialistic assessment of manliness departed considerably from previous views that regarded social status as somewhat independent of wealth. To be respectable in the new capitalist economy, a man needed a stable job with sufficient income to allow him a high degree of autonomy. When possible, he eschewed menial labor, tried to acquire some modern education, and elevated himself by deploying the cultural capital of the new middle class.[28] Literature of the era portrayed this new breed of cosmopolitan man as not just successful but sexually desirable as well.[29]

The fiction of the progressive novelist Lao She illustrates the capitalist masculine ideal. His works laud canny businessmen, particularly those who succeeded abroad, as a new style of Chinese hero.[30] Whereas the traditional hero garnered admiration for exemplary physical prowess or strength of character, the new male role model distinguished himself in the business world. The industrious, flexible, pragmatic businessman was not merely a respectable social type but a patriotic icon. Because Chinese saw themselves as locked in life-or-death competition with other nations, they widely viewed the pragmatic businessman, brash and industrious, as best equipped to cope with the challenge.

Capitalism altered the ways men interacted with those around them. Jürgen Habermas has pointed out that capitalism fundamentally transforms society by engendering the rise of a bourgeois public sphere. In China, the new masculinity emerged together with middle-class institutions as reciprocal social constructions.[31] According to Habermas, prosperity is the prerequisite for full participation in public life in capitalist society. Unlike in precapitalist societies, where groups handle public matters collectively, the atomized individuals of capitalist society are far more likely to put self-interest ahead of group welfare.[32] The influence of this new spirit of individualism on Chinese masculinity was profound. Traditionally manhood had been closely associated with integration into social groups such as kin and village. Under the new capitalist ethos, however, the male subject increasingly viewed himself as an autonomous agent whose identity and interests were not necessarily aligned with others. The writer Lao She summed up this new social type: "Whatever he looked at—people, land, houses, merchandise—was all the same to him. He couldn't care less whether a person had a nose or not. He first determined what you were worth, then figured out his share in brokerage fees. His friendship with people terminated the day he collected his fees."[33] Individualism led men to behave in increasingly varied ways, feeding the dynamism of China's public sphere but also causing disturbing social, political, and cultural dislocations. People had to resolve public matters amid a dense thicket of conflicting individual concerns.

Traditional masculine paradigms had evolved to encourage success within the context of a predominantly agricultural society. Previously it was in a man's best interest to ingratiate himself with family and community and become a harmonious member of the groups structuring rural life. Yet the rise of capitalism rendered many traditional male virtues useless or even counterproductive. Material accumulation and job prestige steadily superseded the communitarian ideal as standards for judging male success.[34] A man no longer gained maximum advantage simply by getting along with those around him. In fact, the successful man was often a lone wolf aggressively pursuing his own interests. It could pay to be a selfish maverick. This increasingly competitive ethos meant that men started to view neighbors and peers as rivals instead of potential allies. Of course, many men failed to thrive in this hypercompetitive environment. Disappointed with their careers, they turned to leisure pursuits and consumerism for fulfillment.

Not everyone welcomed this new breed of brassy businessman. Many of the novels and short stories of Eileen Chang (Zhang Ailing, 1920–1995) explore the disorienting and ambiguous relations between the sexes in the new China. Many of her male characters exemplify modern masculine ideals. While at ease in a wealthy cosmopolitan milieu, these men are far from perfect, and their crassness sometimes drags them down toward outright vulgarity. Many suffer from a disturbing shallowness that demeans them and everyone around them. Deeply selfish, they cynically use women as toys, rendering the relations between the sexes unsatisfying.[35]

Through the businessman archetype, men were no longer saddled with decayed literatus manhood. However, this unfamiliar model of masculinity raised considerable new challenges that many men failed to resolve. And from the male perspective, increasingly liberated women who copied Western values and mannerisms could seem unattractive and desexualized.[36] Both sexes would have to adjust to disturbing new gender norms.

MANLY BODIES, MASCULINE PLACES

Despite the uncertainty engendered by the modernization of masculinity, the transformation of Chinese manhood remained an unstoppable trend. To cope with the threats posed by imperialism and international capitalism, Chinese culture remade key aspects of masculinity along Western and Japanese lines to make men more competitive in the international arena.[37] One result was an unprecedented enthusiasm for sports and physical fitness. As early reformers debated the causes of China's decay, forward-minded thinkers such as Kang Youwei concluded that many of the nation's failures stemmed from the physical weakness of Chinese men, which resulted from their enervating, unhealthy lifestyle.[38] A concern with male strength persisted into the twentieth century, when strong male bodies became closely identified with nationalism.

Lu Xun was extremely disturbed by what he considered a dearth of manliness. Although Chinese had previously considered gentleness and cultivation admirable male traits, this sort of manhood seemed alarmingly effeminate when judged by new standards.[39] In particular, Lu derided the traditional custom of female impersonation on the stage as decadent and uncivilized.[40] Instead of imitating feminine behavior, he believed that men should accentuate stereotypically manly traits and strengthen their bodies.

As progressives rebuilt cities to accommodate a self-consciously modern lifestyle, athletic venues became standard elements of urban planning. For example, in the 1920s the prosperous industrial city of Nantong was rebuilt around five parks. Not only did these leafy oases make the city more attractive, but exercise also became far more convenient. Park facilities included a swimming pool, tennis court, and exercise equipment.[41] Modern public spaces provided physical fitness apparatus to encourage a stronger and healthier man.

The rising popularity of mass sporting events further signaled changing attitudes toward the male body.[42] Seen as a progressive activity integral to social reform and modernization, athletics became a standard component of the modern school curriculum. People believed that athletics taught the value of competition and encouraged homosociality within a manly physical environment. However, as Chinese were unfamiliar with team sports, competitive athletics were slow to gain popularity. Instead military drills became the most common way to express male physicality.[43] Students marching in unison and conducting military drills not only articulated the militaristic values of an era

Students marching in military formation. *Source:* Feng Keli, ed., *Lao Zhaopian* (Jinan: Shandong huabao, 2008), 60:155.

plagued by civil war and foreign incursions but also displayed strong male bodies as symbols of national pride.

As renovated cityscapes guided men toward participating in the new manhood, social critics began to denigrate traditional masculine spaces. The teahouse was previously a popular place for men to spend their free time, conduct business, and socialize. However, these venues implicitly reflected the values of imperial society. The owner seated his patrons according to traditional views of relative social status, facilitating interaction between men in ways that reinforced the social boundaries of imperial society. Even if a businessmen or Western-educated customer had more money than other patrons, the owner would not necessarily allot him the most prestigious seat, instead reserving pride of place for those at the top of the traditional hierarchy, such as landlords and officials. By preserving imperial social boundaries, teahouses did not allow progressive men to display the prestige due to them as exemplars of modern manhood.

Because teahouses did not suit the new elite, progressives excoriated these places as dens of iniquity. Teahouses became associated in the popular imagination with prostitution, gambling, and traditional performances, all of which Chinese increasingly disparaged as backward pursuits that encouraged laziness and dissipation. Just as they demonized traditional venues, reformers sought to remake cities by providing modern spaces amenable to progressive social practices. They encouraged men to spend their leisure time in the growing

Not modern—a traditional-style teahouse. *Source:* Chen Min, *Chapu* (Shanghai: Shanghai jinxiu wenzhang, 2007), 21.

number of westernized venues, such as cinemas, parks, libraries, museums, and restaurants, instead of dissipating themselves in teahouses, bordellos, and opium dens.[44] A major goal of the modernization of urban planning in the early twentieth century was the creation of spaces amenable to modern masculinity.

The rise of the cinema, one of the most popular new urban spaces, exemplifies how the changing urban fabric influenced manhood. During the 1920s the ideal of female chastity went into steep decline, earning women freedom of movement. Henceforth an unmarried woman could acceptably leave the house alone and mingle informally with men.[45] As men started asking women out on dates, the cinema became a popular place for couples to socialize in a safe and respectable (but romantically dark) environment. Notably, cinemas sported a conspicuously modern atmosphere, which allowed a man to demonstrate his sophistication to his girlfriend and others by showing himself at ease in au courant surroundings.

Modern spaces demanded novel codes of conduct. In old-fashioned venues, patrons would chat during performances, eat dinner, noisily slurp tea, and sometimes even get into fistfights over prime seats. In contrast, the cinema management enforced strict rules to maintain a quality environment in often posh surroundings. The art deco Grand Cinema in Shanghai, for example, boasted a spacious lobby, three fountains, and spacious sofa-style seats.[46] As cinemas became common, the audience internalized what was initially an entirely alien etiquette. Moviegoers were supposed to help maintain the clean and tidy environment and watch the film in absolute silence.[47] Although early Chinese films were mostly just cinematic remakes of traditional legends and opera plots, the environment was conspicuously modern.[48]

By embracing new rules that embodied middle-class values, cinemas allowed men to gain a reputation for honor through conspicuous public displays of their bourgeois virtues. Although the society still maintained an honor culture, the definition of honor had changed enormously. The exigencies of capitalism redirected honor away from group loyalty and redefined it largely as an

Cinema in Shanghai. *Source:* Xu Guoxing, Zu Jianping, and Hu Yuanjie (eds.), *Lao chengxiang—Shangai chengshi zhi gen* (Shanghai: Tongji daxue, 2011), 166.

expression of individual moral autonomy.[49] A man was now responsible for his own reputation, and his behavior redounded on himself, not the group. Highly regulated public spaces provided men with opportunities to acquire a reputation for honor by displaying middle-class rectitude, above all a capacity for self-discipline.[50] Men carefully restrained their actions when around women, behaving gallantly and engaging them in gentle conversation. These sorts of social performances flaunted a man's ability to control his behavior, the key to honorable bourgeois manhood. Middle-class spaces also allowed lower-status men to learn the new rules of manhood by giving them opportunities to observe the behavior of men who had mastered this prestigious new code of behavior.[51]

At an even higher cultural level, many reformers portrayed science as nothing less than the key to national salvation.[52] A scientific mind-set also characterized the new manhood. Some feminist critics have described science as a masculinist form of knowledge, in contrast to feminine emotion and intuition, so associating oneself with science became an accepted strategy for a man to boost his masculine credentials.[53] The rise of scientism upended previous ideas about masculine knowledge. Although the Confucian classics had traditionally served as the paradigm of masculine knowledge, scientific education replaced the imperial canon as a source of male prestige.

Even in the late nineteenth century, when few Chinese had a clear understanding of scientific principles, scientific discourse nevertheless began to acquire esteem. Late Qing authors even created the new genre of science fantasy to explore how this new field of knowledge might possibly influence the world. Although this genre arose in response to translations of the works of Jules Verne, Chinese science fantasy differed from Western science fiction in that authors showed little fidelity to actual scientific laws. Plots ostensibly inspired by science were often little more than exotic flights of fancy.[54] Even though these works betray a poor understanding of science, they nevertheless show popular respect for this imported body of knowledge. People increasingly saw mastery of science as a source of male power, and men sought to associate themselves with this paradigmatic body of modern knowledge to gain status and influence.

The founding of museums in major cities provided men with a new kind of elite modern space legitimized by an association with science. The science museum built in Nantong, which opened to the public in 1912, exemplifies how scientific education became consciously integrated into the community. As with other aspects of this carefully planned city, reformists hoped that this model public space would mold people's character. They assumed that a modern city would produce modern citizens, and science held a prime place in their progressive urban vision. The Nantong Museum comprised several Western-style buildings set in a didactic botanical garden, the trees labeled with their scientific names in Latin. There was also a small zoo, provided not for entertainment but as an educational facility for teaching biology through

firsthand observation. The museum's exhibits included a meteorological station and astronomical observatory, displays of plants, animals, and fossils, and
archaeological artifacts and artworks.[55]

Although ostensibly dedicated to teaching science, these sorts of museums
in fact imparted far more practical lessons to visitors as well. As with cinemas
and other modern public spaces, museums were carefully regulated environments that forced visitors to conform to a highly restricted code of civility. By
imposing strict etiquette on visitors, museums helped promulgate a new code
of manners appropriate to middle-class life. And as with cinemas, museums
provided men with an opportunity to display their familiarity with these new
rules of conduct, gaining honor as men at ease in the modern world.

FAMILY LIFE

The family was a major target of reform in the early twentieth century. Debates
over the relevance of traditional Chinese kinship customs to the modern world
were intense, eventually resulting in a comprehensive restructuring of family
life. A major impetus for reform of the family was the desire of educated young
urban men to increase their autonomy. In light of the spirit of individualism
fostered by capitalism, they wanted to be able to choose wives, jobs, and hous-
ing free from the interference of parents and meddlesome relatives. Previously,
in an agrarian society where land was scarce, a man could not hope to achieve
independence until he had inherited his father's fields. Lacking his own means of
subsistence, he had no choice but to maintain close ties with father and brothers
whether he wanted to or not. The promotion of Confucian values such as filial
piety and brotherly love helped smooth relations between kinsmen forced by
economic necessity into close long-term bonds and even extended cohabitation.
However, capitalism liberated sons from their families. A job in a factory, office,
or shop offered a man early economic independence. Once the extended family
lost its economic rationale, it became a prime target for social reform.

Generally speaking, reformers wanted to "modernize" Chinese family life
by modeling it on Western norms. They rejected the traditional ideal of an
extended family of multiple generations living under one roof, not to mention
a bevy of concubines with bound feet. The new ideal was a nuclear family con-
sisting of a father, mother, and children living in their own home apart from
other kin. The ambitious man also wanted the freedom to select his own wife
so that he could choose a spouse who fit his modern urban lifestyle. As men
increasingly competed with one another for status, disassociating themselves
from conservative kinsmen and gaining control over an independent conjugal
family became important prerequisites for upward mobility. Autonomy over
family matters allowed men to control the image they presented to the world.

Reformers presented conjugal family life as a morally superior alternative to the extended family, as it fostered modern virtues such as self-reliance and individualism. They thereby justified the transformation of the kinship system to suit their own interests by claiming that new domestic arrangements served the cause of economic growth and national progress.[56]

To appreciate the modernized Chinese manhood advocated by reformists, it is useful to examine an exemplary figure who embodied these ideals with his own values and conduct. The reformist intellectual Hu Shih (also Hu Shi, 1891–1962) was a key leader in the movement to popularize written vernacular Chinese. Inspired by his time studying at Columbia University under the pragmatist philosopher John Dewey, Hu strove to break the stranglehold of outmoded ideas by promoting an accessible style of writing much closer to the spoken language. Despite his reformist views, the establishment accepted Hu. He served as China's ambassador to the United States and chancellor of Peking University before following the Nationalist army into exile in Taiwan.

Hu Shih.

In hindsight, Hu seems to have carefully calculated much of his oeuvre and conduct to put forward the image of a thoroughly modern man. He was very careful about what he wrote. In contrast to the casualness of the Internet age, his was a time of formal and deliberate social and intellectual interactions. His writings selectively disclosed facts about himself to create an impression of modern manhood, making him seem cosmopolitan, scientific, pragmatic, and forward-looking. Due to his embrace of American middle-class values, he stressed the importance of temperance and criticized tobacco, alcohol, gambling, and prostitutes as unworthy of the respectable man. Hu Shih also believed that men should behave in a chivalrous manner toward women, an utterly alien concept at the time. Even though he and his wife had little in common, he treated her with politesse in public, signaling his devotion to modern manhood. We can read Hu Shih's actions as a public performance intended to lead by example. In particular, he hoped that other men would imitate his reformed mode of masculinity, thereby transforming China into a more progressive society.[57]

Extremism and chaos ultimately thwarted the bold experiment to modernize China by reforming gender. Although masculine traits of the Western middle class initially attracted reformers, endemic violence led many to look to a militarized masculine identity as the most appropriate response to China's difficulties. So instead of imitating the American inventor or European businessman, Chinese men increasingly saw a Japanese-style militarization of society as the best strategy for rapid national strengthening. This led to a reordering

Military-style school uniforms. *Source:* Xu, Zu, and Hu, *Lao chengxiang—Shangai chengshi zhi gen*, 63.

of priorities. While middle-class reformers had advocated exercise as way to maintain individual health, militarists saw it as a useful way to prepare the nation for war.[58]

Moral views also became increasingly conservative, as sexual propriety became a symbol of nationalism and ethnic pride. "Correct" masculine and feminine behavior was no longer a matter of individual choice, as people believed it to have profound implications for the nation as a whole.[59] In this increasingly restrictive atmosphere, a consensus that the state should closely regulate gender norms and sexuality steadily supplanted the previous freewheeling ethos. The New Life Movement, which began in 1934 as a mélange of reactionary Confucian and Christian values, promoted constricted gender roles for both sexes. Government functionaries lambasted the capitalist lifestyle of consumerism and leisure, decrying middle-class pastimes as dangerous decadence. China's leaders began to endorse a dour fascist puritanism intended to harden the populace and thereby strengthen it to meet the nation's collective challenges.[60]

Not everyone agreed with these growing limits on individual behavior. The realization that the clock was turning backward dismayed many progressive thinkers, and intellectuals contemplated a future marked by steadily shrinking horizons. Not coincidentally, depression and related mental illnesses, described by the general term "neurasthenia," became common among university students in the 1930s.[61] By the 1940s, gender was no longer a hot topic of social and political discourse. It was clear to everyone that China's future would be decided not through the reformation of male and female behavior but on the battlefield.[62]

NOTES

1. Appiah, *The Honor Code*, 60.

2. Susan Naquin and Evelyn S. Rawski, *Chinese Society in the Eighteenth Century* (New Haven, CT: Yale University Press, 1989), 106, 111.

3. Pitt-Rivers, "Honour and Social Status," 25–26.

4. Joanna Bourke, *Dismembering the Male: Men's Bodies, Britain and the Great War* (Chicago: University of Chicago Press, 1996); Jon Swain, "How Young Schoolboys Become Somebody: The Role of the Body in the Construction of Masculinity," *British Journal of Sociology of Education* 24, no. 3 (2003): 299–314.

5. Amy Kaplan, "Romancing the Empire: The Embodiment of American Masculinity in the Popular Historical Novel of the 1890s," *American Literary History* 2, no. 4 (1990): 659–90.

6. Peter Zarrow, "He Zhen and Anarcho-Feminism in China," *Journal of Asian Studies* 47, no. 4 (1988): 796–800.

7. Frank Dikötter, *Sex, Culture, and Modernity in China: Medical Science and the Construction of Sexual Identities in the Early Republican Period* (London: Hurst, 1995).

8. Joane Nagel, "Ethnicity and Sexuality," *Annual Review of Sociology* 26 (2000): 111.

9. Appiah, *The Honor Code*, 55–100, argues convincingly that honor was a major motivation for China's reforms in the late imperial and republican eras. The identification of masculinity with the nation is not unique to China and in fact is usually present in honor cultures. Pitt-Rivers, "Honour and Social Status," 35.

10. John Fitzgerald, *Awakening China: Politics, Culture and Class in the Nationalist Revolution* (Stanford, CA: Stanford University Press, 1996), 33.

11. Rogers Brubaker and David D. Laitin, "Ethnic and Nationalist Violence," *Annual Review of Sociology* 24 (1998): 444; Tamar Mayer, "Gender Ironies of Nationalism: Setting the Stage," in *Gender Ironies of Nationalism: Sexing the Nation*, ed. Tamar Mayer (London: Routledge, 2000), 11.

12. Sally Taylor Lieberman, *The Mother and Narrative Politics in Modern China* (Charlottesville: University Press of Virginia, 1998), 76.

13. For a discussion of the relation between nationalism and patriarchal politics, see Joseph S. Alter, "Celibacy, Sexuality, and the Transformation of Gender into Nationalism in North India," *Journal of Asian Studies* 53, no. 1 (1994): 61.

14. For the general dynamics of the connection between imperialism and feminization of the conquered, see Mayer, "Gender Ironies of Nationalism," 14–15. For a specific example, see Alter, "Celibacy, Sexuality, and the Transformation of Gender into Nationalism in North India," 55.

15. For the relation between nationalism and homosociality, see Joanna de Groot, "'Brothers of the Iranian Race': Manhood, Nationhood, and Modernity in Iran c. 1870–1914," in *Masculinities in Politics and War: Gendering Modern History*, ed. Stefan Dudink, Karen Hagemann, and John Tosh (Manchester: Manchester University Press, 2004), 142–43.

16. For a useful parallel with Korean nationalism, see Vladimir Tikhonov, "Masculinizing the Nation: Gender Ideologies in Traditional Korea and in the 1890s–1900s Korean Enlightenment Discourse," *Journal of Asian Studies* 66, no. 4 (2007): 1032.

17. For an example of this phenomenon, see Robert Morrell, "Of Boys and Men: Masculinity and Gender in Southern African Studies," *Journal of Southern African Studies* 24, no. 4 (1998): 616–20.

18. Jenner, *A Knife in the Ribs for a Mate*, 29–30.

19. Zhang Ming, "Yihetuan yishi de wenhua xiangzheng yu zhengzhi yinyu," *Kaifang shidai* 9 (2000): 42–45.

20. David Der-wei Wang, *Fin-de-Siècle Splendor: Repressed Modernities of Late Qing Fiction, 1849–1911* (Stanford, CA: Stanford University Press, 1997), 125–37.

21. Joseph R. Levenson, *Confucian China and Its Modern Fate*, Vol. 1, *The Problem of Intellectual Continuity* (London: Routledge and Kegan Paul, 1958), 95–96.

22. Fan Xueqing, "Qingmo Yue, Gang diqu geming dangren de jianfa yifu yulun," *Xueshu yanjiu* 5 (2007): 101–9.

23. Joseph Levenson, *Liang Ch'i-ch'ao and the Mind of Modern China* (Berkeley: University of California Press, 1970), 93.

24. Lu Xun, "Kong Yiji," in *Lu Xun quanji* (Beijing: Renmin, 1998), 1:434–39.

25. Kam Louie, "Constructing Chinese Masculinity for the Modern World: With Particular Reference to Lao She's *The Two Mas*," *China Quarterly* 164 (2000): 1067–68.

26. Xueping Zhong, *Masculinity Besieged? Issues of Modernity and Male Subjectivity in Chinese Literature in the Late Twentieth Century* (Durham, NC: Duke University Press, 2000), 128. Lu was certainly not the first major thinker to blame masculinity for China's

ills. Liang Qichao considered male weakness a major problem that China would have to address if it were to survive the Darwinian struggle among nations. Sakamoto Hiroko, "The Formation of National Identity in Liang Qichao and Its Relationship to Gender," in *The Role of Japan in Liang Qichao's Introduction of Modern Western Civilization to China*, ed. Joshua A. Fogel (Berkeley: Institute of East Asian Studies, University of California, Berkeley, and Center for Chinese Studies, 2004), 277–80.

27. John K. Chang, *Industrial Development in Pre-Communist China: A Quantitative Analysis* (Edinburgh: University Press, 1969), 79, 84.

28. For a discussion of the impact of capitalism on definitions of masculinity in a developing country, see Raka Ray, "Masculinity, Femininity, and Servitude: Domestic Workers in Calcutta in the Late Twentieth Century," *Feminist Studies* 26, no. 3 (2000): 692, 695–96.

29. Tani Barlow, with Gary J. Bjorge, ed., *I Myself Am a Woman: Selected Writings of Ding Ling* (Boston: Beacon Press, 1989), 55.

30. Louie, "Constructing Chinese Masculinity for the Modern World," 1976.

31. For the idea that masculinity and the social sphere can be reciprocal social constructions, see Linda Kerber, "Separate Spheres, Female World, Women's Place: The Rhetoric of Women's History," *Journal of American History* 75, no. 1 (1988): 39.

32. Jürgen Habermas, *The Structural Transformation of the Public Sphere: An Inquiry into a Category of Bourgeois Society*, trans. Thomas Burger and Frederick Lawrence (Cambridge, MA: MIT Press, 1989).

33. Lao She, "Also a Triangle," in *Blades of Grass: The Stories of Lao She*, ed. William A. Lyell, Sara Wei-Ming Chen, and Howard Goldblatt (Honolulu: University of Hawaii Press, 1999), 74.

34. Michael Kimmel, *Manhood in America: A Cultural History* (New York: Free Press, 1996), 9, develops the thesis that capitalist competition supersedes an agrarian communitarian ethos.

35. Liu Xiaonan, "Shilun Zhang Ailing bixia de nanxing xingxiang," *Hunan jiaoyu xueyuan xuebao* 14, no. 4 (1996): 27.

36. Jane Hunter, *The Gospel of Gentility: American Women Missionaries in Turn-of-the-Century China* (New Haven, CT: Yale University Press, 1984), 204–16.

37. The appropriation of imperial masculinity to cope with the incursions of imperialism is a common strategy men use to allow them to thrive under foreign domination. For a classic example, see T. M. Luhrmann, "The Good Parsi: The Postcolonial 'Feminization' of a Colonial Elite," *Man* (New Series) 29, no. 2 (1994): 333–57.

38. Huang Jinlin, *Lishi, shenti, guojia: jindai Zhongguo de shenti xingcheng (1895–1937)* (Taipei: Lianjing, 2005), 49.

39. Mann, *Gender and Sexuality in Modern Chinese History*, 108–9.

40. David Der-wei Wang, "Impersonating China," *Chinese Literature: Essays, Articles, Reviews (CLEAR)* 25 (2003): 133–34; D. E. Mugello, *Western Queers in China: Flight to the Land of Oz* (Lanham, MD: Rowman & Littlefield, 2012), 31–32, 35.

41. Qin Shao, *Culturing Modernity: The Nantong Model, 1890–1930* (Stanford, CA: Stanford University Press, 2004), 57–62.

42. Susan Brownell, *Training the Body for China: Sports in the Moral Order of the People's Republic* (Chicago: University of Chicago Press, 1995).

43. Qin, *Culturing Modernity*, 162–66.

44. Qin Shao, "Tempest over Teapots: The Vilification of Teahouse Culture in Early Republican China," *Journal of Asian Studies* 57, no. 4 (1998): 1014–15, 1024, 1033–34.

45. Louise Edwards, "Policing the Modern Woman in Republican China," *Modern China* 26, no. 2 (2000): 121.

46. Leo Ou-fan Lee, *Shanghai Modern: The Flowering of a New Urban Culture in China, 1930–1945* (Cambridge, MA: Harvard University Press, 1999), 84.

47. Zhiwei Xiao, "Movie House Etiquette Reform in Early-Twentieth-Century China," *Modern China* 32, no. 4 (2006): 518–20, 522.

48. Lee, *Shanghai Modern*, 94–95.

49. Karen Harvey, "The History of Masculinity, circa 1650–1800," *Journal of British Studies* 44, no. 2 (2005): 303.

50. For the bourgeois redefinition of masculine honor, see Robert A. Nye, *Masculinity and Male Codes of Honor in Modern France* (Oxford: Oxford University Press, 1993), 32.

51. In this respect China closely followed trends pioneered in the West. Glenn Hendler, "Pandering in the Public Sphere: Masculinity and the Market in Horatio Alger," *American Quarterly* 48, no. 3 (1996): 415.

52. Zuoyue Wang, "Saving China through Science: The Science Society of China, Scientific Nationalism, and Civil Society in Republican China," *Osiris* (Second Series) 17 (2002): 291–322.

53. Allison Kelly, "The Construction of Masculine Science," *British Journal of Sociology of Education* 6, no. 2 (1985): 133–54.

54. Wang, *Fin-de-Siecle Splendor*, 252–312.

55. Qin, *Culturing Modernity*, 145–46, 151–52.

56. Susan L. Glosser, "'The Truths I Have Learned': Nationalism, Family Reform, and Male Identity in China's New Culture Movement, 1915–1923," in *Chinese Femininities, Chinese Masculinities: A Reader*, ed. Susan Brownell and Jeffrey N. Wasserstrom (Berkeley: University of California Press, 2002), 121, 123, 139–40. Many early revolutionaries also rejected arranged marriage, often because their parents had selected for them a traditional rural wife who could not appreciate their radical ideology. Christina Gilmartin, "Gender in the Formation of a Communist Body Politic," *Modern China* 19, no. 3 (1993): 306–8.

57. Yung-chen Chiang, "Performing Masculinity and the Self: Love, Body, and Privacy in Hu Shi," *Journal of Asian Studies* 63, no. 2 (2004): 305–32.

58. Huang, *Lishi, shenti, guojia*, 58.

59. This attitude is a common expression of ethnic identity and nationalism. Nagel, "Ethnicity and Sexuality," 113.

60. Edwards, "Policing the Modern Woman in Republican China," 119–20.

61. Arthur Kleinman, *Social Origins of Distress and Disease: Depression, Neurasthenia, and Pain in Modern China* (New Haven, CT: Yale University Press, 1986), 26.

62. Edwards, "Policing the Modern Woman in Republican China," 121.

8

꧁꧂

Revolution, Reform, and Beyond

Neither the Nationalist revolution nor rapid industrialization could assuage the humiliation of bullying at the hands of foreign powers. To the contrary, integration into the global capitalist system only exacerbated the general mood of cultural crisis. China was finally engaging with other countries, but not from the previous position of lofty superiority or even as an equal partner. According to the standards used by the world's great powers to judge a country's worth, China remained vastly inferior to the West. Whether assessed according to the level of economic development, science and technology, or political sophistication, China found itself reduced to a junior member of the community of nations. Some ardent nationalists reasoned that playing by the rules of international capitalism and democracy, already mastered by other nations, simply put China at a disadvantage. Using foreign standards to judge success made Chinese look bad by comparison. Stricken by a sense of national emasculation, intellectuals and activists began to search for ideologies that could put their nation back on its pedestal, thereby restoring collective honor to Chinese men.

REVOLUTION

This search for a quick fix to male self-esteem helps explain China's unlikely embrace of Marxism. Karl Marx expected revolutions to occur in the most developed capitalist countries, not the most backward. The revolutions conducted in his name, first in Russia and then in China, where capitalism was still inchoate, surely would have shocked him. Revolutions led by communist parties at the outer fringes of the industrial world demanded considerable revision of Marxist theory. Nevertheless, embracing this radical ideology had the advantage of instantly placing China at the vanguard of human progress. When judged from the standpoint of socialist dogma, China was now the leader and could deride western Europe and the United States as laggards. Although capitalist democracy had failed to provide Chinese men with the feeling of honor they craved, it seemed that socialism might allow them to hold their heads high once again.[1]

The civil war that followed World War II soon culminated in the flight of Chiang Kai-shek and his defeated Nationalist army to Taiwan. By 1949 Mao Zedong's victorious communists had reunited the country and instituted the People's Republic of China. This victory represented far more than just the dawn of a new political system. More fundamentally, the Chinese Communist Party envisioned an entirely new society and culture. With capitalism dismissed as decadent and backward, it was necessary to remake every aspect of human endeavor it had tainted. Men could no longer stake a claim to honor by succeeding in a competitive job market, engaging in conspicuous consumption, or devoting their free time to the cultivation of middle-class leisure activities. Socialist man would be entirely different. Remaking the nation would require transforming both manhood and womanhood along revolutionary lines.

The Red Army served as the blueprint for this new society. The party systematically reorganized every aspect of life, from work to cooking to recreation, along military lines. Ordinary workers and peasants abandoned traditional clothing for identical military-style uniforms. Authorities pulled down private homes, and families moved into dormitories. Cooking vessels were confiscated and collective canteens established. Farmers no longer tilled their own land but served in military-style labor brigades on communal farms. Local party cadres, like officers commanding troops, stamped out every sign of individuality and personal autonomy.

The revolution sought to militarize masculinity as an antidote to China's previous humiliations. Civilians learned to emulate the communist soldier, brave and strong, as the new model man. Imitating soldiers allowed civilians to demonstrate their commitment to the nation and also to gain a feeling of dignity and citizenship.[2] Society lauded those who sacrificed themselves for the sake of the nation as heroes and paragons of masculinity.

The semimythic Lei Feng became most famous example of the manly socialist hero. The real Lei Feng (1940–1962) was an orphan raised by the Communist Party who grew up to become a soldier. After his untimely accidental death at an early age, the party propaganda apparatus canonized him as a revolutionary paragon to whom they attributed superhuman achievements. As the perfect soldier, Lei came to symbolize every socialist virtue. Because the party so exaggerated his life story, he perfectly exemplifies the ideals of revolutionary masculinity.

Lei Feng. *Source:* Anchee Min, Duo Duo, and Stefan R. Landsberger, *Chinese Propaganda Posters* (Hong Kong: Taschen, 2008), 120.

Most important, the mythic Lei Feng dedicated himself to the welfare of the nation, gladly sacrificing himself for the sake of others. Lei exhorted those around him to display absolute obedience to the Communist Party and Chairman Mao in particular. This unquestioning subservience to the party went far beyond the deference traditionally shown to those in power. In the imperial era, although men of letters treated those in office with respect, they also expected the powerful to exhibit virtue and felt justified remonstrating about moral lapses in government. In contrast, Lei Feng's new model man slavishly followed orders. He owed absolute allegiance to an authoritarian system that transcended conventional ethics. As the lyrics to one revolutionary song declared, "Study the good model Lei Feng; loyal to the revolution, loyal to the party!"[3] The new orthodoxy measured masculine honor according to unquestioning subservience to political authority. And elevation of Chairman Mao into a universal father figure directed the exigencies of filial piety away from the family and toward the party and its fatherly symbol, justifying absolute obedience to the nation's leader.[4]

SOCIALIST ANDROGYNY

The Communist Party reorganized gender relations as a whole, transforming both manhood and womanhood in unprecedented ways. Since antiquity the most basic principle of Chinese gender relations had always been separation of the sexes. Not only were men and women kept physically apart to some extent, but authorities deemed it proper that the sexes be distinguished by behavior, clothing, ritual roles, and even the virtues each pursued. The Communist Party rejected traditional gender distinctions as backward anachronisms and called for male and female behavior to converge. Gender uniformity had a practical goal. Having both sexes assume similar roles in society and the workplace would maximize the productive capacity of female workers.

The ideal socialist woman. *Source:* Min, Duo, and Landsberger, *Chinese Propaganda Posters*, 206.

This unisex ideal was not an androgynous compromise between stereotypical masculinity and femininity. Instead the party took masculinity as the normative standard and encouraged women to adopt traits previously considered masculine. This was not the first time that a society had pursued the masculinization of women as a strategy for building socialism. The Soviets attempted a similar plan to raise female status by encouraging women to behave like men in the early years of the Soviet Union. Revolutionaries there saw the adoption of male traits by women as a form of liberation, raising female status by opening up an unprecedented range of opportunities. However, Soviet women never warmed to the idea of dressing and acting like men, and the party quietly abandoned the plan. As time went on, Stalin and other Soviet leaders retreated to conservative views of gender, emphasizing women's maternal role as their primary contribution to the revolution.[5]

The socialist transformation of femininity took a much more radical turn in China, where a party slogan declared, "The times have changed; men and women are the same."[6] The party did not expect men to become more feminine but encouraged women to take up traditionally masculine occupations and assume male traits. They donned men's clothing and cut their hair short. Dressing like a man demonstrated a revolutionary zeal that showed contempt for frivolous bourgeois and "feudal" fashions.[7] According to this reasoning, anything overtly feminine was backward and hence counterrevolutionary. Although some women claimed that a deliberately simple appearance represented a new style of revolutionary beauty, this radical reimagining of the feminine had a clear masculine inspiration.[8] Most important, women entered many new lines of work. The party expected them to abandon traditional modesty and labor outside the home, even assigning them physically taxing menial tasks such as road construction. Although most cadres were male, women sometimes gained political authority, particularly during the Cultural Revolution, when female Red Guards became a common sight.

MANHOOD IN CHAOS

Over the course of the Cultural Revolution from 1966 to 1976, fanaticism reigned supreme. The Red Guards unleashed pandemonium through random violence, minutely scrutinizing every aspect of life from the standpoint of doctrinal purity and punishing anyone who failed to conform. Ambitious young people realized that in the midst of such insanity, success in life as measured by any conventional standard was simply impossible. Violent radicalism paralyzed every institution, making it impossible to pursue a career or improve one's lot. In fact, any display of ambition was extremely dangerous, as political campaigns targeted the most prominent members of society.

The disorientation fostered by continual bedlam and sterile political campaigns evoked a wide range of responses from young men. While some threw themselves into revolutionary activity, others became apathetic. For example, some youths from well-connected families joined gangs. Although inspired to band together by the example of the Red Guards, these disaffected youth lacked any political agenda. To the contrary, their shared apathy in the face of endless political sloganeering and demonstrations united them. Gang members affected crude mannerisms to prove their toughness, but these displays of strength lacked any real purpose. The impossibility of envisioning a good future for themselves led to nihilism. They devoted their days to meaningless activities with no goal other than killing time.[9] These rebels without a cause embraced bored apathy in rejection of the shallow Lei Feng model of manhood, but they were unable to create a positive alternative.

Revolutionary chaos spurred some workers to organize groups in imitation of fictional bandit gangs such as the paradigmatic heroes of *Water Margin*. Members of these gangs came from diverse backgrounds, making it difficult for them to find common ground, so they bound themselves together through the time-tested metaphor of brotherhood. Like their more privileged counterparts in nihilistic youth gangs, these men were also disappointed by pointless anarchy. However, instead of responding with apathy, these bands of brothers revived the imperial narrative that society had sunk into crisis because a virtuous emperor had unknowingly surrounded himself with evil officials. They considered themselves true loyalists to the godlike Chairman Mao but scorned the Communist Party, which they believed self-interested cadres had corrupted.[10] These men rejected the unthinking loyalty of Lei Feng. Instead of naive obedience to the party, they redirected their absolute fealty to Chairman Mao personally while critiquing party personnel and policies. To justify this critical attitude to state institutions, they adopted the masculine archetypes popularized by fictional imperial rebels.

RECONSTRUCTING MASCULINITY

After the Cultural Revolution ended in 1976, China entered a period of recovery. The revolution had so discredited radicalism that Deng Xiaoping (1904–1997) managed to gain acceptance for a policy of reform and openness that combined political authoritarianism, increased individual autonomy, and economic pragmatism. Recuperation from the mistakes of the previous era included a search for masculinities suitable to the new climate. The radical reign of terror, together with a general sense of powerlessness under an arbitrary totalitarian system, had left many men feeling emasculated.[11] The sexual act had become officially identified with procreation, and authorities deemed sexual excess detrimental to men, robbing them of a clear sexual identity.[12] Ironically, even though women had emulated stereotypical male traits, outwardly bolstering the masculine atmosphere of society, men themselves were left feeling insufficiently manly. Opening to the outside world further exacerbated the problem. Chinese were once again able to compare the state of their own masculinity with slick images of idealized manhood transmitted by Western and Japanese media—and found their own men inadequate in comparison.[13]

Literature and popular entertainment in the 1980s and early 1990s often depicted men as disturbingly effeminate, revealing a widespread craving for a new type of masculinity.[14] The new manhood would have to be strong and compatible with political realities, yet relevant to a constantly changing society propelled by rapid economic growth. Although material progress improved people's lives in many ways, a disorienting rate of change also brought fundamental challenges. As Émile Durkheim famously pointed out, the instability and dizzying opportunity of modern life erodes moral authority. People often end up feeling alienated, empty, and directionless. Although Chinese men now enjoyed unprecedented possibilities, these did not necessarily bring happiness or fulfillment.

China's increasing connections with the rest of the world thrust local masculinity into a much broader context. No longer could people judge Chinese manhood solely within the parochial framework of native culture. Instead they would have to position male identity vis-à-vis the flood of masculine images pouring in from all over the world via movies, television, pop music, magazines, and the Internet. Henceforth hegemonic Chinese masculinity would have to function on three different social levels. First, within the traditional venue of local society, a man needed to appear normative and honorable within his family, grassroots organizations, and community. Second, manhood had to fit the political imperatives of an authoritarian nation-state legitimized by nationalistic ideology. By employing masculine rhetoric such as national strength and will, the government tied vibrant manhood to national well-being, associating Chinese manliness with revanchism and military strength.[15] Finally, China's emergence onto the world stage lent masculinity a transnational dimension. Chinese men would have to act out their gender with an eye to international politics and commerce.

Foreign masculinities were themselves often subtle and conflicted, making them difficult for Chinese to comprehend. A look at contemporary American masculinity helps highlight the complexity of the foreign images pouring into China. American mass media typically promote three main archetypes of manhood: the breadwinner, the man of action, and the rebel.[16] The incongruity of these diverse ideals can puzzle outsiders. For example, constancy and conservatism mark the responsible breadwinner, making this form of manhood completely incompatible with that of the rebel. And while the man of action directs his energies toward positive goals, the rebel rejects mainstream pursuits. How were Chinese men supposed to assimilate such contradictory models of manhood? And of course the United States was just one source of influence. Images from Japan and Europe, not to mention the far more direct impact of media from Hong Kong and Taiwan, subjected mainland Chinese men to a barrage of confusing new priorities and opportunities.

SEARCHING FOR MASCULINE STRENGTH

Some of the most creative new expressions of masculinity were pioneered on television in the 1980s and 1990s. Rapidly rising prosperity made the television set the focal point of the average Chinese living room. The novelty of this medium, together with the thrill of escape from decades of sterile revolutionary propaganda, gave these early TV programs an enormous psychological impact. The first major soap opera on Chinese television, called *Yearnings* (*Kewang*), aired in 1991. This wildly popular series pioneered compelling new images of manhood by depicting heroic protagonists who displayed toughness of spirit and physical strength. Portrayals of virile manhood fascinated a society haunted by a widespread sense of emasculation.[17]

One result of this search for authentic manhood was the rise of the rough man, related to the *Water Margin* bandit hero, as a postrevolutionary masculine ideal. Although the term *haohan* had become obsolete, Chinese culture resurrected traits associated with this model, in particular the use of brotherly righteousness (*yiqi*) to express masculine honor, to construct a contemporary version of the virile man.[18] This sort of revitalized masculinity is a focal point of the works of Wang Shuo, a prolific popular novelist and scriptwriter for *Yearnings*. His novels and short stories captured the public's imagination in the early 1990s, in part because he addressed the problems facing the psychologically castrated man. Although his characters embodied the realities of contemporary society, they were nevertheless a throwback to the fictional bandit hero. Unlike the selfless workers and soldiers of official propaganda, Wang's protagonists were low-class hooligans (*liumang*) and punks (*pizi*). Wang Shuo based these colorful characters on his own firsthand encounters with men living on the margins of society during the Cultural Revolution, which accounts for the vividness of his descriptions. Although these cynical outlaws inhabit the lowest rungs of society, they nevertheless repeatedly prove themselves brave and clever survivors. Lacking education and connections, they have nothing to rely on but their wits. Most important, these hooligans display an unshakable devotion to rough justice. This unexpected streak of idealism appealed to readers living in a time of rapid change and feeling disoriented by shifting values and priorities.[19]

Despite the opportunities offered by economic opening, most men lacked specialized skills or connections, condemning them to a life of endless struggle. Those who failed to thrive in this new environment could not possibly emulate new hegemonic images of masculinity such as the prosperous businessman or happy consumer. Instead they embraced alternate forms of manhood that were readily accessible, taking the *haohan* as a particularly useful template. For example, migrant workers tend to admire men who prove themselves brave, strong, and pugnacious.[20] They consider hedonism a mark of the happy-go-lucky man who demonstrates his autonomy by placing himself above the values of conventional middle-class behavior, proudly rejecting prudence and moderation as unmanly. So by romanticizing low-status characters and taking their conduct to exemplify masculine virtue, Wang Shuo represented the norms of working-class masculinity as embodying authentic manhood.[21] In a manner in keeping with the African American counterculture's masculine ideal of "cool," Wang's hooligans deliberately keep themselves emotionally removed from what is happening around them. This aloofness gives them an air of superiority, even though others might regard them as failures by conventional standards.

During the early reform era, cinema also explored the new manhood. The creation of compelling images of manliness became a way for directors to attract attention and acclaim, as virile male characters fascinated audiences endlessly. Zhang Yimou's 1988 film *Red Sorghum* (*Hong gaoliang*) won both critical acclaim and box office success for a story that romanticizes rough rural men as paragons of manhood.[22] However, this film and the novel by Mo Yan on which

Poster for the 1987 movie *Red Sorghum* (*Hong gaoliang*) featuring a strong man.

it is based have received sharp criticism as a step backward in terms of gender relations. Although the novel and film trumpet male strength and sexual potency, they also depict violence, sadism, murder, and domination of women as signs of a rejuvenated manhood.[23] The new man was not necessarily someone a woman would want to meet, much less marry.

As the censor's grip on popular culture loosened, films from Hong Kong became wildly popular throughout the Chinese mainland. Not only did Hong Kong movies have superior production values and action plots that catered to popular tastes, but their directors also knew how to intrigue audiences with appealing images of strong manhood. In particular, an endless stream of martial arts movies fed the nationalistic desire for images of strong Chinese men. The fact that many of these films were period pieces set in the imperial past encouraged viewers to link manhood with China's history, intensifying the idea that the nation's fate was tied to virility.

The Hong Kong gangster film also exerted enormous influence over Chinese ideas about contemporary masculinity. This genre became popular by raiding traditional narratives such as *Water Margin* for stock characters and themes, then updating them into a contemporary cinematic vernacular. The slick films of director John Woo (Wu Yusen) exemplify the best of the gangster genre. Although Woo eventually achieved success in Hollywood, his depictions of men differ considerably from mainstream American cinema. Whereas the Hollywood style emphasizes the male body, showing protagonists as strong and muscular, Woo focuses on men's emotional lives. In this respect he follows the conventions of *haohan* narrative, which emphasize the relationships among men and the sense of righteousness (*yiqi*) that binds them together.

As in *Water Margin*, women are unimportant in these movies, which reserve a man's key relationships and his most intense emotions for other men. The protagonists primarily exist in a homosocial world of male peers, superiors, and enemies. The threat that violence and greed might destroy the bonds of loyalty among comrades provides the central theme propelling the plot forward. Even the happy ending stresses purely male concerns. Instead of the customary Hollywood denouement featuring heterosexual romance, Woo's films culminate in a strengthening of male bonds, as buddies look forward to working together again in the future.[24]

MANLY MONGOLS, TOUGH TIBETANS

Ethnic complexity complicates the link between masculinity and the nation in the popular imagination. Chinese culture defines mainstream manhood not just in relation to masculinities abroad but also with an eye toward the gender

A strong Tibetan. *Source:* Feng Wei, *Xizang mijing* (Beijing: Zhongguo sheying, 2010), 56.

diversity within China's own borders. Stereotypes about ethnic minorities influence perceptions of the masculinity of China's Han ethnicity, which makes
up more than 90 percent of the population. Although comparatively small in
number, minority peoples nevertheless constitute an important foil for all aspects of Han identity, including male identity. Moreover, simmering tensions
between the Han and certain minorities confound the mutual influences of
their masculinities, guaranteeing that this will remain a significant issue well
into the future.

The Chinese media tend to exoticize minority peoples, portraying them as
colorful, quaint, amusing, and primitive and widely representing them as re-
positories of history and tradition, not as active participants in China's march
toward modernization. In addition, depictions showing them wearing skimpy
clothing and assuming sexually suggestive poses often eroticize minorities.
Merchants commoditize their material culture and offer it for sale to conde-
scending tourists, passing off gaudy souvenirs as authentic tokens of cultural
identity. By purchasing these items, domestic tourists gain a sense of ownership
over minority culture. In other words, Chinese discourse toward minorities
exhibits an attitude of internal orientalism. The Han-dominated media present
images of minorities that make them seem like distant and inferior "others" in
contrast with modern and progressive Han.[25]

Despite the generally patronizing attitude toward minorities displayed by
the Chinese media, ironically the media often put forward men from some
minority peoples as icons of authentic masculinity. Although the media usually
use women to represent the minority groups of Yunnan and other southern
regions, making those peoples seem gentle and effeminate, male imagery more
often exemplifies northern and western ethnicities. Photographs and television routinely depict Tibetans and Mongols engaging in stereotypically manly
activities such as horseback riding and hunting, perhaps clad in animal skins
and furs, exhibiting muscled bare chests, and wearing an expression suggesting
strength of spirit.[26]

The portrayal of Tibetan and Mongol men as hypermasculine is more than
just a media stereotype. Minority men also often consider themselves more authentically masculine than their Han counterparts. For example, Tibetan men
do not generally define their own masculinity in contrast to Tibetan women.
Instead they compare themselves to Han men, find the latter inadequately
masculine, and conclude that Tibetan men are more genuinely manly.[27] In this
respect, the exoticization of China's minorities has ended up producing an
internal critique of mainstream masculinity. If ethnic minorities, whom Han
Chinese treat as distant and irrelevant, exemplify the most authentic expressions of manhood, then masculinity itself seems to reside somewhere beyond
the reach of most men.

THE MATERIAL MAN

Rapid economic growth since the end of the Cultural Revolution has brought unprecedented opportunities to those with power, skills, connections, or plain good luck. In this dynamic atmosphere, many people have embraced the bread-winner model of manhood, measuring a man's success by his ability to hold a good job and provide his family with a high standard of living. According to this way of thinking, money represents the essence of masculinity; a higher income represents superior manliness. Mesmerized by materialism, many Chinese men now devote themselves to climbing the ladder of success, maximizing income, and flaunting their wealth. The goal is not just higher social status in general but, more specifically, the construction of a positive masculine image grounded in material success. The confident businessman, prosperous and powerful, has once again become a captivating model of masculine performance.[28]

Whereas both imperial scholar-officials and communist revolutionaries once derided merchants, rapid growth has unexpectedly made the businessman the new standard bearer of heroic Chinese masculinity. However, economic reforms have unleashed ruthless competition, and many men find themselves unable to meet the challenges of the marketplace. The disappointments of those who fail only amplify the accomplishments of the winners. Fawning profiles of successful businessmen, written in a tone reminiscent of imperial didactic biography, fill newspapers and magazines. But whereas traditional biographers lauded a man for government service, literary accomplishment, or filial devotion, magazine writers now celebrate businessmen for their financial success.

As seen in early soap operas, the model businessman has become a manly hero who can help restore national pride. In the 1990s, popular TV programs often depicted dramatic head-to-head confrontations between Chinese businessmen and foreign rivals in a fight to defend China's honor. Victory represented not merely a personal achievement but a symbolic triumph on behalf of the nation. The many dramas depicting Chinese businessmen succeeding in the international arena have helped assuage the deep sense of humiliation that has festered since the Opium Wars.[29]

Under this materialist mind-set, men win approval not just for obtaining wealth but also by displaying it through conspicuous consumption. This value system has its roots in the nihilism fostered by the pointless chaos of the Cultural Revolution. Disillusionment with politics created a moral vacuum exacerbated by a profound sense of apathy. Even during the Cultural Revolution, some rebels defied the era's irrationality by embracing hedonism.[30] However, poverty limited their ability to seek solace from consumption. As the economy has grown, however, men have gained exciting new opportunities to consume material goods, both for personal gratification and to display a successful persona to the world.

Consumption can have various social functions. For some it is a way to project a manly image by displaying material tokens associated with prestigious manhood. Sometimes a man's appearance can matter far more to observers than his inner qualities. In contemporary China, the material symbols of male success include a large house, a sports car, designer clothing, expensive watches, famous French wines, and other foreign-branded luxury goods. Unlike imperial literati, who emphasized taste and cultivation, contemporary businessmen emphasize an item's cost as the primary symbol of their success. These acquisitions can also have a therapeutic psychological value. The world of business is stressful and unsentimental. While a career can provide fulfillment, it also brings immense anxiety. Untrammeled materialism allows men to construct a fantasy world into which they can occasionally retreat to escape the pressures of the workplace.

Spending money with abandon is also a way for men to display a gutsiness associated with *haohan* masculinity. When the fictional *haohan* has money, he

Dressed in designer brands, amid cognac and cigars. *Source:* Jason Capobianco and Jacky Tam, "Nanren julebu," *GQ Zhizu* 224 (May 2012): 314.

does not hesitate to splash it around. An attitude of insouciance, unconcerned with prudence or moderation, is a hallmark of the traditional tough guy. Daring consumption differs from ordinary conspicuous consumption in fulfilling short-term desires while showing contempt for long-term consequences. A willingness to take unnecessary risks makes a man appear powerful, charismatic, and free. It also avoids passive integration into institutions that subject members to hierarchy and control.[31] Many men in China today indulge in daring consumption. They spend money freely to transcend restrictive social rules, thereby displaying what they consider a superior form of manhood.

THE GENTLE MAN

Another influential masculine archetype of recent decades is the gentle (*wenrou*) man popularized by cultural productions from Taiwan, particularly pop music. Although the mainland dwarfs Taiwan in size and population, within the Chinese-speaking world Taiwan nevertheless enjoys the status of a pop culture superpower. Taiwan's music assembly line churns out glossy musical confections popular with listeners throughout China, and top-forty radio stations in Shanghai or Chongqing feature a stream of melodies sung with the distinctively soft Taiwanese accent.

Mandarin pop music from Taiwan, known as Mandopop, has disseminated a distinctive style of masculinity associated with its singers. In contrast with the tough guy or crass businessman, Taiwanese male singers frequently evoke a style of gentleness and emotional tenderness known as *wenrou*. In Taiwan this quality is also called *siwen*, a term implying sophistication and refinement. Androgynous postwar Japanese masculinity has had a profound influence on Taiwan, and Taiwanese have translated Japanese androgyny into a cultural idiom that mainland Chinese find accessible. The ideal gentle man is educated, polite, clean-cut, compassionate, moderate, and low-key in both speech and manners. These singers are usually young and thin; some are even somewhat effeminate, appearing in publicity photos sporting outré clothing and assuming poses that convey emotional vulnerability.

The Taiwanese gentle man presents a complete contrast with the macho imagery of the Beijing rock music scene. In the 1980s a style of consciously manly music developed in Beijing, featuring loud, raucous songs sung with low raspy voices and harsh northern accents. The lyrics of these rough tunes often dealt with nationalistic or grassroots themes. Beijing rockers borrowed stylistic markers from northwestern peasant culture and packaged them so that urbanites could appreciate their performance as an expression of authentic masculinity. When listening to this sort of music, men far removed from rough rural life could nevertheless fancy themselves as authentically manly. During the 1980s

Xiaohu dui (Little Tigers), the most popular Taiwanese boy band of the 1980s.

and 1990s, these sorts of consciously masculine rock groups were at the center of the Beijing underground music scene.

Although Beijing rock can be subversive, it also displays the strong masculine style preferred by the state apparatus. China's government has repeatedly lambasted Taiwanese Mandopop, criticizing it as cultural decadence. The real issue at stake seems to be an implicit refutation of the Communist Party's nationalistic ideology, which demands that men be strong and tough so they can contribute to building a resurgent China. Nevertheless, Beijing-style rock alienates most listeners, who dismiss it as coarse and vulgar.[32] The association with nationalistic discourse also recalls violent political campaigns such as the Cultural Revolution, which most Chinese today regard with embarrassment. So despite active state patronage, the music industry in the People's Republic of China has so far failed to replace Taiwanese pop with ideologically correct alternatives.

The triumph of Taiwanese pop music has had major implications for Chinese manhood, as the contrast between Beijing and Taipei styles of music—and masculinity—makes very clear. The stereotypical Taiwanese Mandopop singer is gentle, polite, sensitive, sophisticated, and globalized. In contrast, the Beijing rocker is loud, angry, crude, tough, and nationalistic. In the battle for the hearts and minds of China's music fans, so far Taipei has vanquished Beijing. Although the authoritarian state prefers aggressive nationalistic manhood, many men gravitate to the gentle Taiwanese alternative because it offers them a degree of liberation from restrictive masculine stereotypes. The sensitive Mandopop male can express a far wider range of emotions than the stereotypical tough guy.

At times the Mandopop man can be strong and forceful, but he also allows himself to feel compassion, self-doubt, and fear. For example, sometimes the Taiwanese musical icon Jay Chou (Zhou Jielun) presents himself to his fans in the guise of the cool basketball player, martial artist, or hard-boiled gangster. Yet in other contexts he puts himself forward as pretty, sensitive, and contemplative. The gentle man does not need to constrict his emotional range for fear that certain feelings might seem unmanly. By allowing himself the freedom to experience a wide spectrum of feelings, he can be more authentic and holistic.[33] Although he might enjoy drinking beer or playing basketball with buddies, he is not afraid to be seen shopping for skin-care products with his girlfriend.

The gentle man is also consciously apolitical, which in China's relentlessly political society is itself a major form of liberation. Ever since the reformist movements of the early twentieth century, Chinese have largely seen masculinity as a tool of nationalism. By divorcing manhood from the state, redefining it in individual terms, and embracing a cosmopolitan globalized identity, the gentle man distances himself from authoritarian politics, thereby increasing his autonomy.[34]

INTO THE FUTURE

Inevitable economic and demographic developments will present fresh challenges to Chinese manhood. Although incomes are rising rapidly, China's society is also aging very quickly. The number of working-age people will decline just as the proportion of elderly surges, making it increasingly difficult to maintain even a modest rate of economic growth in coming decades. Because material success has become a prime criterion for manliness, an end to high growth in gross domestic product will force a reassessment of what it means to be a successful man.

China's unique population structure, a legacy of the One Child Policy, will also challenge current ideas about manhood. Because the government has limited most couples to just one child since 1979, most young Chinese men lack siblings. This means that they must face the traditional filial responsibility of caring for parents and grandparents by themselves. To complicate matters, independent-minded women are increasingly unwilling to make sacrifices for the sake of elderly in-laws. And lengthening life spans have increased the burden of filial devotion considerably. Convergence of these trends will force a reassessment of men's duty toward elder kin.[35] Traditional expectations regarding the care of elders will become untenable, spelling the inevitable decline of filial piety as a centerpiece of Chinese male identity. However, the inability of many men to live up to this basic responsibility will surely give rise to enormous angst, guilt, and soul searching for years to come.

Another legacy of the One Child Policy is a recalibration of relations between the sexes. Limited to just one child, many families aborted female fetuses to guarantee they would have a son, resulting in a skewed sex ratio. Because women are less numerous than men, there is already intense competition for wives. As women can be very choosy about a mate, they have gained bargaining power on the marriage market and a higher status within the family as both wives and daughters-in-law. Moreover, in the numerous families that have a daughter instead of a son, females must now take on stereotypically male roles. In consequence, women are gaining more power and responsibility within the family, giving them higher social worth.[36] The unavoidable encroachment of women on traditional male roles will undoubtedly influence the future development of masculinity.

Finally, Chinese continue to ponder their national identity as they strive to stake out their place within the international community. Interaction with the outside world has elicited intense introspection about what it means to be Chinese. Since antiquity, specific gender norms have been an important constituent of Chinese identity. Yet in recent decades, the meanings of maleness and femaleness have been in constant flux. Now one of the most important goals in the search for contemporary Chinese identity is finding masculinities appropriate to current circumstances. As society continues to change rapidly, manhood will have to respond, guaranteeing that Chinese masculinity will remain highly dynamic well into the future.

NOTES

1. Levenson, *Confucian China and Its Modern Fate*, 1:134.

2. The use of militarization to bolster male esteem is common in developing countries. For an example, see Lesley Gill, "Creating Citizens, Making Men: The Military and Masculinity in Bolivia," *Cultural Anthropology* 12, no. 4 (1997): 527–50.

3. Tao Dongfeng and Lü Heying, "Lei Feng: Shehuizhuyi lunli fuhao de suzao jiqi bianqian," *Xueshu yuekan* 42, no. 12 (2010): 105. This article explains how views toward Lei Feng have evolved in line with ideological shifts.

4. Jongwoo Han and L. H. M. Ling, "Authoritarianism in the Hypermasculinized State: Hybridity, Patriarchy, and Capitalism in Korea," *International Studies Quarterly* 42, no. 1 (1998): 54. This article describes appropriation of filial piety by the authoritarian state in South Korea, a country with a similar heritage of Confucianism.

5. Thomas G. Schrand, "Socialism in One Gender: Masculine Values in the Stalin Revolution," in *Russian Masculinities in History and Culture*, ed. Barbara Evans Clements, Rebecca Friedman, and Dan Healey (Houndmills, UK: Palgrave, 2002), 197, 203.

6. Emily Honig, "Maoist Mappings of Gender: Reassessing the Red Guards," in *Chinese Femininities, Chinese Masculinities: A Reader*, ed. Susan Brownell and Jeffrey N. Wasserstrom (Berkeley: University of California Press, 2002), 266.

7. Tina Mai Chen, "Dressing for the Party: Clothing, Citizenship, and Gender Formation in Mao's China," *Fashion Theory* 5, no. 2 (2001): 143–71; Honig, "Maoist Mappings of Gender," 257; Sara L. Friedman, *Intimate Politics: Marriage, the Market, and State Power in Southeastern China* (Cambridge, MA: Harvard University Asia Center, 2006), 74–77.

8. Hung-yok Ip, "Fashioning Appearances: Feminine Beauty in Chinese Communist Revolutionary Culture," *Modern China* 29, no. 3 (2003): 329–61.

9. Yusheng Yao, "The Elite Class Background of Wang Shuo and His Hooligan Characters," *Modern China* 30, no. 4 (2004): 437.

10. Elizabeth J. Perry and Nara Dillon, "'Little Brothers' in the Cultural Revolution: The Worker Rebels of Shanghai," in *Chinese Femininities, Chinese Masculinities: A Reader*, ed. Susan Brownell and Jeffrey N. Wasserstrom (Berkeley: University of California Press, 2002), 270, 277. Edward Friedman et al., *Chinese Village, Socialist State* (New Haven, CT: Yale University Press, 1991), 268–69, discusses how people turned back to tradition to deal with the disorientation brought by revolutionary chaos.

11. Kam Louie, "The Macho Eunuch: The Politics of Masculinity in Jia Pingwa's 'Human Extremities,'" *Modern China* 17, no. 2 (1991): 166, 180. For general trends in changing values and the sense of disorientation during the 1980s, see Jie Fan, Thomas Heberer, and Wolfgang Taubman, *Rural China: Economic and Social Change in the Late Twentieth Century* (Armonk, NY: M. E. Sharpe, 2006), 240.

12. Harriet Evans, "Defining Difference: The 'Scientific' Construction of Sexuality and Gender in the People's Republic of China," *Signs* 20, no. 2 (1995): 366–71, 375–76.

13. Zhong, *Masculinity Besieged?* 5.

14. James Farrer, *Opening Up: Youth Sex Culture and Market Reform in Shanghai* (Chicago: University of Chicago Press, 2002), 102–3, 219–20; Louie, "The Macho Eunuch"; Sheldon H. Lu, *Chinese Modernity and Global Biopolitics: Studies in Literature and Visual Culture* (Honolulu: University of Hawaii Press, 2007), 38. Wei Hui, *Shanghai Baby*, trans. Bruce Hume (New York: Pocket Books, 2001), is an example of a novel that depicts foreign men as manly and desirable in contrast to their weak Chinese counterparts.

15. Han and Ling, "Authoritarianism in the Hypermasculinized State," 64, explores the links between Asian authoritarianism and masculine rhetoric.

16. Douglas B. Holt and Craig J. Thompson, "Man-of-Action Heroes: The Pursuit of Heroic Masculinity in Everyday Consumption," *Journal of Consumer Research* 31, no. 2 (2004): 425–40.

17. Lisa B. Rofel, "'Yearnings': Televisual Love and Melodramatic Politics in Contemporary China," *American Ethnologist* 21, no. 4 (1994): 713. William R. Jankowiak, *Sex, Death, and Hierarchy in a Chinese City: An Anthropological Account* (New York: Columbia University Press, 1993), 168, shows that in the early 1980s many women looked for stereotypical masculine traits in a husband.

18. Jenner, *A Knife in the Ribs for a Mate*, 2.

19. Yao, "The Elite Class Background of Wang Shuo and His Hooligan Characters," 432–35; Zhong, *Masculinity Besieged?* 111–17.

20. Li Zhang, "Migration and Privatization of Space and Power in Late Socialist China," *American Ethnologist* 28, no. 1 (2001): 190.

21. For a description of how these sorts of alternative masculinities arise, see R. W. Connell, "Cool Guys, Swots, and Wimps: The Interplay of Masculinity and Education," *Oxford Review of Education* 15, no. 3 (1989): 295.

22. Sheldon H. Lu, "Soap Opera in China: The Transnational Politics of Visuality, Sexuality, and Masculinity," *Cinema Journal* 40, no. 1 (2000): 30.

23. Zhu Ling, "A Brave New World? On the Construction of 'Masculinity' and 'Femininity' in the Red Sorghum Family," in *Gender and Sexuality in Twentieth-Century Chinese Literature and Society*, ed. Tonglin Lu (Albany: State University of New York Press), 122, 124.

24. Jillian Sandell, "Reinventing Masculinity: The Spectacle of Male Intimacy in the Films of John Woo," *Film Quarterly* 49, no. 4 (1996): 23–34.

25. Ben Hillman and Lee-Anne Henfry, "Macho Minority: Masculinity and Ethnicity on the Edge of Tibet," *Modern China* 32, no. 2 (2006): 253; Louisa Schein, *Minority Rules: The Miao and the Feminine in China's Cultural Politics* (Durham, NC: Duke University Press, 2000), 101–6, 119–31.

26. Hillman and Henfry, "Macho Minority," 254, 258. Jay Dautcher, *Down a Narrow Road: Identity and Masculinity in a Uyghur Community in Xinjiang China* (Cambridge, MA: Harvard University Asia Center, 2009), 63, shows that Han stereotypes of Uyghur men sometimes go even further, depicting them as strong to the point of being animalistic and dangerous.

27. Hillman and Henfry, "Macho Minority," 261.

28. For a general description of the breadwinner model of masculinity, see Holt and Thompson, "Man-of-Action Heroes," 427.

29. Lu, "Soap Opera in China," 31.

30. Yao, "The Elite Class Background of Wang Shuo and His Hooligan Characters," 453, 460.

31. For a discussion of daring consumption, see Walsh, "'Hot Money' and Daring Consumption in a Northern Malagasy Sapphire-Mining Town," 290–305.

32. Marc L. Moskowitz, *Cries of Joy, Songs of Sorrow: Chinese Pop Music and Its Cultural Connotations* (Honolulu: University of Hawaii Press, 2010), 1, 27, 103.

33. Moskowitz, *Cries of Joy, Songs of Sorrow*, 89, 100.

34. Moskowitz, *Cries of Joy, Songs of Sorrow*, 115; Lisa Rofel, *Desiring China: Experiments in Neoliberalism, Sexuality, and Public Culture* (Durham, NC: Duke University Press, 2007).

35. Heying Jenny Zhan and Rhonda J. V. Montgomery, "Gender and Elder Care in China: The Influence of Filial Piety and Structural Constraints," *Gender and Society* 17, no. 2 (2003): 209–29.

36. Vanessa L. Fong, "China's One-Child Policy and the Empowerment of Urban Daughters," *American Anthropologist* (New Series) 104, no. 4 (2002): 1098–109.

Glossary

A Q zhengzhuan	阿Q正傳
Anqing	安清
bao (recompense)	報
benye (basic occupations)	本業
Bo Ji	伯姬
Cai Zun	蔡遵
Chen Gang	陳綱
chi (shame)	恥
Chunqiu	春秋
cike (assassin)	刺客
Cui	崔
Dangkouzhi	蕩寇志
dao (way)	道
Daoheng	道恆
Daowen	道溫
di (Earth)	地
Dong Zhongshu	董仲舒
Faguang	法曠
Fang Rufu	房孺復
Fasheng	法乘
Faxian	法顯
Fayuan	法瑗
Fotudeng	佛圖澄
fu (wealth)	富
fugui	富貴

171

gaojie (lofty purity)	高潔
gaomingren (high ranking famous men)	高明人
gaoren (high ranking men)	高人
Gaoseng zhuan	高僧傳
Gaoxing	高行
gegu (cutting flesh from the thigh)	割股
Gongyang	公羊
guan (capping)	冠
Guan Yu	關羽
gui (exalted, high rank)	貴
Han (dynasty)	漢
Han Gaozu	漢高祖
Han Xin	韓信
Han Yu	韓愈
Hanshu	漢書
haohan (good fellow)	好漢
haozu (gentry)	豪族
heli (noncontested divorce)	和離
Hong gaoliang	紅高粱
Hou Hanshu	後漢書
huahu (flower household)	花戶
Huan Tan	桓譚
Huanglao	黃老
Huichi	慧持
Huijiao	慧皎
Huishao	慧紹
jian (base)	賤
jiashi (distinguished gentleman)	佳士
Jin (dynasty)	晉
Jing Ke	荊軻
Jiu Tangshu	舊唐書
Juexian	覺賢
junzi (gentleman)	君子
Kang Senghui	康僧會
Kewang	渴望
kun	坤
Lao She	老舍
Lei Feng	雷鋒
li (ritual propriety, rites)	禮
Li (marquis)	鯉
Li (state)	黎
liang (exalted)	良

Liang (state)	梁
Liang (dynasty)	梁
Liang Qichao	梁啟超
Lienü zhuan	列女傳
liumang (rogue)	流氓
Liu Penzi	劉盆子
Liu Xiang	劉向
liang (exalted)	良
Lü (empress)	呂
Lu Xun	魯迅
mianzi (face)	面子
minggong (famous notable)	名公
Mingshi	明史
mingshi (famous gentlemen)	明士
Mo Di	墨翟
Mo Yan	莫言
Mozi	墨子
mudan (peony)	牡丹
Mulian	目連
nan (man, male)	男
nangeng nüzhi (men plow, women weave)	男耕女織
nannü youbie (separation of the sexes)	男女有別
nei (inner)	內
nü (woman, female)	女
nüguan (Daoist nun)	女冠, 女官
Ouyang Xiu	歐陽修
Pan Jinlian	潘金蓮
Peiligang	裴李崗
pizi (punk)	痞子
qi (vital force)	氣
qian	乾
Qin Ming	秦明
Qin Shihuang	秦始皇
qing (sentiment)	情
qinpi zhi xie (musical harmony)	琴琵之諧
ren (benevolence)	仁
rong (honorable reputation)	榮
ru (insult)	辱
ru (scholar)	儒
Rencheng	任城
Sangfu	喪服
Sanguo yanyi	三國演義

Sengdu	僧度
Sengrou	僧柔
Shang Yang	商鞅
Shangjun shu	商君書
shanjing (mountain sprite)	山精
shaoyao (peony)	芍藥
Shennong	神農
shi (gentleman)	士
Shijing	詩經
shiyou (gentleman friends)	士友
shuangju (chaste widow)	孀居
Shuihu zhuan	水滸傳
Shouguang	壽光
siwen (gentle and sophisticated)	斯文
Song Huizong	宋徽宗
Song Jiang	宋江
Song Shenzong	宋神宗
Song Zhezong	宋哲宗
Tanwuchan	曇無懺
tian (Heaven)	天
Tong Guan	童貫
wai (outer)	外
Wang Shuo	王朔
Wei (dynasty)	魏
Wei Lang	魏朗
wen (civil)	文
wenrou (gentle)	溫柔
Wu (emperor)	武
wu (martial)	武
Wu Dalang	武大郎
Wu Song	武松
Wu Yusen	吳宇森
xiake ("knight errant")	俠客
xian (worthy)	賢
xiannü (female immortal)	仙女
Xiaohu dui (Little Tigers)	小虎隊
Xiaojing	孝經
xiaoren (inferior men)	小人
xin (fidelity)	信
Xin Tangshu	新唐書
yang	陽
Yang Qiu	陽球

yi (righteousness)	義
Yijing	易經
yijue (righteous separation)	義絕
yin	陰
Yin Yuan	駰瑗
Yu Daosui	于道遂
Yu Wanchun	俞萬春
yuanhu (garden household)	園戶
Yue Fei	岳飛
Xiaojing	孝經
Xiaozong (emperor)	蕭宗
Zhang Quanqi	章全啟
Zhang Quanyi	章全益
zhen (authenticity)	真
zhenjie	貞潔
Zhenzong (emperor)	真宗
Zhixiu	智秀
Zhou (dynasty)	周
Zhou Dang	周黨
Zhou Jielun	周杰倫
Zhuang (duke)	莊
Zhufa Chong	竺法崇
Zou Yan	鄒衍
Zuo zhuan	左傳

Bibliography

Adams, Rachel, and David Savran. "Introduction." In *The Masculinity Studies Reader*, edited by Rachel Adams and David Savran, 1–8. Malden, MA: Blackwell, 2002.

Alter, Joseph S. "Celibacy, Sexuality, and the Transformation of Gender into Nationalism in North India." *Journal of Asian Studies* 53, no. 1 (1994): 61.

An Jinhuai. *Zhongguo kaogu*. Taipei: Nantian, 1996. First published 1992.

Anchee Min, Duo Duo, and Stefan R. Landsberger. *Chinese Propaganda Posters*. Hong Kong: Taschen, 2008.

Anonymous. *Shangjun shu*. Taipei: Taiwan shangwu, 1988.

———. "Ducheng jisheng." In *Yingyin Wenyuange siku quanshu*. Taipei: Taiwan Shangwu, 1983.

Appiah, Kwame Anthony. *The Honor Code: How Moral Revolutions Happen*. New York: Norton, 2010.

Ban Gu. *Hanshu*, annotated by Yan Shigu. Taipei: Dingwen, 1979. First published 1962.

Bao Jialin. "Yinyangxue shuo yu funü diwei." In *Zhongguo funüshi lunji xuji*, edited by Bao Jialin, 37–42. Taipei: Daoxiang, 1991.

Barlow, Tani. "Theorizing Women: Funü, Guojia, Jiating." In *Body, Subject and Power in China*, edited by Angela Zito and Tani E. Barlow. Chicago: University of Chicago Press, 1994.

Barlow, Tani, with Gary J. Bjorge, ed. *I Myself Am a Woman: Selected Writings of Ding Ling*. Boston: Beacon Press, 1989.

Berkowitz, Alan J. *Patterns of Disengagement: The Practice and Portrayal of Reclusion in Early Medieval China*. Stanford, CA: Stanford University Press, 2000.

Bird, Sharon R. "Welcome to the Men's Club: Homosociality and the Maintenance of Hegemonic Masculinity." *Gender and Society* 10, no. 2 (1996): 120–32.

Black, Alison H. "Gender and Cosmology in Chinese Correlative Thinking." In *Gender and Religion: On the Complexity of Symbols*, edited by C. W. Bynum et al., 166–95. Boston: Beacon, 1989.

Blok, Anton. "Rams and Billy-Goats: A Key to the Mediterranean Code of Honour." *Man* (New Series) 16, no. 3 (1981): 434–36.

Bourdieu, Pierre. *Distinction: A Social Critique of the Judgement of Taste,* trans. Richard Nice. London: Routledge, 1984.

———. "Marriage Strategies as Strategies of Social Reproduction." In *Family and Society: Selections from the Annales Économies, Sociétés, Civilisations,* edited by Robert Forster and Orest Ranum, trans. Elborg Forster and Patricia M. Ranum, 117–44. Baltimore: Johns Hopkins University Press, 1976.

———. *Masculine Domination,* trans. Richard Nice. Cambridge, UK: Polity Press, 2001.

Bourke, Joanna. *Dismembering the Male: Men's Bodies, Britain and the Great War.* Chicago: University of Chicago Press, 1996.

Boyarin, Daniel. *Unholy Conduct: The Rise of Heterosexuality and the Invention of the Jewish Man.* Berkeley and Los Angeles: University of California Press, 1997.

Bray, Francesca. "The Inner Quarters: Oppression or Freedom?" In *House Home Family: Living and Being Chinese,* edited by Ronald G. Knapp and Kai-yin Lo, 259–79. Honolulu and New York: University of Hawaii Press and China Institute in America, 2005.

Brod, Harry. "Some Thoughts on Some Histories of Some Masculinities: Jews and Other Others." In *Theorizing Masculinities,* edited by Harry Brod and Michael Kaufman, 82–96. Thousand Oaks, CA: Sage, 1994.

Broughton, Trev Lynn. *Men of Letters, Writing Lives: Masculinity and Literary Auto/Biography in the Late Victorian Period.* New York: Routledge, 1999.

Brown, Judith K. "A Note on the Division of Labor by Sex." *American Anthropologist* 72 (1970): 1073–78.

Brownell, Susan. *Training the Body for China: Sports in the Moral Order of the People's Republic.* Chicago: University of Chicago Press, 1995.

Brubaker, Rogers, and David D. Laitin. "Ethnic and Nationalist Violence." *Annual Review of Sociology* 24 (1998): 444.

Campbell, J. K. *Honour, Family, and Patronage: A Study of Institutions and Moral Values in a Greek Mountain Community.* Oxford: Clarendon Press, 1964.

Cao Wei. "Shiji zhong cike xingxiang suo zaixian de rujia wenhua jingshen qizhi." *Xijiangyue* 1 (2010): 23–24.

Capobianco, Jason, and Jacky Tam. "Nanren julebu," *GQ Zhizu* 224 (May 2012): 314.

Carrigan, Tim, Bob Connell, and John Lee. "Toward a New Sociology of Masculinity." *Theory and Society* 14, no. 5 (1985): 551–604.

Chang, John K. *Industrial Development in Pre-Communist China: A Quantitative Analysis.* Edinburgh: University Press, 1969.

Chang, Shelly Hsueh-lun. *History and Legend: Ideas and Images in the Ming Historical Novels.* Ann Arbor: University of Michigan Press, 1990.

Chen Enlin. "Lun 'Gongyang zhuan' Fuchou sixiang de tedian yu jing jin, guwen fuchoushuo wenti." *Shehui kexue zhanxian* (February 1998): 137–45.

Ch'en, Kenneth K. S. *The Chinese Transformation of Buddhism.* Princeton, NJ: Princeton University Press, 1973.

———. "Filial Piety in Chinese Buddhism," *Harvard Journal of Asiatic Studies* 28 (1968): 81–97.

Chen Li, annotator. *Baihu tongyi.* Taipei: Guangwen, 1987. First published 1875.

Chen Menglei. *Zhouyi qianshu.* Shanghai: Guji, 1983.

Chen Min. *Chapu.* Shanghai: Shanghai Jinxiu Wenzhang, 2007.

Chen Ruoshui. *Tangdai de funü wenhua yu jiating shenghuo.* Taipei: Yunchen, 2007.

Chen Shijiao. *Hualihuo,* edited by Congshu jicheng. Changsha: Shangwu, 1939.

Chen Si. *Haitangpu.* Taipei: Xinxing, 1988.

Chen Xiaoang. "Chunqiu shiqi de zhenjieguan." *Xinan minzuxue xuebao (zhexue shehui kexue ban)* 21, no. 19 (2000): 105–9.

Chen, Tina Mai. "Dressing for the Party: Clothing, Citizenship, and Gender Formation in Mao's China." *Fashion Theory* 5, no. 2 (2001): 143–71.

Cheng Jiangong. "'Yi—Yanwen' de lunli jiazhi ji qi xianshi yiyi." *Hexi Xueyuan xuebao* 26, no. 6 (2010): 38–42.

Cheng Xiaolin and Zhu Jingxia. "Shilun Tang chuanqi xiaoshuo zhong de xiake xingxiang." *Mudanjiang Daxue xuebao* 19, no. 4 (2010): 40–41.

Chodorow, Nancy J. "Gender as a Personal and Cultural Construction." *Signs* 20, no. 3 (1995): 516–44.

Cole, Alan. *Mothers and Sons in Chinese Buddhism.* Stanford, CA: Stanford University Press, 1998.

Connell, R. W. "The Big Picture: Masculinities in Recent World History." *Theory and Society* 22, no. 5 (1993): 598–603.

———. "Cool Guys, Swots, and Wimps: The Interplay of Masculinity and Education." *Oxford Review of Education* 15, no. 3 (1989): 295.

———. *Masculinities,* 2nd ed. Berkeley: University of California Press, 2005.

———. "Theorizing Gender." *Sociology* 19, no. 2 (1985): 263.

Connell, R. W., and James W. Messerschmidt. "Hegemonic Masculinity: Rethinking the Concept." *Gender and Society* 19, no. 6 (2005): 830–32.

Conner, Marlene Kim. *What Is Cool?: Understanding Black Manhood in America.* New York: Crown, 1995.

Cua, Antonio S. "The Ethical Significance of Shame: Insights of Aristotle and Xunzi." *Philosophy East and West* 53, no. 2 (2003): 156–57.

Dautcher, Jay. *Down a Narrow Road: Identity and Masculinity in a Uyghur Community in Xinjiang China.* Cambridge, MA: Harvard University Asia Center, 2009.

Davis, Adrian. "Fraternity and Fratricide in Late Imperial China." *American Historical Review* 105, no. 5 (2000): 1630–31.

Davis, Richard L. "Chaste and Filial Women in Chinese Historical Writings of the Eleventh Century." *Journal of the American Oriental Society* 121, no. 2 (2001): 204–18.

Dawson, David. *Allegorical Readers and Cultural Revision in Ancient Alexandria.* Berkeley: University of California Press, 1991.

de Groot, Joanna. "'Brothers of the Iranian Race': Manhood, Nationhood, and Modernity in Iran c. 1870–1914." In *Masculinities in Politics and War: Gendering Modern History,* edited by Stefan Dudink, Karen Hagemann, and John Tosh, 142–43. Manchester: Manchester University Press, 2004.

Demetriou, Demetrakis Z. "Connell's Concept of Hegemonic Masculinity: A Critique." *Theory and Society* 30, no. 3 (2001): 341.

De Rauw, Tom. "Baochang: Sixth-Century Biographer of Monks . . . and Nuns?" *Journal of the American Oriental Society* 125, no. 2 (2005): 203, 208.

Deslandes, Paul R. "Competitive Examinations and the Culture of Masculinity in Oxbridge Undergraduate Life, 1850–1920." *History of Education Quarterly* 42, no. 4 (2002): 544–78.

Dikötter, Frank. *Sex, Culture, and Modernity in China: Medical Science and the Construction of Sexual Identities in the Early Republican Period*. London: Hurst, 1995.

Di Yanchun and Zhang Yunhui. "Zhongguo fojiao jielü yu xiaodao guannian." *Wenshan Shifan Gaodeng Zhuanke Xuexiao xuebao* 19, no. 2 (2006): 59–60.

Dodd, Peter C. "Family Honor and the Forces of Change in Arab Society." *International Journal of Middle East Studies* 4, no. 1 (1973): 40–54.

Donaldson, Mike. "What Is Hegemonic Masculinity." *Theory and Society* 22, no. 5 (1993): 655.

Du Fangqin. "Ming Qing zhenjie de tedian ji qi yuanyin." *Shanxi Shida xuebao* 10 (1997): 43.

Duan Tali. "Cong fuqi guanxi kan Tangdai funü jiating diwei bianhua." *Lanzhou Daxue xuebao* 6 (2001): 53.

———. "Tangdai nüxing jiating jiaose ji qita diwei." *Zhongguo wenhua yanjiu* (2002): 141–49.

Duan Yucai. *Shuowen jiezi zhu*. Shanghai: Guji, 1981.

Ebrey, Patricia. "Patron-Client Relations in the Later Han." *Journal of the American Oriental Society* 103, no. 3 (1983): 541–42.

Edwards, Louise. "Policing the Modern Woman in Republican China." *Modern China* 26, no. 2 (2000): 121.

———. "Women in Honglou Meng: Prescriptions of Purity in the Femininity of Qing Dynasty China." *Modern China* 16, no. 4 (1990): 411–12.

Elman, Benjamin A. "Political, Social, and Cultural Reproduction via Civil Service Examinations in Late Imperial China." *Journal of Asian Studies* 50, no. 1 (1991): 7–28.

Elvin, Mark. "Female Virtue and the State in China." *Past & Present* 104 (1984): 111–52.

Evans, Harriet. "Defining Difference: The 'Scientific' Construction of Sexuality and Gender in the People's Republic of China." *Signs* 20, no. 2 (1995): 366–71, 375–76.

Evans-Pritchard, E. E. "The Nuer of the Southern Sudan." *Kinship and Family: An Anthropological Reader*, edited by Robert Parkin and Linda Stone, 74–77. Malden, MA: Blackwell, 2004.

Fan Chengda. "Fancun meipu." In *Yingyin Wenyuange siku quanshu*. Taipei: Taiwan Shangwu, 1983.

———. *Wujunzhi*. Shanghai: Shangwu, 1939.

Fan Xueqing. "Qingmo Yue, Gang diqu geming dangren de jianfa yifu yulun." *Xueshu yanjiu* 5 (2007): 101–9.

Fan Ye. *Hou Hanshu*, annotated by Liu Zhao et al. Beijing: Zhonghua Shuju, 1965.

Fan, Jie, Thomas Heberer, and Wolfgang Taubman. *Rural China: Economic and Social Change in the Late Twentieth Century*. Armonk, NY: M. E. Sharpe, 2006.

Fang Jinhua. "'Gegu' ciyi kaoshi." *Taizhou Shizhuan xuebao* 20, no. 4 (1998): 41–43.

Fang Liqing and Wu Weigen. "Daojia 'tian fu di mu' yinyu ji qi shengtai zhihu jiedu." *Zhejiang Nonglin Daxue xuebao* 28, no. 4 (2011): 640–43.

Fang Yan. "Songdai nüxing gegu liaoqin wenti shixi." *Qiusuo* 11 (2007): 210–12.

Farrer, James. *Opening Up: Youth Sex Culture and Market Reform in Shanghai*. Chicago: University of Chicago Press, 2002.

Fei Xiaotong. *From the Soil: The Foundations of Chinese Society*. Berkeley: University of California Press, 1992.

Feng Keli, ed. *Gushi fengwu*. Jinan: Shandong huabao, 2008.

———. *Lao Zhaopian*. Jinan: Shandong Huabao, 2008.

Feng Wei. *Xizang mijing*. Beijing: Zhongguo Sheying, 2010.

Fitzgerald, John. *Awakening China: Politics, Culture and Class in the Nationalist Revolution*. Stanford, CA: Stanford University Press, 1996.

———. "Continuity within Discontinuity: The Case of *Water Margin* Mythology." *Modern China* 12, no. 3 (1986): 372–75.

Folsom, Kenneth E. *Friends, Guests, and Colleagues: The Mu-fu System in the Late Ch'ing Period*. Berkeley: University of California Press, 1968.

Fong, Vanessa L. "China's One-Child Policy and the Empowerment of Urban Daughters." *American Anthropologist* (New Series) 104, no. 4 (2002): 1098–109.

Friedman, Edward, et al. *Chinese Village, Socialist State*. New Haven, CT: Yale University Press, 1991.

Friedman, Sara L. *Intimate Politics: Marriage, the Market, and State Power in Southeastern China*. Cambridge, MA: Harvard University Asia Center, 2006.

Fung, Heidi. "Becoming a Moral Child: The Socialization of Shame among Young Chinese Children." *Ethos* 27, no. 2 (1999): 180–209.

Furth, Charlotte. "Androgynous Males and Deficient Females: Biology and Gender Boundaries in Sixteenth- and Seventeenth-Century China." *Late Imperial China* 9, no. 2 (1988): 1–3.

Gates, Philippa. *Detecting Men: Masculinity and the Hollywood Detective Film*. Albany: State University of New York Press, 2006.

Geaney, Jane. "Guarding Moral Boundaries: Shame in Early Confucianism," *Philosophy East and West* 54, no. 2 (2004): 113–42.

Gill, Lesley. "Creating Citizens, Making Men: The Military and Masculinity in Bolivia." *Cultural Anthropology* 12, no. 4 (1997): 527–50.

Gilmartin, Christina. "Gender in the Formation of a Communist Body Politic." *Modern China* 19, no. 3 (1993): 306–8.

Gilmore, David D. *Honor and Shame and the Unity of the Mediterranean*. Washington, DC: American Anthropological Association, 1987.

———. *Manhood in the Making: Cultural Concepts of Masculinity*. New Haven, CT: Yale University Press, 1990.

Glosser, Susan L. "'The Truths I Have Learned': Nationalism, Family Reform, and Male Identity in China's New Culture Movement, 1915–1923." In *Chinese Femininities, Chinese Masculinities: A Reader*, edited by Susan Brownell and Jeffrey N. Wasserstrom. Berkeley: University of California Press, 2002.

Goldin, Paul Rakita. *The Culture of Sex in Ancient China*. Honolulu: University of Hawaii Press, 2002.

Goldman, Harvey. "Images of the Other: Asia in Nineteenth-Century Western Thought—Hegel, Marx and Weber." In *Asia in Western and World History: A Guide for Teaching*, edited by Ainslie Thomas Embree and Carol Gluck. Armonk, NY: M. E. Sharpe, 1997.

Guizot, François. *The History of Civilization in Europe*, translated by William Hazlitt, edited by Larry Siedentop. London: Penguin, 1997. First published 1846.

Guo Moruo. "You guan Yijing de xin." *Zhongguoshi yanjiu* 1 (1979): 5.

Guo Songyi. "Qingdai funü de shoujie he zaijia." *Zhejiang shehui kexue* 1 (2001): 124–32.

Guoli Gugong Bowuyuan Bianji Weiyuanhui. *Gugong shuhua tulu*. Taipei: Guoli Gugong Bowuyuan, 1989.

Gutmann, Matthew C. "Trafficking in Men: The Anthropology of Masculinity." *Annual Review of Anthropology* 26 (1997): 386.

Habermas, Jürgen. *The Structural Transformation of the Public Sphere: An Inquiry into a Category of Bourgeois Society*, trans. Thomas Burger and Frederick Lawrence. Cambridge, MA: MIT Press, 1989.

Hammond, Charles E. "Waiting for a Thunderbolt." *Asian Folklore Studies* 51, no. 1 (1992): 38–44.

Han, Jongwoo, and L. H. M. Ling. "Authoritarianism in the Hypermasculinized State: Hybridity, Patriarchy, and Capitalism in Korea." *International Studies Quarterly* 42, no. 1 (1998): 54.

Hardy, Grant. "The Reconstruction of Ritual: Capping in Ancient China." *Journal of Ritual Studies* 7, no. 2 (1993): 69–90.

Harrison, Simon. "Cultural Boundaries." *Anthropology Today* 15, no. 5 (1999): 11.

Harvey, Karen. "The History of Masculinity, circa 1650–1800." *Journal of British Studies* 44, no. 2 (2005): 303.

He Jianping. "Shizu shehui yu 'xieqin fuchou,'" *Guizhou shehui kexue* 136, no. 4 (1995): 40–44.

He Rongyi. *Daodejing zhuyi yu xijie.* Taipei: Wuna, 1985.

He Shanmeng. *Wei Jin qinglun.* Beijing: Guangming Ribao, 2007.

He Xiu and Xu Yan, annotators. *Chunqiu gongyanzhuan zhushu.* Taipei: Yiwen, 1955. First published 1815.

Hegel, Robert E. *Reading Illustrated Fiction in Late Imperial China.* Stanford, CA: Stanford University Press, 1998.

Hendler, Glenn. "Pandering in the Public Sphere: Masculinity and the Market in Horatio Alger." *American Quarterly* 48, no. 3 (1996): 415.

Henricks, Robert G. *Lao-Tzu Te-Tao Ching: A New Translation Based on the Recently Discovered Ma-Wang-Tui Texts.* New York: Ballantine, 1989.

Herman, Andrew. *The "Better Angels" of Capitalism: Rhetoric, Narrative, and Moral Identity among Men of the American Upper Class.* Boulder, CO: Westview, 1999.

Herzfeld, Michael. *The Poetics of Manhood: Contest and Identity in a Cretan Mountain Village.* Princeton, NJ: Princeton University Press, 1985.

Hillman, Ben, and Lee-Anne Henfry. "Macho Minority: Masculinity and Ethnicity on the Edge of Tibet." *Modern China* 32, no. 2 (2006): 253.

Hiltebeitel, Alf, et al., eds. *Hair: Its Power and Meaning in Asian Cultures.* Albany: State University of New York Press, 1998.

Hinsch, Bret. "The Criticism of Powerful Women by Western Han Dynasty Portent Experts." *Journal of the Economic and Social History of the Orient* 49, no. 1 (2006): 96–121.

———. "Harmony (*He*) and Gender in Early Chinese Thought." *Journal of Chinese Philosophy* 22 (1996): 109–28.

———. "The Origins of Separation of the Sexes in China." *Journal of the American Oriental Society* 123, no. 3 (2003): 595–616.

Hiroko, Sakamoto. "The Formation of National Identity in Liang Qichao and Its Relationship to Gender." In *The Role of Japan in Liang Qichao's Introduction of Modern Western Civilization to China*, edited by Joshua A. Fogel, 277–80. Berkeley: Institute of East Asian Studies, University of California, Berkeley, and Center for Chinese Studies, 2004.

Ho, David Y. F. "Fatherhood in Chinese Culture." In *The Father's Role: Cross-Cultural Perspectives*, edited by Michael E. Lamb. London: Routledge, 1987.

Ho, David Yau-fai. "On the Concept of Face." *American Journal of Sociology* 81, no. 4 (1976): 867–84.

Holcombe, Charles. "The Exemplar State: Ideology, Self-Cultivation, and Power in Fourth Century China." *Harvard Journal of Asiatic Studies* 49, no. 1 (1989): 98–101.

Holmgren, Jennifer. "The Economic Foundations of Virtue: Widow-Remarriage in Early and Modern China." *The Australian Journal of Chinese Affairs* 12 (1985): 1–27.

Holt, Douglas B., and Craig J. Thompson. "Man-of-Action Heroes: The Pursuit of Heroic Masculinity in Everyday Consumption." *Journal of Consumer Research* 31, no. 2 (2004): 425–40.

Holzman, Donald. "The Place of Filial Piety in Ancient China." *Journal of the American Oriental Society* 118, no. 2 (1998): 185–99.

Honig, Emily. "Maoist Mappings of Gender: Reassessing the Red Guards." In *Chinese Femininities, Chinese Masculinities: A Reader*, edited by Susan Brownell and Jeffrey N. Wasserstrom. Berkeley: University of California Press, 2002.

Hsia, C. T. *The Classic Chinese Novel*. New York: Columbia University Press, 1968.

Hsiao Ching. Taipei: Confucius Publishing, n.d.

Hu Ying. "Angling with Beauty: Two Stories of Women as Narrative Bait in *Sanguozhi yanyi*." *Chinese Literature: Essays, Articles, Reviews* 15 (1993): 99–112.

Hu Zifeng. *Xian Qin zhuzi yishuo tongkao*. Taipei: Wenshizhe, 1974.

Huang Jinlin. *Lishi, shenti, guojia: jindai Zhongguo de shenti xingcheng (1895–1937)* Taipei: Lianjing, 2005.

Huang Qingfa. "Tangdai sengni de chujia fangshi yu shisuhua qingxiang." *Nantong Shifan Xueyuan xuebao (zhexue shehui kexue ban)* 18, no. 1 (March 2002): 91.

Huang, Martin W. *Negotiating Masculinities in Late Imperial China*. Honolulu: University of Hawaii Press, 2006.

———. "Sentiments of Desire: Thoughts on the Cult of Qing in Ming-Qing Literature." *Chinese Literature: Essays, Articles, Reviews* 20 (1998): 163.

Huang, Philip C. *The Peasant Economy and Social Change in North China*. Stanford, CA: Stanford University Press, 1985.

Hulsewé, A. F. P. *Remnants of Ch'in Law: An Annotated Translation of the Ch'in Legal and Administrative Rules of the 3rd Century B.C., Discovered in Yün-meng Prefecture, Hu-pei Province, in 1975*. Leiden: Brill, 1985.

Hung-yok Ip. "Fashioning Appearances: Feminine Beauty in Chinese Communist Revolutionary Culture." *Modern China* 29, no. 3 (2003): 329–61.

Hunter, Jane. *The Gospel of Gentility: American Women Missionaries in Turn-of-the-Century China*. New Haven, CT: Yale University Press, 1984.

Jacka, Tamara. *Women's Work in Rural China*. Cambridge: Cambridge University Press, 1997.

Jameson, Frederic. *The Political Unconscious: Narrative as a Socially Symbolic Act*. Ithaca, NY: Cornell University Press, 1981.

Jankowiak, William R. *Sex, Death, and Hierarchy in a Chinese City: An Anthropological Account*. New York: Columbia University Press, 1993.

Jen-Der Lee. "Conflicts and Compromise between Legal Authority and Ethical Ideas: From the Perspective of Revenge in Han Times." *Renwen ji shehui kexue jikan* 1, no. 1 (1988): 359–408.

Jenner, W. J. F. *A Knife in the Ribs for a Mate: Reflections on Another Chinese Tradition*. Canberra: Australian National University, 1993.

Ji Dejun. "Lishi yanyi xiaoshuozhong 'rujiang' xingxiang de wenhua jiedu." *Guangzhou Shiyuan xuebao (shehui kexue ban)* 21, no. 2 (2000): 13–15.

Jia Gongyan, annotator. *Zhouli zhushu.* Taipei: Yiwen, 1955. First published 1815.

Jia Yanhong. "Tangdai funü lihun leixing qianxi." *Qining Shizhuan xuebao* 4 (2002): 63–65.

Jiao Jie. "Xiannü xiafan—jituo Tangdai nanzi lixiang de wenhua xianxiang." *Lishi yuekan* 4 (1999): 122–26.

Jiao Jie and Geng Guanjing. "Cong 'Liji' kan zhanguo yihou fuquan de qianghua." *Funü yanjiu luncong* 4, no. 106 (2011): 59–64.

Jin Xia. "Qianlun Tangdai houqi hunyin de tedian." *Shandong Jiaoyu Xueyuan xuebao* 91 (2002): 46–48, 51.

Jing Shuhui. *Wei Jin shiren yu zhengzhi.* Beijing: Zhonghua, 2007.

Kao, Karl S. Y. "Bao and Baoying: Narrative Causality and External Motivations in Chinese Fiction." *Chinese Literature: Essays, Articles, Reviews* 11 (1989): 120.

Kaplan, Amy. "Romancing the Empire: The Embodiment of American Masculinity in the Popular Historical Novel of the 1890s." *American Literary History* 2, no. 4 (1990): 659–90.

Karras, Ruth Mazo. *From Boys to Men: Formations of Masculinity in Late Medieval Europe.* Philadelphia: University of Pennsylvania Press, 2003.

Kelly, Allison. "The Construction of Masculine Science." *British Journal of Sociology of Education* 6, no. 2 (1985): 133–54.

Kerber, Linda. "Separate Spheres, Female World, Women's Place: The Rhetoric of Women's History." *Journal of American History* 75, no. 1 (1988): 39.

Kieschnick, John. *The Eminent Monk: Buddhist Ideals in Medieval Chinese Hagiography.* Honolulu: University of Hawaii Press, 1997.

Kim, Joo Yup, and Sang Hoon Nam. "The Concept and Dynamics of Face: Implications for Organizational Behavior in Asia." *Organization Science* 9, no. 4 (1998): 522–34.

Kimmel, Michael. *Manhood in America: A Cultural History.* New York: Free Press, 1996.

Kiritani Seiichi. "Ryō Shaku Keikō ni okeru rekishi ishiki—toku ni kan kai ishiki no igi ni tsuite." *Indogaku butsukyōgaku kenkyū* 20, no. 2 (1972): 298–301.

Kleinman, Arthur. *Social Origins of Distress and Disease: Depression, Neurasthenia, and Pain in Modern China.* New Haven, CT: Yale University Press, 1986.

Knapp, Keith Nathaniel. *Selfless Offspring: Filial Children and Social Order in Medieval China.* Honolulu: University of Hawaii Press, 2005.

Knoblock, John, and Jeffrey Riegel. *The Annals of Lü Buwei.* Stanford, CA: Stanford University Press, 2000.

Kong Lingguang. "Zhongguo shenhua zhong de beiju yingxiong xinjie." *Qiqihaer Shifan Gaodeng Zhuanke Xuexiao xuebao* 104 (2008): 44–45.

Kruger, Steven F. "Becoming Christian, Becoming Male?" In *Becoming Male in the Middle Ages,* edited by Jeffrey Jerome Cohen and Bonnie Wheeler. New York: Garland, 1997.

Lai Xinxia, ed. *Mingke lidai lienü zhuan.* Tianjin: Renmin Meishu, 2004.

Lai Yanyuan. *Chunqiu fanlu jinzhu jinyi.* Taipei: Taiwan Shangwu, 1984.

Lai Zhide. *Zhouyi jizhu,* annotated by Zhang Wanbin (張萬彬). Beijing: Jiuzhou, 2004.

Lao She. "Also a Triangle." In *Blades of Grass: The Stories of Lao She,* edited by William A. Lyell, Sara Wei-Ming Chen, and Howard Goldblatt. Honolulu: University of Hawaii Press, 1999.

Lao Tan. *Shuihu—yizhi bei wudu.* Chongqing: Chongqing Daxue, 2010.

Lau, D. C. *Lao-tsu: Tao Te Ching.* Harmondsworth, UK: Penguin, 1963.

Lee, Leo Ou-fan. *Shanghai Modern: The Flowering of a New Urban Culture in China, 1930–1945*. Cambridge, MA: Harvard University Press, 1999.

Levenson, Joseph. *Liang Ch'i-ch'ao and the Mind of Modern China*. Berkeley: University of California Press, 1970.

Levenson, Joseph R. *Confucian China and Its Modern Fate*. Vol. 1, *The Problem of Intellectual Continuity*. London: Routledge and Kegan Paul, 1958.

Lewis, Mark Edward. *Sanctioned Violence in Early China*. Albany: State University of New York Press, 1990.

Li Diaoyuan, ed. *Huayang guozhi*. Taipei: Hongye, 1972.

Li Zhang. "Migration and Privatization of Space and Power in Late Socialist China." *American Ethnologist* 28, no. 1 (2001): 190.

Li, Wai-yee. *The Readability of the Past in Early Chinese Historiography*. Cambridge, MA: Harvard University Asia Center, 2007.

Liebenthal, Walter. "Chinese Buddhism during the 4th and 5th Centuries." *Monumental Nipponica* 11, no. 1 (1995): 54, 57–58.

Lieberman, Sally Taylor. *The Mother and Narrative Politics in Modern China*. Charlottesville: University Press of Virginia, 1998.

Lin Chuanfang. "Ryō Kōsōden no ikyō ni tsuite." *Indogaku butsukyōgaku kenkyū* 24, no. 2 (1976): 272–75.

Lin Jiali et al., eds. *Xinyi shenjian duben*. Taipei: Sanmin, 1996.

Lin Sujuan. "Chunqiu Zhanguo shiqi wei junfu Fuchou suoshe zhi zhongxiao yiti ji xiangguan jingyi tanjiu." *Hanxue yanjiu* 24, no. 1 (2006): 43.

Lin Yanzhi. "Tangdai shiqi Dunhuang diqu de nüren jieshe." *Zhongguo wenhua yuekan* 6 (2000): 32–50.

Lindman, Janet Moore. "Acting the Manly Christian: White Evangelical Masculinity in Revolutionary Virginia." *William and Mary Quarterly* 57, no. 2 (2000): 393–416.

Liu Chaoqian. "Xiake yu ru wenhua de yizhi duikangxing." *Kongzi yanjiu jikan* 1 (1995): 42–44.

Liu Chunxue. "'Yi' zhi kun yanjiu." *Xingtai Xueyuan xuebao* 26, no. 1 (2011): 113–14.

Liu Guangming. "'Gegu' ciyi de yanbian." *Chizhou Shizhuan xuebao* 16, no. 4 (2002): 60–61.

Liu I-ching. *Shih-shuo Hsin-yü: A New Account of Tales of the Word*, trans. Richard B. Mather. Minneapolis: University of Minnesota Press, 1976.

Liu Jingshen. "An Exploration of the Mode of Thinking in Ancient China." *Philosophy East and West* 35, no. 4 (1985): 387–96.

Liu Liming. "Handai de xiezu fuchou yu 'Chunqiu' jueyu." *Xinan minzu xueyuan xuebao—zhexue shehui kexue ban* 23, no. 3 (2002): 73–74.

Liu Meng. "Liushi jupu." In *Yingyin Wenyuange siku quanshu*. Taipei: Taiwan Shangwu, 1983.

Liu Qing. "'Wenren lun bing' yu Songdai bingxue de fazhan." *Shehui kexue jia* 49, no. 5 (1994): 56–60.

Liu Qiulin and Liu Jian, eds. *Zhonghua jixiangwu datudian*. Beijing: Guoji Wenhua, 1994.

Liu Xiaonan. "Shilun Zhang Ailing bixia de nanxing xingxiang." *Hunan jiaoyu xueyuan xuebao* 14, no. 4 (1996): 27.

Liu Xu, et al. *Jiu Tangshu*, annotated by Liu Jie and Chen Naiqian. Beijing: Zhonghua, 1975.

Liu Yao. "'Gaoseng zhuan' xulu suolun siben shu kao." *Zhongguo wenhua yanjiu* (spring 2007): 87–92.

Louie, Kam. "Constructing Chinese Masculinity for the Modern World: With Particular Reference to Lao She's *The Two Mas.*" *China Quarterly* 164 (2000): 1067–68.

———. "Global Masculine Identities." In *Asian Masculinities: The Meaning and Practice of Manhood in China and Japan*, edited by Kam Louie and Morris Low. London: Routledge Curzon, 2003.

———. "The Macho Eunuch: The Politics of Masculinity in Jia Pingwa's 'Human Extremities,'" *Modern China* 17, no. 2 (1991): 166, 180.

———. *Theorizing Chinese Masculinity: Society and Gender in China.* Cambridge: Cambridge University Press, 2002.

Lu Tongyan. "Cong 'chujia wujia' dao chujia er you 'jia'—Tang dai sengni xiaodao lunli xianxiang luexi." *Linyi Shifan Xueyuan xuebao* 30, no. 4 (2008): 77–81.

Lu Xun. "Kong Yiji." In *Lu Xun quanji*, 1:434–39. Beijing: Renmin, 1998.

Lu You. *Tianpeng mudanpu.* Taipei: Xinxing, 1988.

Lu, Sheldon H. *Chinese Modernity and Global Biopolitics: Studies in Literature and Visual Culture.* Honolulu: University of Hawaii Press, 2007.

———. "Soap Opera in China: The Transnational Politics of Visuality, Sexuality, and Masculinity." *Cinema Journal* 40, no. 1 (2000): 30.

Lu, Sheldon Hsiao-peng. *From Historicity to Fictionality: The Chinese Poetics of Narrative.* Stanford, CA: Stanford University Press, 1994.

Luhrmann, T. M. "The Good Parsi: The Postcolonial 'Feminization' of a Colonial Elite." *Man* (New Series) 29, no. 2 (1994): 333–57.

Luo Yinghuan and Fu Junlian, trans. *The Classified Characters and Political Abilities.* Beijing: Zhonghua, 2007.

Makino Tatsumi. *Chūgoku kazuko kenkyū (shita).* Tokyo: Ochanomizu, 1980.

Makita Tairyō. "Kōsōden no seiritsu (shita)." *(Kyōtō) tōhō gakuhō* 48 (1975): 229–59.

———. "Kōsōden no seiritsu (ue)." *(Kyōtō) tōhō gakuhō* 44 (1973): 101–25.

Mann, Susan. "The Male Bond in Chinese History and Culture." *American Historical Review* 105, no. 5 (2000): 1600–1614.

Mann, Susan L. *Gender and Sexuality in Modern Chinese History.* Cambridge: Cambridge University Press, 2011.

Mao Yangguang. "Cong muzhi kan Tang dai funü de zhenjieguan." *Baoji Wenli Xueyuan xuebao (shehui kexue ban)* 20, no. 2 (2000): 68.

Mayer, Tamar. "Gender Ironies of Nationalism: Setting the Stage." In *Gender Ironies of Nationalism: Sexing the Nation*, edited by Tamar Mayer. London: Routledge, 2000.

McDermott, Joseph P. "Friendship and Its Friends in the Late Ming." In *Jinshi jiazu yu zhengzhi bijiao lishi lunwenji*, 67–96. Taipei: Zhongyang Yanjiuyuan Jindaishi Yanjiusuo and Department of History, University of California, Davis, 1992.

McIsaac, Lee. "'Righteous Fraternities' and Honorable Men: Sworn Brotherhoods in Wartime Chongqing." *American Historical Review* 105, no. 5 (2000): 1641–55.

McMahon, Keith. *Misers, Shrews, and Polygamists: Sexuality and Male-Female Relations in Eighteenth-Century Chinese Fiction.* Durham, NC: Duke University Press, 1995.

Merson, John. *Roads to Xanadu: East and West in the Making of the Modern World.* London: Weidenfeld and Nicolson, 1989.

Miller, William Ian. *Humiliation.* Ithaca, NY: Cornell University Press, 1993.

Mori Mikisaburō. *Rōsō to bukkyō*. Kyoto: Hōsōkan, 1986.

Morrell, Robert. "Of Boys and Men: Masculinity and Gender in Southern African Studies." *Journal of Southern African Studies* 24, no. 4 (1998): 616–20.

Moskowitz, Marc L. *Cries of Joy, Songs of Sorrow: Chinese Pop Music and Its Cultural Connotations*. Honolulu: University of Hawaii Press, 2010.

Mosquera, Patricia M. Rodriguez, Anthony S. R. Manstead, and Agneta H. Fischer. "The Role of Honour Concerns in Emotional Reactions to Offenses." *Cognition and Emotion* 16, no. 1 (2002): 144.

Mou, Sherry J. *Gentlemen's Prescriptions for Women's Lives: A Thousand Years of Biographies of Chinese Women*. Armonk, NY: M. E. Sharpe, 2004.

Mowry, Robert D., et al. *Worlds within Worlds: The Richard Rosenblum Collection of Chinese Scholars' Rocks*. Cambridge, MA: Harvard University Art Museums, 1997.

Mugello, D. E. *Western Queers in China: Flight to the Land of Oz*. Lanham, MD: Rowman & Littlefield, 2012.

Nagel, Joane. "Ethnicity and Sexuality." *Annual Review of Sociology* 26 (2000): 111.

Nakajima Ryūzō. *Rokychyō shisō no kenkyū: shidaibu to butsukyō shisō*. Kyoto: Heirakuji, 1985.

Naquin, Susan, and Evelyn S. Rawski. *Chinese Society in the Eighteenth Century*. New Haven, CT: Yale University Press, 1989.

Niu Zhiping. "Shuo Tangdai junei zhi feng." *Shixue yuekan* 2 (1988): 38.

———. "Tangdai dufu shulun." In *Zhongguo funüshilunji xuji*, edited by Bao Jialin, 55–65. Taipei: Daoxiang, 1991.

———. "Tangdai hunyin de tianmingguan." *Hainan Shiyuan xuebao* 2 (1995): 59–61.

Nye, Robert A. "Kinship, Male Bonds, and Masculinity in Comparative Perspective." *American Historical Review* 105, no. 5 (2000): 1656.

———. *Masculinity and Male Codes of Honor in Modern France*. Oxford: Oxford University Press, 1993.

Nylan, Michael. "Confucian Piety and Individualism in Han China," *Journal of the American Oriental Society* 116, no. 1 (1996): 1–27.

———. *The Five "Confucian" Classics*. New Haven, CT: Yale University Press, 2001.

O'Hara, Albert Richard. *The Position of Woman in Early China: According to the Lieh Nü Chuan "The Biographies of Chinese Women."* Washington, DC: Catholic University of America Press, 1945.

Ōsawa Masaasa. *Tō Sō jidai no kazoku, kekkon, josei: tsuma wa tsuyoku*. Tokyo: Akashi, 2005.

Ouyang Xiu. *Loyang mudanji*. Taipei: Xinxing, 1988.

———. *Xin Tangshu*, annotated by Song Qi et al. Beijing: Zhonghua Shuju, 1975.

Ownby, David. "Approximations of Chinese Bandits: Perverse Rebels, Romantic Heroes, or Frustrated Bachelors." In *Chinese Femininities, Chinese Masculinities: A Reader*, edited by Susan Brownell and Jeffrey N. Wasserstrom, 233–34. Berkeley: University of California Press, 2002.

———. *Brotherhoods and Secret Societies in Early and Mid-Qing China: The Formation of a Tradition*. Stanford, CA: Stanford University Press, 1996.

Peng Zhongde. "Xiao tian fa di, ru 'yi' zhi men." *Hubei Daxue xuebao (zhehui shehui kexue ban)* 38, no. 4 (2011): 82–86.

Peristiany, Jean G., ed. *Honour and Shame: The Values of Mediterranean Society*. London: Wiedenfeld & Nicolson, 1965.

Perry, Elizabeth J., and Nara Dillon. "'Little Brothers' in the Cultural Revolution: The Worker Rebels of Shanghai." In *Chinese Femininities, Chinese Masculinities: A Reader*, edited by Susan Brownell and Jeffrey N. Wasserstrom. Berkeley: University of California Press, 2002.

Pina-Cabral, João de. "The Mediterranean as a Category of Regional Comparison: A Critical View." *Current Anthropology* 30, no. 3 (1989): 399–406.

Pitt-Rivers, Julian. "Honour and Social Status." In *Honour and Shame: The Values of Mediterranean Society*, edited by J. G. Peristiany. Chicago: University of Chicago Press, 1966.

——. "The Kith and the Kin." In *The Character of Kinship*, edited by Jack Goody, 89–106. Cambridge: Cambridge University Press, 1973.

Plaks, Andrew H. "*Shui-hu Chuan* and the Sixteenth-Century Novel Form: An Interpretive Reappraisal." *Chinese Literature: Essays, Articles, Reviews* 2, no. 1 (1980): 43.

Qin Shao. *Culturing Modernity: The Nantong Model, 1890–1930*. Stanford, CA: Stanford University Press, 2004.

——. "Tempest over Teapots: The Vilification of Teahouse Culture in Early Republican China." *Journal of Asian Studies* 57, no. 4 (1998): 1014–15, 1024, 1033–34.

Qiu Guihua. "Tangdai nüxing rezhong rudao yuanyin chutan." *Anhui Daxue xuebao (Zhexue shehui kexue ban)* 24, no. 3 (2000): 55–58.

Qiu Jian. "Qian qiu xia gu xiang—cong 'Shiji' hua xiake." *Yuwen xuekan* 5 (2005): 41–42.

Qiu Xuan. *Mudan rongruzhi*. Taipei: Xinxing, 1988.

Qiu Zhonglin. "Renyao, xieqi yu xiaogan—gegu liaoqi xianxiang zhong de yiliao guannian yu minsu xinyang." Paper presented at *Medicine and Society: A Symposium*, Institute of History and Philology, Academia Sinica, Taipei, Taiwan, 1997.

Raphals, Lisa. *Sharing the Light: Representations of Women and Virtue in Early China*. Albany: State University of New York Press, 1998.

Ray, Raka. "Masculinity, Femininity, and Servitude: Domestic Workers in Calcutta in the Late Twentieth Century." *Feminist Studies* 26, no. 3 (2000): 692, 695–96.

Reed, Carrie E. "Tattoo in Early China." *Journal of the American Oriental Society* 120, no. 3 (2000): 370.

Roddy, Stephen J. *Literati Identity and Its Fictional Representations in Late Imperial China*. Stanford, CA: Stanford University Press, 1998.

Rofel, Lisa. *Desiring China: Experiments in Neoliberalism, Sexuality, and Public Culture*. Durham, NC: Duke University Press, 2007.

Rofel, Lisa B. "'Yearnings': Televisual Love and Melodramatic Politics in Contemporary China." *American Ethnologist* 21, no. 4 (1994): 713.

Ropp, Paul S., Paola Zamperini, and Harriet T. Zurndorfer. *Passionate Women: Female Suicide in Late Imperial China*. Leiden: Brill, 2001.

Rossi, Alice S. "Gender and Parenthood." In *Gender and the Life Course*, edited by Alice S. Rossi. New York: Aldine, 1985.

Ryor, Kathleen. "Wen and Wu in Elite Cultural Practices during the Late Ming." In *Military Culture in Imperial China*, edited by Nicola di Cosmo, 219–42. Cambridge, MA: Harvard University Press, 2009.

Sandell, Jillian. "Reinventing Masculinity: The Spectacle of Male Intimacy in the Films of John Woo." *Film Quarterly* 49, no. 4 (1996): 23–34.

Schaberg, David. *A Patterned Past: Form and Thought in Early Chinese Historiography*. Cambridge, MA: Harvard University Asia Center, 2001.

Schein, Louisa. *Minority Rules: The Miao and the Feminine in China's Cultural Politics.* Durham, NC: Duke University Press, 2000.

Schneider, Jane. "Of Vigilance and Virgins: Honor, Shame and Access to Resources in Mediterranean Societies." *Ethnology* 10, no. 1 (1971): 2.

Schrand, Thomas G. "Socialism in One Gender: Masculine Values in the Stalin Revolution." In *Russian Masculinities in History and Culture*, edited by Barbara Evans Clements, Rebecca Friedman, and Dan Healey. Houndmills, UK: Palgrave, 2002.

Schwartz, Benjamin I. *The World of Thought in Ancient China.* Cambridge, MA: Belknap Press of Harvard University Press, 1985.

Scott, Joan W. "Gender: A Useful Category of Historical Analysis." *American Historical Review* 91, no. 5 (1986): 1053–75.

Sedgwick, Eve Kosofsky. *Between Men: English Literature and Male Homosocial Desire.* New York: Columbia University Press, 1985.

Shi Baocheng. *Fojia de chuanshuo.* Changsha: Yuelu, 2004.

Shi Lei. "Li yi shun tian: 'Liji' zhong de tiandao sixiang shulun." *Jinan xuebao (zhexue shehui kexue ban)* 156 (2012): 134–39.

Shi Nai'an and Luo Guangzhong. *Outlaws of the Marsh*, trans. Sidney Shapiro. Beijing and Changsha: Foreign Languages Press and Hunan People's Publishing House, 1999.

Shi Zhengzhi. "Shishi jupu." In *Yingyin Wenyuange siku quanshu.* Taipei: Taiwan Shangwu, 1983.

Shi Zhu. "Baiju jipu." In *Yingyin Wenyuange siku quanshu.* Taipei: Taiwan Shangwu, 1983.

Shih, Robert, trans. *Biographies des Moines Éminents (Kao Seng Tchouan) de Houei-Kiao.* Louvain: Institut Orientaliste, 1968.

Shinomi Takao. *Ryū Kō Retsujoten no kenkyū.* Tokyo: Tōkai Daigaku, 1989.

Sinha, Mrinalini. *Colonial Masculinity: The "Manly Englishman" and the "Effeminate Bengali" in the Late Nineteenth Century.* Manchester: Manchester University Press, 1995.

Sommer, Matthew. *Sex, Law and Society in Late Imperial China.* Stanford, CA: Stanford University Press, 2000.

Sommer, Matthew H. "Dangerous Males, Vulnerable Males, and Polluted Males: The Regulation of Masculinity in Qing Dynasty Law." In *Chinese Femininities, Chinese Masculinities: A Reader*, edited by Susan Brownell and Jeffrey N. Wasserstom. Berkeley: University of California Press, 2002.

———. "The Uses of Chastity: Sex, Law, and the Property of Widows in Qing China." *Late Imperial China* 17, no. 2 (1996): 77–130.

Song Geng. *The Fragile Scholar: Power and Masculinity in China.* Hong Kong: Hong Kong University Press, 2004.

Sponberg, Alan. "Attitudes toward Women and the Feminine in Early Buddhism." In *Buddhism, Sexuality, and Gender*, edited by Jose I. Cabezon. Albany: State University of New York Press, 1992.

Sun Guangde. *Xian Qin liang Han yinyang wuxing shuo de zhengzhi sixiang.* Taipei: Jiaxin shuini Gongsi Wenhua Jijinhui, 1969.

Sun Ji. *Handai wuzhi wenhua ziliao tushuo.* Beijing: Wenwu, 1991.

Swain, Jon. "How Young Schoolboys Become Somebody: The Role of the Body in the Construction of Masculinity." *British Journal of Sociology of Education* 24, no. 3 (2003): 299–314.

Tadao Yoshikawa. *Rokuchyō seishinshi kenkyū*, 2nd ed. Kyoto: Dōhōsha, 1986.

Tan Jiajian. *Mozi yanjiu.* Guiyang: Guizhou jiaoyu, 1995.

Tang Guizhang, ed. *Quansongci*. Beijing: Zhonghua, 1965.

Tao Dongfeng and Lü Heying. "Lei Feng: Shehuizhuyi lunli fuhao de suzao jiqi bianqian." *Xueshu yuekan* 42, no. 12 (2010): 105.

Theiss, Janet M. *Disgraceful Matters: The Politics of Chastity in Eighteenth Century China*. Berkeley: University of California Press, 2004.

Tikhonov, Vladimir. "Masculinizing the Nation: Gender Ideologies in Traditional Korea and in the 1890s–1900s Korean Enlightenment Discourse." *Journal of Asian Studies* 66, no. 4 (2007): 1032.

Van der Veer, Peter. "The Power of Detachment: Disciplines of Body and Mind in the Ramanandi Order." *American Ethnologist* 16, no. 3 (1989): 459.

van Ess, Hans. "Praise and Slander: The Evocation of Empress Lü in the *Shiji* and *Hanshu*." *Nannü* 8, no. 2 (2006): 221–54.

van Gennep, Arnold. *The Rites of Passage*, trans. Monika Vizedom and Gabrielle L. Caffee. Chicago: University of Chicago Press, 1960.

Veyne, Paul. *Did the Greeks Believe in Their Myths?: An Essay on the Constitutive Imagination*, trans. Paula Wissing. Chicago: University of Chicago Press, 1988.

Walls, Andrew Finlay. *The Cross-Cultural Process in Christian History*. London: Continuum, 2002.

Walsh, Andrew. "'Hot Money' and Daring Consumption in a Northern Malagasy Sapphire-Mining Town." *American Ethnologist* 30, no. 2 (2003): 283.

Wang Guan. "Yangzhou shaoyaopu." In *Yingyin Wenyuange siku quanshu*. Taipei: Taiwan Shangwu, 1983.

Wang Guixue. *Wangshi lanpu*. Taipei: Xinxing, 1980.

Wang Houxiang. "Tangdai jiating caichan ye jicheng zhidu shulun." *Wenshi zazhi* 4 (2003): 66–68.

Wang Jianzhong. *Handai huaxiangshi tonglun*. Beijing: Zijincheng, 2001.

Wang Li. "Xiezu Fuchou yu guiling chongbai." *Shanxi Daxue xuebao* 24, no. 4 (2001): 11–15.

Wang Li and Wu Haiyong. "Zhonggu Hanyi fojing Fuchou zhuti chutan." *Zhonggu bijiao wenxue* 3 (1999): 101–18.

Wang, David Der-wei. *Fin-de-Siècle Splendor: Repressed Modernities of Late Qing Fiction, 1849–1911*. Stanford, CA: Stanford University Press, 1997.

———. "Impersonating China." *Chinese Literature: Essays, Articles, Reviews (CLEAR)* 25 (2003): 133–34.

Wang, Zuoyue. "Saving China through Science: The Science Society of China, Scientific Nationalism, and Civil Society in Republican China." *Osiris* (Second Series) 17 (2002): 291–322.

Watson, James L. "Self-Defense Corps, Violence and the Bachelor Sub-culture in South China: Two Case Studies." *Proceedings of the Second International Conference on Sinology*. Taipei: Academia Sinica, 1989.

Watson, Rubie S. "The Nomad and the Nameless: Gender and Person in Chinese Society." *American Ethnologist* 13 (1986): 619–31.

Wei Hui. "Nüxing pinde xiuyang yanjiu: cong 'Zhouyi' zhi buyi nüde fenxi." *Xuzhou Gongcheng Xueyuan xuebao (shehui kexue ban)* 3 (2010): 88–92.

———. *Shanghai Baby*, trans. Bruce Hume. New York: Pocket Books, 2001.

Wei-hung Lin. "Chastity in Chinese Eyes: *Nan-Nü Yu-Pieh*." *Hanxue yanjiu* 12 (1991): 26.

Wetherell, Margaret, and Nigel Edley. "Negotiating Hegemonic Masculinity: Imaginary Positions and Psycho-discursive Practices." *Feminism & Psychology* 9, no. 3 (1999): 335–56.

Wilhelm, Richard, and Cary F. Baynes. *The I Ching or Book of Changes.* Princeton, NJ: Princeton University Press, 1977.

Wong, Robin R. *Images of Women in Chinese Thought and Culture: Writings from the Pre-Qin Period through the Song Dynasty.* Indianapolis: Hackett, 2003.

Wright, Arthur Frederick. "Fo-t'u-teng: A Biography." *Harvard Journal of Asiatic Studies* 11, nos. 3–4 (1948): 321–71.

Wu Hung. *Monumentality in Early Chinese Art and Architecture.* Stanford, CA: Stanford University Press, 1995.

Wu Pinxian. "Cong Da Xiao Dai Liji kan funü renshen qijian de lisu guifan." *Kongmeng yuekan* 7 (2000): 36–45.

Wu Zimu. *Menglianglu.* Beijing: Zhonghua, 1985.

Wu, Yenna. *The Chinese Virago: A Literary Theme.* Cambridge, MA: Council on East Asian Studies, Harvard University, 1995.

Xu Guoxing, Zu Jianping, and Hu Yuanjie, eds. *Lao chengxiang—Shangai chengshi zhi gen.* Shanghai: Tongji Daxue, 2011.

Xu Jieshun. "Hanzu gudai nangeng nüzhi jingji jiegoulun." *Liaozhou Shifan xuebao* 16, no. 4 (2001): 80–84.

Xu Xiaowang. "Cong 'Mindu bieji' kan gudai dongnan de tongxinglian wenti." *Lishi yuekan* 133 (February 1999): 101–7.

Xu Youwei and Philip Billingsley. "Out of the Closet: China's Historians 'Discover' Republican-Period Bandits." *Modern China* 28, no. 4 (2002): 477–78.

Yang Haiming. "Jianxi 'Gaoseng zhuan' yu 'Xu gaoseng zhuan' cheng shumu de ji zuo zhuan linian zhi yitong." *Xian Shiyou Daxue xuebao (shehui kexue ban)* 16, no. 4 (2007): 86–90.

Yang Kuan. *Zhanguoshi.* Taipei: Taiwan shangwu, 1997.

Yang Yi. *Zhongguo gudian xiaoshuo shier jiang.* Shanghai: Shanghai sanlian, 2007.

Yang, L. S. "The Concept of *Pao* as a Basis for Social Relations in China." In *Chinese Thought and Institutions*, edited by John King Fairbank, 291–309. Chicago: University of Chicago Press, 1957.

Yao Ping. *Tangdai funü de shengming licheng.* Shanghai: Shanghai Guji, 2004.

Yao, Yusheng. "The Elite Class Background of Wang Shuo and His Hooligan Characters." *Modern China* 30, no. 4 (2004): 437.

Ying Shao. *Fengsu tongyi.* Taipei: Zhonghua shuju, 1985.

You Biao. *Songdai siyuan jingjishi gao.* Baoan: Hebei Daxue Chubanshe, 2003.

Yu Jiaxi. *Shishuo xinyu jianshu.* Taipei: Huazheng, 1991.

Yuan Jixi. *Renhai guzhou: Han Wei Liuchao shi de gudu yishi.* Zhengzhou: Henan Renmin, 1995.

Yung-chen Chiang. "Performing Masculinity and the Self: Love, Body, and Privacy in Hu Shi." *Journal of Asian Studies* 63, no. 2 (2004): 305–32.

Zang Zhifei. "Chunqiu Gongyangxue yu Handai Fuchou fengqi fazheng." *Xuzhou Shifan Xueyuan xuebao (zhexue shehui kexue ban)* (February 1996): 23–28.

Zarrow, Peter. "He Zhen and Anarcho-Feminism in China." *Journal of Asian Studies* 47, no. 4 (1988): 796–800.

Zeng Youhe. "Shixi fojiao xiaodaoguan yu rujia xiaodaoguan de chayi ji qi yinying zhi dao." *Shanxi Gaodeng Xuexiao shehui kexue xuebao* 19, no. 11 (2007): 30–32.

Zhan, Heying Jenny, and Rhonda J. V. Montgomery. "Gender and Elder Care in China: The Influence of Filial Piety and Structural Constraints." *Gender and Society* 17, no. 2 (2003): 209–29.

Zhang Bangji. *Chenzhou mudanji.* Taipei: Xinxing, 1988.

———. *Mozhuang manlu.* Beijing: Zhonghua, 1985.

Zhang Daoyi. *Zhongguo tuan daxi.* Qingdao: Shandong Meishu, 1993.

Zhang Gongfu. *Meipin.* Taipei: Xinxing, 1988.

Zhang Guofeng. *Huashuo shuihu.* Guilin: Guangxi Shifan Daxue, 2009.

Zhang Ming. "Yihetuan yishi de wenhua xiangzheng yu zhengzhi yinyu." *Kaifang shidai* 9 (2000): 42–45.

Zhao Huijuan and Guo Yongyu. "Xingbie chayi yanjiu de sizhong quxiang." *Xinan Shifan Daxue xuebao (Renwen shehui kexue ban)* 29, no. 5 (September 2003): 32–36.

Zhao Shigeng. *Jinzhang lanpu.* Taipei: Xinxing, 1988.

Zhao, Henry Y. H. *The Uneasy Narrator: Chinese Fiction from the Traditional to the Modern.* Oxford: Oxford University Press, 1995.

Zheng Zhimin. "Tang dai shiren yu jinü guanxi de yanbian—yi 'Quan Tang shi' wei zhongxin." *Zhongxing shixue* 12 (1994): 65–85.

Zhiqiao, Dong. "'Gaoseng zhuan' de shiliao, yuliao jiazhi ji chongxin jiaoli yu yanjiu." *Dongnan Daxue xuebao (zhexue shehui kexue ban)* 6, no. 4 (2004): 111–16.

Zhiwei Xiao. "Movie House Etiquette Reform in Early-Twentieth-Century China." *Modern China* 32, no. 4 (2006): 518–20, 522.

Zhong, Xueping. *Masculinity Besieged? Issues of Modernity and Male Subjectivity in Chinese Literature in the Late Twentieth Century.* Durham, NC: Duke University Press, 2000.

Zhou Mi. *Guixin zazhi.* Beijing: Zhonghua, 1985.

Zhou Shihou. *Luoyang mudanji.* Taipei: Xinxing, 1980.

Zhou, Yiqun. *Festivals, Feasts, and Gender Relations in Ancient China and Greece.* Cambridge: Cambridge University Press, 2010.

Zhu Dake. *Liumang de shengyan: dangdai Zhongguo de liumang xushi.* Beijing: Xinxing, 2006.

Zhu Hengfu, Wang Xuejun, and Zhao Yi. *Xinyi Gaoseng zhuan.* Taipei: Sanmin, 2005.

Zhu Ling. "A Brave New World? On the Construction of 'Masculinity' and 'Femininity' in the Red Sorghum Family." In *Gender and Sexuality in Twentieth-Century Chinese Literature and Society,* edited by Tonglin Lu (Albany: State University of New York Press).

Zhu Yi. "Han Tang jian xia de geren xingxiang he shehui neihan." *Zhongguo shehui lishi pinglun* 6 (2006): 165–68.

Zito, Angela. *Of Body and Brush: Grand Sacrifice as Text/Performance in Eighteenth-Century China.* Chicago: University of Chicago Press, 1997.

Index

A Q zhengzhuan. See True Story of Ah Q, The
adultery, 50, 72, 74
African American, 111–2, 159
agency, 6, 53, 61, 72, 87, 138
agriculture, 14–5, 24, 34, 50, 132, 138, 144, 152
An Lushan Rebellion, 79, 85
Analects, 135
ancestor, 35, 54
androgyny, 6, 139, 154, 165
Anqing, 58
assassination, 38, 42, 115

bandits, 39, 111, 114, 117, 121–3, 126, 135
Beijing, 165–6
Biographies of Eminent Monks, 47, 51, 57
Biographies of Women, 74, 77
biography, 49, 52, 57, 63, 74, 81, 116, 163
biology, 3, 13
Bo Ji, 77
body, 16, 50, 55, 72, 77, 81, 133, 139–40, 147, 160
Bourdieu, Pierre, 92–3
Boxers, 134
Britain, 131, 133
brother, 7, 39–40, 49, 63, 81, 120, 122, 125, 127, 144, 156, 167

Buddhism, 2, 9, 47–65, 84, 96, 118, 123, 134
bureaucracy, 63–4, 91, 94
businessman, 137–8, 140, 146, 158, 163, 165

cannibalism, 80–1, 116
capitalism, 9, 92–3, 132, 137–9, 142, 144, 147, 151–2
capping, 30
celibacy, 54, 65, 126
Chang, Eileen, 138
chastity, 71–87, 93, 126–7, 141
Chen Gang, 39
Chiang Kai-shek, 152
child, 50, 57, 61, 84, 124–5, 144
Chou, Jay, 167
Christianity, 53, 147
Chunqiu. See Springs and Autumns of the State of Lu
Classic of Changes, 16, 21–5
Classic of Filial Piety, 58
Classic of Poetry, 16
coming-of-age ritual, 29–30
communism. *See* socialism
concubine, 82, 85, 99, 126, 133, 144
Confucianism, 8, 9, 16, 22–4, 33, 35, 64, 93, 97, 116, 118, 122–4, 135, 143–4, 147

Confucius, 33
connoisseurship, 94, 97–9, 104–7
cool, 111–2, 159
cosmology, 13, 19–25
courage, 31, 50, 55, 111, 118–9, 122, 158
courtesan, 85–7, 104–5
cultural capital, 63, 92–4, 99, 104, 107, 137
Cultural Revolution, 155–6, 158, 163, 166

Dangkouzhi. See Quell the Bandits
dao, 21
Daoheng, 61
Daoism, 23, 84
Daowen, 58
de Beauvoir, Simone, 3–4
definitions of masculinity, 3–6
Deng Xiaoping, 156
Dewey, John, 145
divorce, 83–4
Dong Zhongshu, 24, 38
dowry, 74
Durkheim, Emile, 56–7, 157

earth, 20–1
economy, 7, 9, 13, 18, 61, 91–2, 99, 101, 131, 133, 137, 144–5, 151, 157–8, 163, 167
education, 5, 13, 50, 57, 91, 93–5, 97, 99, 105–7, 123–4, 133, 135, 137, 139, 143, 158, 165
effeminacy, 6, 53, 134, 139, 157, 165
emasculation, 151, 156, 158
emperor, 52, 80, 98, 131, 156
Europe, 6, 7, 53, 66, 131–3, 146, 152, 157
examination, 94

face, 32, 42
Faguang, 61
family, 8, 16, 19, 31–2, 35, 37–9, 50, 54–5, 58, 62, 65, 72, 76, 81, 92–3, 95, 124, 126, 138, 144–5, 152, 168
Fang Rufu, 83
Fasheng, 57
father, 7, 35, 41, 50, 72, 81, 92, 107, 124, 144, 153
Faxian, 54
Fayuan, 58

feminism, 13, 143
filial piety, 7–8, 35, 37, 50, 53–4, 55–8, 61, 63, 80–1, 85, 116, 119, 124–5, 134, 144, 153, 163, 167–8
film, 7, 141–2, 144, 157, 159–60
flower, 94–107
footbinding, 132–3, 144
Fotudeng, 47, 49
France, 131
friend, 39, 86, 117, 125, 138, 160, 167

gang, 7, 37, 40, 117–27, 155–6
Gao Meimei, 81
Gaoseng zhuan. See Biographies of Eminent Monks
Gaoxing of Liang, 76
garden, 94, 97, 99, 101–4
gentleness, 139, 143, 165–7
gentry, 62, 91, 94, 97, 99, 101, 105, 114, 140
Gilmore, David, 4
Gongyang, 36, 38, 42
government, 8, 62, 64, 80, 93, 97, 114, 116, 122–3, 131–2, 147, 156, 163, 167
grandson, 41
Guan Yu, 115, 122
Guizot, François, 62
Guliang, 42

Habermas, Jürgen, 137
hagiography, 47, 50, 58
hair, 50, 55, 135, 155
Han dynasty, 8, 16, 29–43, 51, 62, 79, 115, 116
Han Gaozu, 82, 116
Han Guangwu, 40
Han Xiaozong, 39
Han Xin, 116
Han Yu, 65
Hanshu. See Records of the Han
haohan, 111–2, 116–27, 134, 158, 160, 164
heaven, 20–1, 42, 74
Hegel, G.W.F., 6
hegemonic masculinity, 4, 92, 94, 96, 101–2, 104, 107, 111–2, 122, 136, 157–8
hero, 52, 55, 114–7, 121–7, 135, 137, 158
heterosexuality, 54, 125, 160

homosexuality, 7
homosocial, 18, 125, 127, 133–4, 139, 160
Hong gaoliang. See Red Sorghum
Hong Kong, 157, 160
honor, 2, 18, 29–43, 50, 71, 76–7, 79–85,
    93, 97, 101–4, 116, 122–5, 127, 134,
    142–4, 152–3, 157
honor culture, 30–1, 71, 76, 81, 82, 85, 142
horticulture. *See* garden
Hou Hanshu. See Records of the Later Han
Hu Shih, 145–6
Huan Tan, 40–1
Huanglao, 23
Huichi, 57
Huijiao, 47, 49, 51, 55, 58, 63
Huishao, 56
hunting, 14
husband, 72, 76, 79, 80–3, 124, 127, 168

ideology, 5, 49, 52, 62, 64, 79, 96, 121, 152,
    155, 157, 166
immortal, 84–5
imperialism, 9, 131–4, 139–40, 151
India, 49, 50, 54, 58
individualism, 19, 53, 87, 99, 116, 133, 136,
    138, 143–5, 147, 152, 167
infanticide, 41, 126
inheritance, 32
in-laws, 19, 57, 72, 81, 127, 167

Japan, 139, 146, 157, 165
Jing Ke, 114
Jiu Tangshu. See Old Tang History
Judaism, 53
Juexian, 57

Kang Senghui, 58
Kang Youwei, 132, 139
Kewang. See Yearnings
kinship, 5, 7–8, 34, 39, 63, 72, 81–2, 93,
    125–6, 138, 144, 167–8
Kong Yiji, 135
Kumārajīva, 57
kun, 20–5

Lao She, 135, 137–8
Laozi, 21

law, 13, 37–42, 73–4, 93, 114, 116, 122, 123
Legalism, 15
Lei Feng, 152, 156
Lévi-Strauss, Claude, 72
Li, Marquis of Shougang, 40
Liang Qichao, 135
Lienü zhuan. See Biographies of Women
Liji. See Records of Rites
literatus, 63, 91–3, 95, 99, 101, 103, 105,
    107, 111, 117, 121, 123–4, 136, 138,
    163–4
Liu Penzi, 40
Liu Xiang, 74, 76
Lotus Sutra, 55
loyalty, 31, 35, 37, 57, 71, 117, 122–3,
    125–6, 142
Lü, Empress, 82
Lu Xun, 134–6, 139

Manchus, 135
Mao Zedong, 152–3, 156
marriage, 7, 50, 54–5, 58, 62, 72, 74, 79,
    84–5, 93, 126
martial arts, 160, 167
Marx, Karl, 6, 151
Marxism, 121, 151
Mediterranean model, 30–2
Mencius, 33
merchant, 91, 93, 97, 99, 101–5, 107,
    127, 163
metaphysics, 13, 20–5, 99, 123
middle class, 136–7, 142–4, 146–7, 159
militarism. *See* war
Ming dynasty, 79, 111–27
Ming History, 79
Mingshi. See Ming History
misogyny, 54, 71, 126, 160
Mo Di, 15
Mo Yan, 159
modern, 132–4, 136–46, 157, 162
Mongol, 162
monk, 47, 49, 53–65
mother, 7, 33, 37, 54, 57–8, 61, 81, 116,
    134, 144, 155
mourning, 54, 58, 61
Mourning Costume, 58
Mozi. See Mo Di

Mulian, 134
museum, 143–4
music, 165–7
mutilation, 50, 55, 76, 80, 81, 87, 116, 119

Nantong, 139, 143
nationalism, 133–5, 137, 139–40, 145–7,
    151–3, 157, 160, 163, 165–8
nature, 94
Neolithic, 14, 34
New Life Movement, 147
New Records of the Tang, 81
nomad, 9, 51, 80, 115, 131
Northern and Southern dynasties, 51, 61
nun, 84

officials, 33, 35–9, 42, 50, 64, 80, 91, 94,
    97, 99, 103, 114, 116–7, 135, 140, 147,
    152, 155–6, 163
Old Tang History, 83
opium, 131–2, 141
Opium Wars, 131, 133, 163
ordeal, 29–30
Orientalism, 6, 162
Ouyang Xiu, 97, 99

Pan Jinlian, 127
parent, 7–8, 49, 54–5, 58, 61, 65, 80, 144, 167
patriarchy, 71, 80, 85, 112
patron, 49, 62, 94, 115
Peiligang culture, 14
peony, 96–107, 132
philosophy, 80, 96
politics, 5, 18, 20, 24–5, 35, 42, 49, 61, 87,
    96, 114, 117, 121, 126, 133, 151, 157,
    163, 167
portents, 24–5
poverty, 83–4, 112, 126, 163
property, 32, 50, 62–3, 72, 74
prostitute, 82, 85, 133, 140, 146

qian, 20–5
Qin dynasty, 41, 94
Qin Shihuang, 114
qing, 117–8
Qing dynasty, 131–5, 143
Quell the Bandits, 135

racism, 6–7, 132–3
recluse, 8–9, 96, 104
Records of Rites, 16, 19
Records of the Han, 38
Records of the Later Han, 34, 36
Red Guard, 155
Red Sorghum, 159
religion, 13, 18, 115, 134
Rencheng, Prince of Wei, 55
revolution, 2, 135, 137, 151–2, 155–6
righteousness, 33, 35–6, 74, 76–7, 118,
    122–4, 134, 158, 160
Rites of Zhou, 42
ritual, 13, 16, 18–9, 21, 29–30, 32–3, 35,
    50, 63–4, 77, 80, 82, 94, 118, 124, 154
Romance of the Three Kingdoms, 117, 122
Russia, 151, 154–5

Sangfu. See Mourning Costume
Sanguo yanyi. See Romance of the
    Three Kingdoms
science, 131–2, 135–6, 143, 146, 151
Sedgwick, Eve, 125
Sengdu, 58
shame, 31, 33–4, 72, 131–2, 135
Shang Yang, 15
Shang dynasty, 1
Shanghai, 1, 9, 142, 165
Shangjun shu. See Writings of Lord Shang
Shen Cunzhong, 83
Shennong, 15
Shijing. See Classic of Poetry
shrew, 81–3
Shuihu zhuan. See Water Margin
siwen, 165
slave, 41, 82, 85, 119
social Darwinism, 132–3, 137
socialism, 151–6, 163
son, 8, 33, 35, 41, 54, 58, 65, 80, 92–3, 107,
    114, 116, 124, 134, 167–8
Song Jiang, 118
Song dynasty, 91–107, 116
Soviet Union. *See Russia*
space, 16–8, 73, 154
sport, 4, 133, 139, 147
Springs and Autumns of the State of Lu,
    36, 38

Stalin, 155
stepmother, 57, 61
symbolic capital. *See* cultural capital
suicide, 52, 55–6, 81, 87, 116
Sui dynasty, 51

Taipei, 167
Taiwan, 145, 157, 165–7
Tang dynasty, 58, 65, 71–87, 97, 114, 125
Tanwuchan, 58
tattoo, 118–9
teahouse, 140–1
television, 157–8, 162–3
Tibet, 161–2
True Story of Ah Q, The, 136

uncle, 54, 61
United States, 145–6, 152, 157

vengeance, 2, 31–2, 34–43, 93, 111, 114,
    122–3, 127, 158
Verne, Jules, 143
virginity, 72, 82

Wang Shuo, 158–9
war, 2, 32, 34, 36, 51, 91–3, 111, 131, 133,
    139, 146–7, 152
Warring States era, 32
Water Margin, 117–20, 126–7, 134–5,
    156, 158, 160
wealth, 33, 63, 92–3, 94, 96–7, 100–102,
    104, 111, 114–5, 123, 126, 137–8, 163
Weber, Max, 6
Wei dynasty, 39
Wei Lang, 39
West, 6–7, 53, 66, 131–3, 135–6, 139–40,
    143–6, 152, 157
widow, 74–7, 79, 84, 93
wife, 54, 75–6, 79, 80–3, 93, 126–7, 144,
    146, 168
woman, 1–2, 4, 13–25, 54–5, 63, 71–87,
    93, 124–7, 132–3, 139, 141, 143, 146–7,
    152, 154, 156, 160, 167–8

women's history, 1–2
Woo, John, 160
work, 5, 8, 9, 13–4, 32, 54, 84, 133, 137–8,
    144, 152, 155, 158, 163–4
Writings of Lord Shang, 15
Wu Dalang, 127
Wu of Liang, Emperor, 64
Wu Song, 120
Wu Yusen. *See* Woo, John

xiake, 114, 122, 125
Xiang, Duke of Qi, 36
Xiaojing. See Classic of Filial Piety
Xinhai Revolution, 137
Xin Tangshu. See New Records of the Tang
Xun Yue, 42

yang, 20, 22–5
Yang Qiu, 37
Yearnings, 158
Yijing. See Classic of Changes
yin, 20, 22–5
Yin Yuan, 39
Yongjia chaos, 51
You, King of Zhou, 18
Yu Daosui, 61
Yu Wanchun, 135
Yue Fei, 116
Yunnan, 162

Zhang Ailing. *See* Chang, Eileen
Zhang Quanyi, 81
Zhang Yimou, 159
Zhenzong, Emperor, 102
Zhixiu, 55
Zhou Dang, 36
Zhou Jielun. *See* Chou, Jay
Zhou dynasty, 14–25, 32–4, 74
Zhouli. See Rites of Zhou
Zhuang, Duke of Li, 76
Zhufa Chong, 54
Zou Yan, 23
Zuo commentary, 38, 42

About the Author

Bret Hinsch is professor in the Department of History, Foguang University, Taiwan.

2 8 MAY 2025

York St John
Library and Information Services
Normal Loan

Please see self service receipt for return date.

Fines are payable for late return